OUT OF

Left Field

OVER 1,134
NEWLY DISCOVERED
AMAZING BASEBALL
RECORDS, CONNECTIONS,
COINCIDENCES, AND MORE!

JEFFREY LYONS AND DOUGLAS B. LYONS

TIMES 𝕿 BOOKS

RANDOM HOUSE

Copyright © 1998 by Jeffrey Lyons and Douglas B. Lyons

All rights reserved under International and Pan-American Copyright Conventions.
Published in the United States by Times Books, a division of Random House, Inc., New
York, and simultaneously in Canada by Random House of Canada Limited, Toronto.

Library of Congress Cataloging-in-Publication Data

Lyons, Jeffrey.
Out of left field : over 1,134 newly discovered amazing baseball records, connections,
coincidences, and more / Jeffrey Lyons and Douglas B. Lyons. — 1st ed.
    p.   cm.
ISBN 0-8129-2993-4
  1. Baseball—Miscellanea.   2. Baseball players—Miscellanea.
I. Lyons, Douglas B. II. Title.
GV873.L84   1998
796.357—dc21   97-34006

Random House website address: www.randomhouse.com
Printed in the United States of America on acid-free paper

9 8 7 6 5 4 3 2

First Edition

INTRODUCTION

OKAY, LET'S MAKE THIS BRIEF so you can get to the good stuff. Stuff that will amuse and amaze. Stuff that will start and settle arguments. Stuff that may stump you at first, but that you can use to show off later. Stuff that will enhance your social standing or get you thrown out of the room, depending on your ability to gauge your surroundings. Stuff that is to some as fascinating as the musings of Casey Stengel. And to others as pointless as the musings of . . . well, Casey Stengel.

This is baseball stuff. Real good baseball stuff. Who knew that five big leaguers came from Lebanon (sort of)? Not me. Who knew that Babe Ruth wasn't the only wayward lad turned superstar who spent his formative years at St. Mary's Industrial School for Boys? Know who else pulled a stretch there? Al Jolson, that's who. Oh, Mammy, I never would have known that.

Now, right there this book has paid for itself, especially if you haven't really purchased it yet, and you're just loitering in the bookstore, leafing through introductions. But there's lots more, and the store will be closing soon. So head for the register and come across with the cash. You'll be glad you did, and so will I, because maybe we'll find ourselves on an airplane together sometime. Then, if you have read Jeff and Doug's book, you'll be able to offer up a conversational icebreaker like this: "So, Bob, who was the only palindromic manager in big league history?" I'll be so impressed I'll pretend I've forgotten the answer, just so you can supply it. It's in here, trust me.

I have ulterior motives, I must admit. I'm pointing toward the time when people no longer approach me with a look that says, "I'm certain you've never heard this before," and then ask, "Who's the only person to play for the Yankees, the Knicks, and the Rangers in the same season?" Being the eternal good sport, I smile vacantly and shrug, then brace myself for the side-splitting answer: "Why, it was Gladys Gooding. She played the organ at the games. Get it, Bob?" This information is often accompanied by a slap on the back, which sends me lurching forward as I contemplate summoning Security.

People. People. I don't care what your brother-in-law tells you. You need some new stuff, good stuff. Here it is. Enjoy.

Bob Costas

Acknowledgments

_____

W HILE THIS BOOK IS THE WORK of the authors, we have consulted with a number of people who have detailed and specific knowledge of particular events, facts, or people.

Tim Wiles, Director of Research at the National Baseball Library & Archive at the Hall of Fame in Cooperstown, Scot Mondore, Senior Researcher, and their staff have provided invaluable support, encouragement, and help in tracking down obscure facts and sources.

Special thanks to Bob Costas, Rosie O'Donnell, Stan Musial, Billy Crystal, Richard Zitzmann, and Danny Gardella.

Thanks also to Steve Fink of the Royals; Glen Serra of the Atlanta Braves; Marty Pérez; John Olguin of the Dodgers; the Canadian Baseball Hall of Fame; Paul Siminovsky; Ken Kondo; Walt Wilson; Paula Homan, Curator of the Cardinals Hall of Fame Museum; Erv Fisher, the Cardinals' historian; Bob Broeg of the *St. Louis Post-Dispatch;* Richard Beverage of the Pacific Coast League Historical Society; Rich Johnson of the *Seattle Times;* Dean Miller of the Jacksonville Suns; Thomas H. Smith, Director of the Legends of the Game Baseball Museum & Learning Center at the Ballpark in Arlington, Texas; Connie Riley of the Bronx Department of Highways; Larry Pansino for information about baseball monuments in Pittsburgh; Joe Williams and Catherine Lyons (no relation to the authors) of the Wappingers Falls Historical Society, for information on Dan Brouthers; Jim Charlton; Tom Darow; Pat Herman of the Orlando Rays; Jon Light, author of *The Cultural History of Baseball;* Lewis Scheider;

Charles W. Bevis; Kathy Gardner; Jack Little; Russ Lake; William Delaney; David Smith; Len Zaslowski; Jason Young of the Whiskey Jacks; Jim Tessmer of the Macon Braves; Eugene N. Harley; Nick and Tina Kazymirczuk; Lyle Spatz; and Bill Plummer III of the Amateur Softball Association.

Special recognition is in order for John Williams; Lawrence Jordan, our agent; Stanley Newman, our editor at Times Books, who always believed in this project; and Stephanie Landis and Andrew Linker, for keeping us honest.

We are also grateful to our oldest brother George, who knows more about baseball than most people have forgotten, and our brother Warren—the best ballplayer in the family, and the best accompanist Stan Musial ever had!

To Nancy, my MVP.

Douglas B. Lyons

B ASEBALL HAS HAD a profound influence on my life. It has kept me young; it has given me day-to-day excitement half the year and longing for that thrill the other half. It has crammed my brain with thousands of names I'd otherwise never need, and facts no rational human being ought to know, and it has been such a part of my life that it's hard to thank everyone who either got me started in the game or has sustained my interest.

First are my father, Leonard Lyons; my mother, Sylvia, who always hit to right field; and my oldest brother George, who instilled in me the knowledge of the game, the love of its history, and the ability to remember batting averages and trivia before anyone called it trivia. I was the only kid in my school who knew who Walt Moryn, Bill Sarni, and Purnal Goldy were; that Casey Stengel once studied dentistry; and that Mickey Mantle had twin brothers named Ray and Roy.

My father's soft yet tricky overhand pitches to me in our daily softball-hitting sessions in Central Park, and George's lofty flies, were the basis for whatever ability I was able to muster to make the high school team as starting center fielder and to keep playing the game to this day, as the cofounder of the N.Y. Showbusiness Softball League, where I still patrol right field from April to late August.

I also dedicate this book to my teammates for the last 27 years—*my* "Boys of Summer"—including Mike Griffith, Jim Hart, Steve Drooker, Bill Evans, Rod Friedman, Richard Curtis, Dave Foster, Jimmy Dos Santos, Ira Resnick, Andy Watkins, Larry Terese, Morty Gilbert, Eddie Rodriguez, Mort Fleischner, David Rios, Jamie Delson, Moose, and Ted Liebowitz. The times I spend with them in the park each spring and summer are among the happiest hours of my life. Our opponents keep getting younger, but we keep having more fun.

I also dedicate this book to Joe Castiglione, my Red Sox buddy, one of the world's most decent people and the Voice of the Old Towne Team, who, with Jerry ("We Owe You a Station Break") Trupiano, forms the best play-by-play radio team of them all. These two are made "from the best stuff on Earth." Ken Coleman, who first let me stumble through half an inning on the air in 1987, and Bob Starr, "The Burly Broadcaster," who manned the Fenway mike all too briefly in Boston, are also in my thoughts; so are Hector Martinez and Bobby Serrano, who each summer let me broadcast a few innings of Red Sox games in Spanish. *¡Gracias, amigos!*

This is also for Phil Rizzuto, the most colorful of them all (who may some-day learn to pronounce *Yom Kippur*); Bobby Murcer, who tried in vain to teach this New Yorker how to chew tobacco; Bill White, whom I revere; and Ken "Hawk" Harrelson, who made 1968 at Fenway so memorable. Steve August, Dick Bresciani, and the legendary "Uncle Lou" Gorman, of the Red Sox, and Lou's successor as general manager, Dan Duquette, have always treated us roy-ally on our annual pilgrimages to Mecca. And Johnny Pesky, who was Nomar before Nomar.

Joe Morgan, the best manager the Red Sox have ever had, is a fountain of knowledge about baseball and life and should still be in the dugout.

Phyllis Mehridge, Vice President of the American League, flattered me by urging me to apply for the job of President, and I'll never forget that. I live in hope.

And finally, this book is for Andy Kasper, a onetime catcher in the Giants' system, whose friendship I will always treasure. He was part of our family for only about eight seasons, but since his untimely passing, I have never watched a baseball game without thinking of him.

Jeffrey Lyons

RESEARCH NOTES

SOME OF OUR SOURCES were not all that unusual—the New York Public Library; The White Plains and Scarsdale, New York Public Libraries; the National Baseball Library in Cooperstown; the media relations departments of the National and American Leagues and of every big-league team, and virtually all minor-league teams as well; village historians and historical societies in the hometowns of every Hall of Famer; state departments of historic preservation; and numerous publications from the Society for American Baseball Research (SABR).

But delving into the vast history and lore of baseball has also taken us to out-of-the-way places and sources, such as the historian of the West Laurel Hill Cemetery in Bala Cynwyd, Pennsylvania, where Harry Wright is buried; the Bronx Department of Highways; the historian at West Point; the archivist of the California Department of Correction, and the historian of San Quentin; the National Aeronautics and Space Administration; the Slo-Pitch Softball Hall of Fame; the Lions Club in Dunsmuir, California; Sherry Smith's daughter; the curator of the Arlington National Cemetery; Phil and Joe Niekro's mother Ivy; the high school art teacher in Wahoo, Nebraska, whose students decorated Sam Crawford Stadium; the Prague Chamber of Commerce; and two Lord Mayors' offices; and to such unusual sources, at least for baseball research, as *Gentlemen's Quarterly, Overdrive* magazine, *Library Journal, Foundry* magazine, *International Boxing Digest*, a film festival in Indianapolis, and a law clerk in the United States District Court.

Without exception, our sources were eager to offer assistance and encouragement. Baseball fans are everywhere—thank you all!

CONTENTS

———

FOREWORD

E VER SINCE I WAS A LITTLE BOY, I've been collecting baseball trivia of one sort or another. From an imitation I used to do of DiMaggio dusting himself off after a slide—which my father, in turn, did for Joe D. one night at Toots Shor's restaurant, much to DiMag's amazement—to odd facts and incidents, the endless supply of baseball lore has always fascinated me. I remember knowing at a very early age, for instance, that Jackie Jensen's wife was a diver named Zoe Anne Olson and that they both feared flying. I wasn't even ten when I knew that Ted Williams' middle name is Samuel, or that Elmer Valo was born in Ribnik, Czechoslovakia, or that Ralph Terry was born in a place called Big Cabin, Oklahoma. Baseball fans who collect such trivia defy those who detest the sport by treasuring these facts, and feel privileged to have collected them; these are gems that belong only to us.

There are already vast numbers of baseball trivia books—many of which Douglas and I own. But over the years, we've uncovered many fascinating facts that neither of us had ever seen before. About three years ago, Douglas and I set out to compile a book of these "new" facts—trivia and unusual incidents, quirks and coincidences that might otherwise have been lost forever.

This may sound like we took our task very seriously. Not at all! Often we'd exchange newfound facts with glee, as if we were paleontologists uncovering a valuable fossil. Or we'd play "Can You Top This?" *Hey, I found another big leaguer married at home plate! So what? I found the only lefty to hit three home runs in a single game off a lefty pitcher!*

Alas, my teenage son Ben prefers basketball. Lately, he's even taken up golf! Only during the baseball season does he think about the old game and its infinite facts, incidents, and odd occurrences. And, thank goodness, he gets into it. He has a Rotisserie Baseball team and knows all of today's players, but I want him to know that among the thousands of players who came before his time, many would be stars today. Yes, there was a Ken Griffey Sr. My daughter, Hannah, for her part, is a Derek Jeter fan who has learned to throw quite effectively, fears no ball, no matter how high it is hit or how fast it is tossed at her, and has quite a pickoff move.

This book is also a bond with our oldest brother, George, who gave us our love for baseball with his vast knowledge and appreciation for the game, albeit through the eyes of a rare New York–based St. Louis Cardinals fan. The trove of facts tucked in George's head would fill five books like ours.

I hope this book will explain to my wife and all non-baseball fans, in some part, that I am not absolutely insane between April and October and that yes, there can be some fascinating events as well as interesting characters who don baseball uniforms and play a game for a living. I cherish those rare moments when my wife asks me a Red Sox score—about three times a season if I'm lucky. I never consider that she might simply be wondering when the game will be over, rather than how the team I have loved for fifty years has fared. Though I don't expect to find her thumbing through these pages, I hope she'll have a better understanding of those who love the greatest game ever invented and cherish the unusual, the amazing, the odd and memorable events that have made baseball a joy for six generations of fans.

Jeffrey Lyons

WHAT MAKES BASEBALL DIFFERENT from all other sports, and makes it—as Babe Ruth called it in his 1948 farewell speech at Yankee Stadium—the "only real game," are the memories beyond who won, who lost, or who scored. It's the spectacular or botched plays, amazing feats, historic firsts and lasts, streaks, errors, and the endless stream of players. Only baseball creates this fascination.

Not all the memorable players were great, of course. Is there a hockey equivalent of Marv Throneberry (Marvin Eugene Throneberry, whose initials spell MET), a basketball counterpart for Harvey Haddix or one-armed Pete Gray, or a football player to rival 3'7" Eddie Gaedel?

In baseball, there are thousands of moments, memorable events, great catches, weird plays, and odd names. New ones are created every season. Odd names? Consider Charlie Manlove, Whoops Creeden, Bevo LeBourveau, Silver King, Urbane Pickering, Toots Shultz, Nikco Riesgo, Phonney Martin, Tricky Nichols, Memo Luna, Nick Goulish, Mysterious Walker, Earl Huckleberry,

Drungo Hazewood, Blix Donnelly, Ed Kenna ("The Pitching Poet"), Hercules Burnett, Moxie Divis, Ice Box Chamberlain, and Al Orth ("The Curveless Wonder").

Who caught Roger Maris's 61st home run? New Yorkers might know it was Sal Durante, a fan (in section 33, box 163D, seat 4). Too easy? Okay: who caught *Babe Ruth's* 60th home run? Joe Forner, also a fan. For whom did midget Gaedel pinch hit? Frank Saucier.

Mediocre players have had moments of fame. Take Bucky Dent—the first major-league game he saw, he played in! Dropped balls, errors (just ask Bill Buckner!), strikeouts, no-hitters, crazy pitches (Dave LaRoche befuddling Gorman Thomas), unhittable pitches (John Kruk laughing in the 1993 All-Star Game as Randy Johnson struck him out on three straight invisible pitches); weird plays—Germany Schaefer stealing *first* base, Jimmy Pearsall running the bases *backward* after his 100th home run, a nearsighted and probably hungover Ryne Duren throwing his last warmup pitch over the catcher's head; Joe Morgan cocking his arm as a reminder to keep his elbows out, Mike Hargrove ("The Human Rain Delay") taking forever to readjust each and every item of clothing before every pitch, or Joe Page jumping over the bullpen fence on his way in to pitch.

Baseball is full of such delightful players and episodes. So is this book. Some of the names mentioned will bring back memories, while others will be ones you've never heard of. You'll meet forgotten players whose unusual feats or backgrounds add to the rich flavor of the game. You may think you're pretty good if you can name the Hall of Famer born on a train, or the only adoptee in Cooperstown. But who is the only player born at sea?

Out of Left Field is meant primarily to be read for pleasure. That's why the answers are given right after the questions instead of in the back. You might also enjoy reading the questions to your favorite baseball experts—just to show them they don't know as much as they thought!

There are a few trick questions, but most are clearly labeled. Few questions deal with minor leaguers, and only a handful involve pre-1900 players. "Modern," at least here, means post-1900. We have made every effort to be up-to-date through the end of the 1997 season.

If you have a favorite baseball question that you think would be suitable for the next edition of this book, please send it to us with your name, address, phone number, a self-addressed stamped envelope—and the answer! We'll acknowledge your contribution in the next edition if we use it. Send it to: Times Books Puzzles & Games, 201 East 50th Street, New York, NY 10022-7703. E-mail: BASBALINFO@aol.com.

Douglas B. Lyons

THE FABULOUS BABE

W HILE OTHER PLAYERS POP UP in many different chapters in this book, Babe Ruth is the only one with his own chapter. No other player has influenced the game or the country as powerfully as Ruth. As Red Smith wrote, "He transcended records and his place in the American scene was no mere matter of statistics." Some of his records have been broken. But as a pitcher, a high-average hitter, the highest-paid player of his time, a consummate slugger, the restorer of the country's faith in the integrity of the game during its darkest hour after the Black Sox scandal, and a *bona fide* American character, Ruth's status is unique. Sure, Hank Aaron hit more home runs, and Ty Cobb stole more bases. Lots of pitchers have won more games. But Ruth's shadow still falls across the game of baseball. He deserves his own chapter.

When Babe Ruth set the single-season record by hitting 29 home runs in 1919, whose record did he break, and what was it?

Clifford Carlton "Gavvy" Cravath held the record of 24, set in 1915 with the Phillies.

In 1927, when Ruth set the home run record yet again, with 60 in a single season, how many were grand slams?

Two. On September 27, Ruth connected for a grand slam at Yankee Stadium off future Hall of Famer Lefty Grove of the A's (home run #57). On September 29, Ruth hit another grand-slam homer (#59) in the fifth inning off Paul Hopkins of the Senators.

The only future Hall of Famer besides Grove to give up a home run to Ruth in 1927 was Ted Lyons of the White Sox, who surrendered #54 in New York on September 21.

How many games did the Yankees play that year?

In a 154-game season, they played 155. The April 14 game ended in a 9-9 tie because of darkness. Ruth did not homer in that game.

How many games did Ruth play that year?

151.

How many batting titles did Ruth win in his career?

Although he was a lifetime .342 hitter, he won only one batting crown, with a .378 average in 1924.

Who is the only pitcher to face both Babe Ruth and Mickey Mantle?

Al Benton. His career with the Athletics, Tigers, Indians, and Red Sox spanned the years from 1934 to 1952. Benton was with the Philadelphia A's in 1934 when he faced Ruth, who was still a Yankee. Benton was with the Red Sox when he pitched to Mantle in 1952.

Benton is also the only man with two sacrifice bunts in the same inning—a very strange third inning, complete with 17 batters—on August 6, 1941. He picked up a win as his Tigers beat the Indians 11-2.

How many MVP awards did Ruth win?

None. The modern award was first given in 1931. Although he hit .373 that year, with 46 home runs and 163 RBIs(!), Ruth lost to Lefty Grove, who was 31-4 with a 2.06 ERA.

How heavy was Ruth's bat?

42 ounces.

By contrast, how heavy was Hank Aaron's bat?

Only 33 ounces.

Who was the Red Sox manager in 1914, Ruth's first season?

Bill Carrigan.

Who was Ruth's last manager?

Hall of Famer "Deacon" Bill McKechnie, of the Boston Braves, 1935.

Ruth led the American League in home runs every year from 1918, when he hit just 11, to 1931, when he tied with Lou Gehrig at 46, averaging 39.3 per year during that span—except in 1922 and 1925.

Who led the league in home runs in 1922?

Ken Williams of the Browns, with 39. Ruth had 35.

In 1925, the home run champ was a Yankee outfielder, but it was not Ruth. Who was it?

Bob Meusel, who had 33. Ruth had 25 that year, in a season marked by a suspension and surgery.

Ruth led the American League in RBIs in every year between 1919 and 1923, averaging 132.5 in each of those years—except for 1922. Who won the RBI title that year?

Ken Williams again. He drove in 155 runs to Ruth's 99. Ruth played only 110 games that year because he was suspended for barnstorming.

Off whom did Ruth hit his first home run?

Jack "Crab" Warhop of the Yankees, on May 6, 1915. Two weeks later, Warhop gave up Ruth homer number two.

Who scored more runs, Ruth or Hank Aaron?

It's a tie: 2,174 for both—second on the all-time list to Cobb's 2,245.

Is this a beautiful game, or what?

In how many seasons did Ruth strike out 100 times or more?

Never, although only 36 men struck out more in their careers than he did. In all, he whiffed 1,330 times. His season high was 93 in 1923.

This mediocre pitcher (29-48 lifetime, 4.63 ERA) somehow had a knack for striking Ruth out. In fact, he struck him out 10 times in their first 14 meetings. What was his name, and what did he do after his baseball career ended?

Hubert "Shucks" Pruett of the Browns. He struck out Ruth three times in one game (June 12, 1922, as the Browns beat the Yankees 7-1). After the 1932 season Pruett became a doctor, earning his M.D. from St. Louis University.

How many times did Ruth hit homers in both games of a doubleheader?

25.

Ruth's second wife, Claire, had a cousin who could play some. In fact, he played his way into the Hall of Fame. Who was he?

Johnny Mize.

Ruth died on August 16, 1948. Who is the only big leaguer born on that date?

Mike Jorgensen, first baseman and occasional outfielder, playing from 1968 to 1985 for the Mets, Expos, Athletics, Rangers, Braves, and Cardinals. He managed the Cards in 1995.

How many games did Ruth pitch for the Yankees?

Five—he won them all. He pitched one in 1920, two in 1921, and one each in 1930 and 1933. The last two were complete games.

How many times did Ruth hit two home runs in one game?

A record 72! Next on the list is Willie Mays, with 63.

As a batter, Ruth led the American League in both strikeouts and walks in four seasons. Only one other man has ever led the American League in both categories in the same season even once. Who is he?

Mickey Mantle. In 1958, Mantle had 129 walks and 120 strikeouts.

		BB	SO
Ruth:	1923	170	93
	1924	142	81
	1927	138	89
	1928	135	87

Four National Leaguers have also achieved this unusual double. Who are they?

	BB	SO
Hack Wilson, Cubs, 1930	105	84*
Dolf Camilli, Dodgers, 1939	110	107
Mike Schmidt, Phillies, 1983	128	148
Dale Murphy, Braves, 1985	90	141

*In 1930, Wilson hit 56 homers and drove in 190 RBIs. Nearly 70 years later, he still holds the record for most home runs in a National League season and the major-league record for most RBIs in a season, which in

1930 was just 154 games. He had a slugging average of .723 that year, and a batting average of .356.

Some year, right? Why didn't Wilson win the Triple Crown? Because Bill Terry hit *45* points higher—.401—the last National Leaguer to hit .400!

What was Ruth's record as a pinch hitter?

Not so good: 13 for 67, a .194 average.

"Hey, Skip, I gotta start!"

Which outfielder hit the most career home runs? How many?

Babe Ruth—692.

Yes, Hank Aaron had more total homers, but he also played 210 games at first, 43 games at second, and 7 games at third, and he hit 22 homers in his two years with the American League Milwaukee Brewers, where he was a designated hitter for 202 games. As an outfielder, Aaron hit 661 home runs.

Ruth had nine homers in his first four big-league seasons, when he was used exclusively as a pitcher. Over the next 11 years, he pitched only 42 games and played 2,238 games in the outfield, plus another 31 at first base.

Who is the only Hall of Famer to homer off Babe Ruth?

Sam Rice of the Senators, a three-run shot at Fenway Park on June 25, 1919.

What did Ruth do in his last major-league at bat?

Ruth should have retired after May 25, 1935, when he hit three home runs for the Boston Braves—including the longest shot ever in Forbes Field—over the right-field wall. (Ruth hit three homers in a game twice during regular season play and twice in the World Series.) After his last home run, he sat down in the dugout—the *other team's* dugout—next to Pirate rookie pitcher Mace Brown.

Babe Ruth Days had been scheduled around the league, and Ruth hung on for two more weeks. His last game was against the Phillies in Philadelphia on May 30, 1935. In his last at bat, he struck out. On June 2, Ruth announced his retirement.

How many home runs did Ruth hit in the minor leagues?

One.

Which state can claim to be the site of Ruth's first professional home run?

It wasn't hit in a state. On September 5, 1914, while pitching a 9-0 win for the Providence Grays over the Toronto Maple Leafs, Ruth homered in Toronto. This was the first official homer of his professional career.

When Ruth retired after the 1935 season, only two other living players had hit over 300 home runs. Who were they?

Lou Gehrig, with 378, and Rogers Hornsby, with 300.

ALL IN THE FAMILY

Name the only two brothers to hit over 150 career home runs apiece.

Ken (282) and Clete (162) Boyer.

Which brothers were teammates the longest?

Hall of Famers Paul and Lloyd Waner, who played together for 14 years (1927–1940) with the Pirates.

Who are the only three brothers with at least 1,000 career hits each?

The Alous: Felipe (2,101), Jésus (1,216), and Matty (1,777).

On September 22, 1963, the brothers shared the same outfield for the San Francisco Giants, as the Giants beat the Mets 13-4. In the seventh inning, Matty played left, Felipe was in center (replacing Willie Mays), and Jesus played right. In the eighth inning, Jesus, Matty, and Felipe were retired 1, 2, 3.

Which future Hall of Famers besides Mays were also in the game?

Duke Snider (with the Mets) and Willie McCovey, who hit three homers!

Name the DiMaggio brothers.

Joe, Tom, Mike, Dom, and Vince. Tom and Mike were not ballplayers. Their sisters are Marie, Mamie, and Nellie. Joe's the eighth child, and Dom's the youngest.

When Phil and Joe Niekro faced each other, who won more games?

Joe, with five wins to Phil's four.

Who were the first two brothers to manage simultaneously in the modern big leagues?

Rene (Marlins) and Marcel (Angels) Lachemann, in 1994. So far, no brothers in this century have managed in the same league at the same time.

In 1879, future Hall of Famers George Wright and his brother Harry managed the Providence Greys and Boston Red Caps, respectively, in the National League.

This family had more brothers play in the big leagues than any other. How many and who?

The five Delahantys: Hall of Famer Big Ed, plus brothers Frank, Jim, Joe, and Tom.

How many sets of twins have played in the big leagues since 1900?

Seven.

The Cliburns: catcher Stan (Angels, 1980) and pitcher Stewart (Angels, 1984–1985, 1988).

The Edwardses: Mike (Pirates, A's, 1977–1980) and Marshall (Brewers, 1981–1983). Younger brother Dave was an outfielder for the Twins and Padres from 1978 to 1982.

The Grimeses: Ray (Red Sox, Cubs, Phillies, 1920–1926) and Roy (Giants, 1920).

The Shannons: Joe (Braves, 1915) and Red (Braves, A's, Red Sox, Senators, Reds, 1915, 1917–1921, 1926).

The Jonnards: Claude (Giants, Browns, Reds, 1921–1929) and Clarence James "Bubber" (White Sox, Pirates, Phillies, Cardinals, 1920–1935).

The O'Briens: Eddie was an infielder and occasional pitcher for the Pirates from 1953 to 1958, and Johnny, also an infielder, was Eddie's teammate from 1953 to 1958. Johnny finished his career with the Cardinals and Milwaukee Braves.

The Cansecos: José (A's, Rangers, Red Sox, 1985–) and Ozzie (A's, Cardinals, 1990, 1992–93). They were teammates with the Oakland A's in 1990.

Name two sets of three brothers who were all big-league pitchers.

The Clarksons—John (328-178), Dad (39-39), and Walter (18-16). John pitched in the National League from 1882 to 1894. Dad also pitched in the National League, from 1891 to 1896, while Walter toiled in the American League from 1904 to 1908.

More recently, the Perez brothers, Melido, Carlos, and Pascual, all pitched in the big leagues.

Who was the first father to manage two sons in the big leagues *at the same time?*

Cal Ripken Sr. He managed sons Cal Jr. and Billy when they played for the Orioles in 1987.

He pitched for the Senators from 1909 through 1912, compiling a 25-31 record. In 1911, he hit .303. His brother was an outfielder with the Browns from 1913 to 1915. He had two sons, both of whom won batting championships. Who are they?

Ewart Gladstone "Dixie" Walker was the pitcher. His brother Ernie was the Brownie.

Dixie's sons were Harry and Dixie (real name Fred, known—at least in Brooklyn—as "The People's Cherce"). In 1944, with the Dodgers, the younger Dixie led the National League with a .357 batting average.

Harry "The Hat" led the National League with a .363 average in 1947, when he was with the Cardinals and Phillies.

Which brothers hit the most home runs in big-league history?

The Waners	Paul (112), Lloyd (28)	140
The Meusels	Bob (156), Irish (106)	262
The Alous	Jésus (32), Matty (31), Felipe (206) Total	269
The Allens	Richie (351), Hank (6), Ron (1)	358
The Nettleses	Graig (390), Jim (16)	406
The Mays	Lee (354), Carlos (90)	444
The Boyers	Ken (282), Clete (162), Cloyd (0)	444
The DiMaggios	Dom (87), Vince (125), Joe (361)	573
The Aarons	Tommie (13), Hank (755)	768!

Who are the only brothers to finish in the top five in MVP voting in the same year?

Mort and Walker Cooper, 1943 Cardinals. Walker finished second in the 1943 voting to Stan Musial, while Mort was fifth. (Mort was National League MVP in 1942.)

Which Hall of Fame pitcher gave up home runs to all three Alou brothers?

Ferguson Jenkins, Cubs: to Jesus on July 23, 1967 (Giants) and May 31, 1973 (Astros); to Felipe on April 25, 1968 (Braves); to Matty on September 5, 1971 (Cardinals).

Who are the only father-and-son major leaguers to play in Japan?

The Keoughs: Marty (outfield/first base, 1956–1966) and his son Matt (pitcher, 1977–1986). Marty played in Japan in 1968, as did Matt from 1987 to 1990.

Name the only father and son to umpire in the big leagues in the last century.

> *Hint #1: They both played in the big leagues. Hint #2: One is a Hall of Fame player.*

Dad Clarkson and his son, Hall of Famer John.

These brothers finished first and second in the National League batting race in the same year—the only brothers to do this. Who were they?

Matty and Felipe Alou. In 1966, Matty, with the Pirates, hit .342 to lead the league, while Felipe, with the Braves, came in second at .327.

When did brothers first oppose each other in an All-Star game?

July 23, 1969. Carlos May, of the American League White Sox, was a pinch hitter. His brother Lee, of the National League Reds, played first base. The National League beat the American League 9-3 at RFK Stadium in Washington, D.C.

They both gave up home runs to Ted Williams—the only father-and-son pitchers to do so. Who were they?

Thornton and Don Lee.

Place them in order of age, oldest to youngest: Joe, Vince, and Dom DiMaggio; Jesus, Matty, and Felipe Alou; Ken, Clete, and Cloyd Boyer; Luke, Joe, and Tommy Sewell.

Felipe, Matty, Jésus Alou
Vince, Joe, Dom DiMaggio
Cloyd, Ken, Clete Boyer
Joe, Luke, Tommy Sewell

Name the only brothers to win the Cy Young Award.

Jim (Twins, 1970) and Gaylord (Cleveland, 1972) Perry.

Who are the only brothers to lead the American League in triples and runs scored (not necessarily in the same year)?

Dom and Joe DiMaggio. In 1950, Dom (Red Sox) led all American Leaguers with 11 triples and 131 runs scored.

Joe led the American League in triples in his rookie year, 1936, with 15. In 1937, when he led the league with 46 home runs, he also led in runs scored with 151.

Which brothers had the most hits in one season?

Paul and Lloyd Waner. In 1927, Paul led the league with 237 hits and Lloyd had 223—a total of 460. They finished their careers with a total of 5,611 hits!

She played in the All-American Girls Professional Baseball League from 1946 to 1949, stealing 354 bases. Her son became a big leaguer. Who was she?

The late Helen Callaghan St. Aubin. (Her sister, Marge, was her teammate at Ft. Wayne in 1945, 1946, and 1948.) Her son, Casey Candaele, played for the Expos and Astros from 1986 to 1993 and for the Indians in 1996–97.

Which father-and-son combo hit the most home runs?

Bobby and Barry Bonds—706 through the 1997 season (332 for Bobby, and a still-growing 374 for Barry).

The Bells, Gus and Buddy, and the Berras, Yogi and Dale, are tied for second place with 407 homers each.

Which pitching brothers won the most games in the same season—for the same team?

Dizzy and Daffy Dean (Cardinals, 1934). Dizzy won 30 and Daffy 19, for a total of 49.

Name the only uncle-nephew teammates.

Marv Grissom and Jim Davis of the 1954 Giants. (Dwight Gooden has never been a teammate of his nephew, Gary Sheffield.)

Who were the first brothers to play in the same outfield?

Jim and John O'Rourke, for the 1880 Boston Red Caps.

Which brothers played the most total years?

The Niekro brothers—46. In second place are the five Delahantys with 41, just beating out the three DiMaggios, who played a total of 34 major-league seasons.

Who is the only man to play all nine positions and pitch against his cousin in the same game?

Bert Campaneris, Kansas City A's. On September 8, 1965, with his team in last place, the first batter Campaneris faced was his cousin, José Cardenal, then of the Angels.

Which pitching brothers combined for the most career wins in the big leagues?

The Niekros: Phil, with 318, and Joe, with 221, for a total of 539. In second place, just 10 wins behind, are Gaylord and Jim Perry.

Who were the first brothers in the National League to hit homers for opposing teams in the same game?

The Cuccinellos, on July 5, 1935. Tony blasted one for the Dodgers, and Al connected for the Giants. The Dodgers won, 14-4.

Who were the first father and son to play in the big leagues?

No, not the Griffeys. They were the first to play on the same team in the same year. The first big leaguer whose son also became a big leaguer was Herm Doscher, who played 80 games, mostly at third base, for Troy, Chicago, and Cleveland in the National League (1879, 1881–1882). His son Jack was a 2-11 pitcher with the Cubs, Dodgers, and Reds (1903–1908).

Who were the first brothers to hit home runs in the same game?

Paul and Lloyd Waner of the Pirates, on September 24, 1927. In fact, each hit his home run in the fifth inning, off Dolf Luque of the Reds, thus making Luque the first pitcher to give up home runs to brothers in the same game— and in the same inning!

Name a big leaguer whose sister was an Olympic champion.

Scott Bullett (Pirates and Cubs, 1991, 1993, 1995, 1996). His sister Vicky won a gold medal in basketball in the 1988 Seoul Olympics.

In a Toronto-Baltimore game on September 20, 1996, both teams' starting third basemen were married to Olympic champions. Name the ballplayers and their wives.

Ed Sprague Jr.–himself a member of the USA's 1988 Olympic baseball team—started at third base for the Blue Jays. His wife is Kristin Babb, gold medalist in solo synchronized swimming for the United States, 1992.

The Orioles' starting third baseman was Todd Zeile, married to gymnast Julianne McNamara. She won a gold medal in Los Angeles in 1984 on the uneven parallel bars and a silver medal in floor exercise. She also shared the U.S. team's silver medal.

Who is the only big leaguer whose daughter-in-law was an Olympic champion?

Ed Sprague Sr., A's, Reds, Cardinals, Brewers, 1968–1976.

When was the first time rookie brothers faced each other as starting pitchers?

September 29, 1986. Greg Maddux of the Cubs beat his brother Mike of the Phillies 8-3.

Which big leaguer had the most siblings?

Probably Willie Horton of the Tigers, Rangers, Indians, A's, Blue Jays, and Mariners. He is the youngest of 21 children. (He has two sons named John.) Runner-up is Marquis Grissom, one of 15. (As of this writing, Grissom has purchased houses for 11 of his siblings.) Both Ron Jackson and Gerald Williams have 12 siblings. The Boyer brothers, Clete, Cloyd, and Ken, had six sisters and four more brothers. Lou "The Mad Russian" Novikoff was one of 12 children, while Mariano Duncan and Tony Fernandez each had 10 siblings.

The Hall of Famer with the most siblings is probably Satchel Paige, one of 12 children. Satchel himself had seven children, the last of which was born when he was 57.

Gus Bell had 12 children. Only Buddy made the majors.

Gary Thurman has a twin sister and three siblings (a brother and two sisters) who are triplets.

Name three sets of fathers and sons to pitch in a World Series.

Mel Stottlemyre, 1964, Yankees; Todd Stottlemyre, 1992, 1993, Blue Jays
Jim Bagby Sr., 1920, Indians; Jim Bagby Jr., 1946, Red Sox
Pedro Borbon Sr., 1972, 1975, 1976, Reds; Pedro Borbon Jr., 1995, Braves

Which brothers hit the most home runs as teammates in a single season?

Tony and Billy Conigliaro, 1970 Boston Red Sox. Tony had 36 to Billy's 18, for a total of 54.

This big leaguer married his teammate's sister. Who were they?

Roy Smalley Sr. and Gene Mauch were teammates on the Cubs in 1948 and 1949. Smalley married Mauch's sister.

Roy Jr. later played for the Twins, where from 1976 to 1980 he was managed by Uncle Gene.

When we spoke to Ivy Niekro, mother of Phil and Joe, she noted that on September 30, 1979 her boys did something that no pitching brothers had ever done before or were likely to do again. What was it?

On that date, the Niekro brothers each won their 21st and final game of the season. In fact, that tied them for the league lead in wins. Phil won for the Braves against the Reds, while Joe and the Astros beat the Dodgers.

On September 14, 1990, pitcher Kirk McCaskill of the California Angels did something that no other pitcher had ever done before. It will probably never be done again. What was it?

He surrendered home runs—in fact, back-to-back home runs—to a father and son, Ken Griffey Sr. and Jr. of the visiting Seattle Mariners.

"I played in the World Series. My aunt is in the Softball Hall of Fame. Who am I?"

Jim Thome, who played for the Indians in the 1995 and 1997 World Series. His father's sister, the late Carolyn Thome Hart, was a 1970 inductee into the National Softball Hall of Fame in Oklahoma City. During her 15-year career, she played on 10 national championship teams and was named an All-American in 1950, 1951, 1952, and 1959. In 1950, 1951, 1952, and 1958 she was on the All-World tournament team. She is also a member of the Greater Peoria Sports Hall of Fame.

"The day I pitched a no-hitter, I retired my brother three times. Yet *he's* the one in the Hall of Fame. Who are we?"

Pitcher Wes Ferrell of the Indians pitched a 9-0 no-hitter on April 29, 1931 against the hapless St. Louis Browns. Wes also hit a two-run homer in the fourth inning and doubled to right to drive in another two runs in the eighth.

His brother, future Hall of Famer Rick, went hitless in three trips to the plate.

Who is the first big leaguer who had two sons play in the big leagues?

James Joseph Cooney (Cubs, 1890–1892). His sons were Jimmy "Scoops" and Johnny Cooney.

You're Pat Underwood. It's May 31, 1979. You've struggled and sacrificed to make it to the big leagues, and now you're going to pitch in your big-league debut for the Cleveland Indians. Who is your pitching opponent?

Your brother Tom of the Blue Jays. (The Indians won 1-0.)

BLOOD IS THICKER THAN WATER DEPARTMENT

These Hall of Famers were father-in-law and son-in-law. Who were they?

Clark Griffith and Joe Cronin. Cronin married Griffith's daughter Mildred.
Family or no, Griffith traded Cronin to the Red Sox on February 26, 1934 for Lyn Lary and $225,000.

On April 17, 1976, Mike Schmidt hit four homers in one game against the Cubs. He hit one off Mike Garman and two off Rick Reuschel. Off whom did he hit the fourth?

Rick's brother Paul.

Which father-and-son pair have played for the most teams?

Tito and Terry Francona—13. Tito played for the Orioles, White Sox, Tigers, Indians, Cardinals, Phillies, Braves, Oakland A's, and Brewers between 1956 and 1970. His son Terry, who went on to manage the Philadelphia Phillies in 1997, played for the Expos, Cubs, Reds, and Indians between 1981 and 1990.

Who are the only father and son to each hit three home runs in a game?

Ken Griffey Sr. and Jr.

Ken Sr.'s came on July 22, 1986, when he was with the Braves, against the Phillies in Atlanta. (The Braves lost.)

Ken Griffey Jr.'s first three-homer game was on May 24, 1996, against the Yankees.

By the way, no brothers have ever hit three homers apiece in a game.

How many sets of three or more brothers played in the big leagues?

17.

Allen	Hank, Richie, and Ron
Alou	Felipe, Jésus, Matty
Boyer	Clete, Cloyd, Ken
Clarkson	Dad, **John,** Walter
Cross	Lafayette "Lave," Frank, and Amos
Cruz	Hector, José, Tommy
Delahanty	**Ed,** Frank, Jim, Joe, Tom
DiMaggio	Dom, **Joe,** Vince
Edwards	Dave, Marshall, Mike
Mansell	John, Mike, Tom
O'Neill	Jack, Jim, Mike, Steve
Paciorek	John, Tom, and Jim (one game only)
Perez	Carlos, Pascual, Melido
Sadowski	Bob, Eddie, Ted
Sewell	**Joe,** Luke, Tommy
Sowders	Bill, John, Len
Wright	**George, Harry,** Sam

Note: Hall of Famers are in **boldface.**

Name four men who managed their own sons in the major leagues.

Connie Mack, who managed his son Earle; Yogi Berra—Dale; Cal Ripken Sr.—Cal Jr.; Hal McRae—Brian.

On June 20, 1997, Aaron Boone (son of Bob Boone, and grandson of Ray Boone), was called up from Indianapolis (AAA) to play for the Cincinnati Reds. Was this a happy day or a sad day for the Boone family?

Both. To make room for Aaron Boone, the Reds briefly demoted his brother, Bret, who was hitting just .205.

Hit Records

Only two men have led their league in batting while playing for last-place teams. Who are they?

Dale Alexander, 1932, Boston Red Sox (.367). Alexander also played briefly for the Detroit Tigers in 1932.

Edgar Martinez, 1992, Seattle Mariners (.343).

What is unusual about Stan Musial's 3,630 career hits?

He hit the same number at home as on the road: 1,815.

# # #

Hitting for the cycle—getting a single, a double, a triple, and a homer in one game—is not a monumental accomplishment like a no-hitter or four home runs in one game. It's just an oddity. Many players have had a single, a double, and a homer in one game, but because the triple—a blend of power and speed—is the rarest hit in the game (unless you count inside-the-park home runs), hitting for the cycle is quite rare.

Who is the only man to hit for the cycle in both leagues?

Bob Watson, on June 24, 1977 for the Astros and September 15, 1979 for the Red Sox.

Too easy? Try these next few questions about hitting for the cycle.

Who is the only player to hit for the cycle twice in one season?

Floyd Caves "Babe" Herman, Dodgers—May 18 and July 24, 1931.

Only two men have hit for the cycle three times in a career. Who are they?

Babe Herman did it for the third time on September 30, 1933 as a Cub. Bob Meusel did it with the Yankees on May 7, 1921, July 3, 1922, and July 26, 1928.

# # #

On August 16, 1978, the first four Twins to bat hit for the cycle, sort of. In the first game of a twin bill against the Royals at home, the leadoff batter was Hosken Powell. He singled. Next up was Roy Smalley Jr., who doubled. Rod Carew then hit a triple, and Glenn Adams followed with a home run.

Who had the most career at bats against all-time strikeout leader Nolan Ryan without ever striking out?

Fernando Valenzuela—12.

He is the only man to bat at least .400 in a major-league season *without 200 hits*. Who is he?

Ted Williams, who had 185 hits in his .406 year of 1941. In fact, Williams walked so often (2,019 times, #2 on the all-time list), he *never* had a 200-hit season. His maximum was 194, in 1949.

Of the 25 players who have hit 400 or more home runs, how many stole home 10 or more times?

Only two. Lou Gehrig stole home 15 times and Babe Ruth 10 times.

Off which pitcher did Mickey Mantle hit the most home runs?

Hall of Famer and 300-game winner Early Wynn—13.

In 1972, Rod Carew—the only Hall of Famer born on a train—accomplished a feat no one else in American League history has ever done or cared to do. What was it?

He led the American League in batting (.318) but had *no* home runs.

Two National Leaguers have been homerless batting champions: Clarence "Ginger" Beaumont of the Pirates in 1902, batting .357, and Hall of Famer Zack Wheat of the Dodgers in 1918, batting .335.

How many consecutive pitches can a batter take in one official at bat without swinging the bat?

Eleven. Batter comes up with two outs and a runner on base. The count goes to 3 and 2—still no swing. Then the runner is thrown out while trying to steal, and the inning ends. At the start of the next inning, the same batter comes up again with no count—but it's still considered the same at bat—and he goes to 3 and 2 again. That's 10 pitches and still no swings. The next pitch is the 11th—either a swing, strike three, or ball four.

Which National Leaguer—a Hall of Famer—won the most home run titles, is regarded as the best *ever* at his position, was named "Player of the Decade" for the 1980s, and yet was not mentioned at all in Ken Burns's 18½-hour television documentary, *Baseball*?

Mike Schmidt.

Who are the only players to homer from both sides of the plate in one game *in both leagues*?

Reggie Smith and Eddie Murray.

Smith did it for the Red Sox in 1967, 1968, 1972, and 1973 and for the Cardinals in 1975 and 1976.

Murray did it in 1982 and in 1987, when he was an Oriole, and in 1990, with the Dodgers.

Who is the only man to hit .400 and draw 100 walks in the same season?

Ted Williams, who hit .406 and drew 145 walks in 1941.

This Brave came to bat 581 consecutive times (1981–1983) without a home run. Then in 1983 he homered in two consecutive games! Who was he?

Brett Butler.

Oriole "Diamond" Jim Gentile had a big day on May 9, 1961. What did he do?

He became the first player to hit grand slams in consecutive innings (the first and second), as the visiting Orioles beat the Twins 13-5 (the first off Pedro Ramos and the second off Paul Giel). Gentile then added another RBI, bringing his total for the day to nine!

Who had the lowest batting average in a season in which he drove in at least 100 runs?

Tony Armas. In 1983, he had 107 RBIs, but batted only .218, for the Red Sox. Ironically, his pet phrase that year was: "You got to see the ball to hit the ball."

Eddie Mathews hit 512 home runs and drove in 1,453 runs during his 17-year Hall of Fame career. How many RBI titles did he win?

None. His high was 135, in his second year, 1953 (the Braves' first year in Milwaukee)—good enough only for second place to Roy Campanella's 142.

Who is the only man to drive in over 100 runs, yet score fewer than 50 in the same season?

Vic Wertz, 1960 Red Sox, who had 103 RBIs and 45 runs.

Who experienced the biggest drop in batting average from one season to the next?

Norm Cash. In 1961, as a Tiger, he hit .361 and led the league. The next year, after changing where he stood in the batter's box, his average fell to .243—a drop of 118 points!

Norm, I think I see a problem developing here.

On July 3, 1966, Tony Cloninger, pitching for the Atlanta Braves against the Giants, did something no other National League pitcher had ever done—and it had nothing to do with pitching. What did he do?

He hit two grand slams in the same game. The first, in the first inning, was off Bob Priddy, and in the fourth inning he slammed another off Ray Sadecki. He finished the day with an RBI single—nine RBIs.

In the 1970s, Cloninger played slow-pitch softball for Howard's Furniture of Denver, North Carolina. In 1977, he hit .615 with 195 homers.

Bryan Harvey, also a pitcher, played for Howard's from 1980 to 1984, hitting .557 (456 hits) with 205 homers in 818 at bats.

After nine and a half years in the big leagues and over 300 games, Joe Niekro finally hit his first home run, as an Astro, on May 29, 1976. Who was the pitcher?

His brother Phil Niekro, of the Braves.

GOOD NEWS, GOOD NEWS, BAD NEWS DEPARTMENT

In four different years, he led the American League in homers, walks, and strikeouts. Who was he?

Babe Ruth.

YEAR	HR	BB	SO
1923	41	170*	93
1924	46	142	81
1927	60	138	89
1928	54	135	87

*The all-time record—over 70 years old!

Who had the highest batting average during his last full year with his team?

Nap Lajoie. In 1901, he hit .422 for the A's, leading the American League. The following June he was sold to the Indians.

"Sorry, Nap, you're just not getting the job done!"

Was Lajoie the only batting champ traded or sold the year after he won the batting crown?

No. On November 7, 1928, the Boston Braves traded Rogers Hornsby, who had led the league that season with a .387 average, to the Cubs for Socks Seibold, Percy Jones, Lou Legett, Freddie Maguire, Bruce Cunningham, and $200,000.

"If the A's can trade Lajoie, what makes you think we can't trade you?"

On August 28, 1916, Heinie Zimmerman of the Cubs was traded to the Giants for Larry Doyle in an exchange that involved three other players. Zimmerman was the 1912 National League batting champion, and Doyle was the 1915 champ.

And on April 17, 1960, Rocky Colavito, the 1959 American League home run champion (with 42), was traded by the Indians to the Tigers for Harvey Kuenn, who batted .353 to lead the American League in batting in 1959.

This is the only time a defending home run champion was traded for a defending batting champion.

The next year, 1960, Colavito hit .249 with 35 home runs, while Kuenn's batting average fell to .308.

Who succeeded Connie Mack in 1951 after his remarkable 50 years as manager of the Philadelphia Athletics?

Jimmy Dykes, who never won a pennant in his 21 years as a manager.

Before his illustrious managing (and owning) career began, Mack was primarily a catcher for the Washington Senators and Pittsburgh Pirates in the National League, and the Buffalo Bisons in the Players League, from 1886 to 1896.

In 1953, Shibe Park, home of the Philadelphia A's and onetime home of the Phillies, was renamed Connie Mack Stadium, making Mack (known to his friends as "Mr. Mack") only the second big leaguer to have a big-league stadium named after him in his lifetime. (Charles Comiskey was the other.) Connie Mack Stadium closed in 1970 and was demolished in 1976.

Who are the only catchers to hit 300 homers, drive in 1,000 runs, and score 1,000 runs?

Carlton Fisk, Yogi Berra, and Johnny Bench.

	HOMERS	RBIs	RUNS
Fisk	376	1,330	1,276
Berra	358	1,430	1,175
Bench	369	1,376	1,091

Did anyone ever pinch-hit for Stan Musial?

Hall of Fame writer Bob Broeg of the *St. Louis Post-Dispatch* provides the answer exclusively for this book.

> Back in 1955, acting with trick rule book chicanery, [Cardinal manager] Harry Walker had Pete Whisenant bat for Musial at a time Stan was ailing with a bad wrist, hopeful of giving "The Man" a day off. With Musial listed third, Pete batted for him and took the outfield. Brooklyn's Johnny Podres hit Musial on the wrist in the fourth inning on August 29, 1955. Musial thus maintained his 594-consecutive-game streak, then the longest in the majors.
>
> I traveled with the Cards then. Stan was embarrassed and felt he could have played. Later, statistical rules were changed requiring a player similarly pinch hit to play a defensive position, too, though that could be academic with the DH.
>
> About other pinch hitting, it was done for Musial early in his career by Coaker Triplett—May 8, 1942 [in the ninth inning. Musial was 0-for-4, and

Triplett was no better, going 0-for-1. But the Cardinals beat the Reds 5-2.] and September 17, 1942 [Cards beat the Boston Braves, 6-4]—a solid right-handed hitter. And with Musial's grace and understanding, he said he never resented [Cards' manager Billy] Southworth's decision because Triplett was good against left-handed pitching, and obviously no one knew then how great Musial would be.

Did anybody ever pinch-hit for Joe DiMaggio?

No!

What was Mike Cubbage's first big-league hit?

As a Texas Ranger, he hit a grand slam off Angel Bill Singer—The Singer Throwing Machine—on June 20, 1975.

"One season, I hit six grand slams. Three times, I hit at least 30 home runs in a season. Although I played for 12 seasons and was an All-Star during 6 of them, I never hit another grand slam. Who am I?"

Don Mattingly of the Yankees. His six grand slams all came in 1987, when he hit 30 homers.

Which batting champion once led the American League in ERA?

Babe Ruth. As a Red Sox pitcher in 1916, his record was 23-12, and he pitched to a league-leading ERA of 1.75. Ruth was the American League batting champion in 1924, with a .378 average.

Who hit the most home runs in the 1950s?

Duke Snider of the Dodgers, with 326.

How many batting titles did Willie Mays win?

Only one—in 1954, when he hit .345.

Only four righties have won four or more battling titles in the National League since 1900. Three are Hall of Famers Honus Wagner (8), Rogers Hornsby (7), and Roberto Clemente (4). Who is the fourth?

Bill Madlock (4).

Who had the most at bats without ever hitting a home run?

Tom Oliver (Red Sox, 1930–1933): 1,931 at bats, no homers.

Al Bridwell (shortstop, 1905–1915) had over 3,600 at bats before hitting his first home run on April 30, 1913. He hit just one more in his career (in 1914): 4,169 at bats, two home runs.

Which Hall of Famer has the most career at bats without ever hitting a home run?

"Iron Man" Joe McGinnity. During his 10-year career (1899–1908), mostly with the Giants, he came to bat 1,297 times, hit .194 (not bad for a pitcher), but never connected for a homer.

Waite Hoyt is a close second, with 1,287 at bats and no homers.

Who is the only American Leaguer to drive in fewer than 40 runs in the same year in which he won the batting championship?

"Pistol" Pete Runnels, 1960 Red Sox. He led the league with a .320 average, but drove in only 35 runs.

SWITCH-HITTING DOES NOT ALWAYS HELP DEPARTMENT

Only one switch-hitter has won a league batting title three times. Who was he?

Pete Rose, Reds, 1968 (.335), 1969 (.348), and 1973 (.338).

Who has the most lifetime home runs for a player whose last name begins with the letter *Q*?

Jamie Quirk, with 43. He played for Kansas City, Milwaukee, St. Louis, Cleveland, the Yankees, Oakland, and Baltimore from 1975 to 1992.

Of the thousands of men who have played in the majors and minors, who hit the most home runs in one season?

Joe Bauman, of Roswell, New Mexico, in the Longhorn League. In 1954, he clubbed 72 homers, drove in 224 runs, and hit .400. The 6'5" 240-pounder did not make it to the big leagues.

Who had the longest hitless streak in big-league history?

Pitcher Bob Buhl went 0-for-1962: no hits in 69 at bats for the Cubs and one for the Braves. His career batting average was .089.

Which rookie had the most hits?

Future Hall of Famer Lloyd Waner, 1927 Pirates, with 223!

"Who *is* this kid?"

Who is the only man to win four home run crowns while playing for three different teams?

Reggie Jackson.

YEAR	TEAM	HR
1973	Oakland	32
1975	Oakland	36*
1980	Yankees	41*
1982	California	39*

*Tie.

Who are the last players in the American and National Leagues to win the home run crown three consecutive years?

American League: Harmon Killebrew, Twins, 1962–64.
National League: Mike Schmidt, Phillies, 1974–76.

Who had the most strikeouts the year he won a batting title?

Dave "The Cobra" Parker. With a .338 average for the 1977 Pirates, he struck out 107 times.

Who had the most hits in a decade of the twentieth century?

Rogers Hornsby. Between 1920 and 1929, he had 2,085 hits.

Who led the legendary 1927 Yankees in hits?

Earle Combs, with 231. He hit .356 that year, batting leadoff. Second with 218 was Lou Gehrig, who batted .373. These two Yankees finished 1 and 2 in the league in hits.

Who had the highest lifetime batting average without ever winning a batting title?

Hall of Famer Eddie Collins. His career average, over 25 years, was .333. His high was .369 in 1920, but he finished fifth behind George Sisler of the Browns, who won the American League title that year by hitting .407.

If you had Eddie Collins and 73 points, *you lost*!

In 1922, George Sisler batted .420 to lead the American League. What was his batting average in 1923?

Sisler did not play in 1923—he had double vision as a result of poisonous sinusitis.

Who had the fewest RBIs in the season in which he won the batting title?

Hall of Famer Richie Ashburn, the pride of Tilden, Nebraska. In 1958, the Phillies star, batting leadoff, hit .350—tops in the National League—but had only 33 RBIs. Ernie Banks led the league with 129 RBIs.

Off whom did Roberto Clemente get his 3,000th and final hit on September 30, 1972?

Jon Matlack of the Mets—Clemente hit a double.

What is the lowest RBI total to lead a league?

73—Hi Myers, 1919 Dodgers.

Between 1903 and 1911, the Pirates' Honus Wagner won the batting title every year except 1905 and 1910. Who won in those years?

1905—Cy Seymour, Cincinnati, .377 (Wagner hit .363). 1910—Sherry Magee, Philadelphia, .331 (Wagner hit .320).

Who *are* these guys?

Who was the shortest home run champion?

Hack Wilson. Although he was 5'6", he led the National League in 1926 (21), 1927 (30), 1928 (31), and 1930 (56)—that 56 is still the National League record. Hack weighed 190 pounds, had an 18-inch neck, and wore size 6 shoes.

During his 56-game hitting streak in 1941, Joe DiMaggio scored 56 runs and hit 56 singles. How many RBIs did he collect?

55.

How many grand slams did Roger Maris hit in 1961, when he hit 61 homers?

Although Maris hit 9 three-run homers that year, he did not hit a single grand slam. Thus Maris's claim to the record for Most Home Runs in a Single Season without a Grand Slam should stand for some time.

How many games did the Yankees play that year?

163. One ended in a tie on April 22. Maris did not homer in that game.

How many games did Maris actually play in that year?

161.

Who won the American League batting championship in 1906, the year before Ty Cobb's first of 12 batting crowns?

George Stone, who hit .358 for the St. Louis Browns.

How many batting titles did Lou Gehrig win?

Only one—in 1934, his Triple Crown year, when he batted .363. Charlie Gehringer of the Tigers was second with an average of .356.

What are the odds of two men, *whose last names start with the same five letters,* finishing 1 and 2 in the batting race? And what if Henry Gehring, a pitcher who retired in 1908, had still been playing in 1934!

But one year, two men whose names started and ended with the same *four* letters did finish 1 and 2. Who were they?

Matty and Felipe Alou. In 1966, they came in 1 and 2 in the National League batting race. Matty, with the Pirates, hit .342, and Felipe, of the Braves, hit .327.

Between 1907 and 1919, Ty Cobb won 12 batting titles, including 9 in a row (1907–1915). In 1916, although he batted .371, he did not win. Who did?

Tris Speaker of Cleveland, hitting .386.

What was Ty Cobb's lowest batting average for a full season?

.324, in 1908—but, oddly in an era of high averages, it was still good enough to lead the league.

In 1930, Hack Wilson had one of the greatest years in the history of the game—56 homers (still the National League record), 190 RBIs (still the major-league record), and a .356 batting average.

What kind of year did Wilson have in 1931?

Lousy—112 games, 61 RBIs, 13 homers, and a .261 batting average. In fact, his drops from 190 RBIs to 61 (a difference of 129) and from 56 home runs to just 13 (a drop of 43) are the largest single-season declines ever.

Who are the last two switch-hitters to lead the National League in home runs?

Howard Johnson, 1991 Mets, with 38, and Ripper Collins, 1934 Cardinals, with 35.

What did Joe DiMaggio do in his first big-league at bat?

Grounded out to Browns' third baseman Harlond Clift, May 3, 1936.

Who is the only man to walk twice in an inning *four times*?

George "Twinkletoes" Selkirk of the Yankees.

Who hit the most home runs in his final season?

Dave Kingman. In 1986 with Oakland, he batted .210 and drove in 94 runs with 35 home runs and 118 hits.

Kingman, whose dog was named "Homer," will also retire the title for most home runs in a career (442) for someone who is not, *and will never be,* in the Hall of Fame. No friend of the media, he once gave a female reporter a gift-wrapped dead rat.

Only one man has hit 50 or more home runs for a last-place club. Who is he?

Ralph Kiner, 1947 Pirates (51).

What was the count when Boston's Tracy Stallard gave up Roger Maris's 61st home run on October 1, 1961?

2 and 0.

What modern player has the most hits without ever appearing in a World Series?

Rod Carew—3,053.

What did Frank Robinson do his first day as manager of the Cleveland Indians, April 7, 1975?

He inserted himself in the lineup and hit a home run to help his team to a 5-3 win over the Yankees.

He came to bat twice in his entire one-day major-league career—and had two triples. Who is he?

Ed Irvin, an amateur replacement for the Tigers on May 18, 1912, when the entire regular team struck in sympathy with Ty Cobb, who had been suspended for assaulting a fan at a game.

Who stopped the longest consecutive-game hitting streak in Joe DiMaggio's professional career?

> *Hint: It was not Ken Keltner, Jim Bagby, or Al Smith of the Indians in 1941.*

Ed Walsh Jr.—son of the Hall of Fame White Sox pitcher—stopped DiMaggio's *61*-game hitting streak on July 26, 1933. It was after Walsh's own four-year major-league career had ended, when the 18-year-old DiMaggio was with the San Francisco Seals in the Pacific Coast League.

Who is the only man to win batting titles in his first two full seasons?

Tony Oliva, Twins, 1964 (.323) and 1965 (.321). Oliva came up to the Twins in 1962, but played only nine games. He played another seven in 1963, so he was still considered a rookie in 1964. Injuries curtailed what would have been a brilliant career.

Who hit the first pinch-hit home run in World Series history?

Yogi Berra, pinch-hitting for Sherm Lollar in Game 3 (vs. Brooklyn), October 2, 1947, off Ralph Branca in the seventh inning. (The Yankees eventually lost that game 9-8.)

Among the other World Series records held by Yogi Berra:

Most Series played	14
Most consecutive Series played	5*
Most Series as a catcher	12
Most games	75
Most at bats	259
Most hits	71
Most times hit by pitch in a World Series career	3*
Most times hit by pitch in a game	2*
Most singles	49
Most doubles	10*

*Tie.

Does Yogi's son Dale (infielder, 1977–1987, .236 batting average, 49 homers) hold any records?

Yes. He holds the National League single-season record for reaching base the most times through catcher's interference—seven, set with Pittsburgh in 1983. Dale did it 18 times in his career, #2 behind Pete Rose, who did it 29 times.

Ironic, isn't it, that Yogi Berra's son holds a record involving *bad* catching?

Who is the only player to win the home run, RBI, and batting titles more than twice?

Ted Williams. He was home run champ in 1941, 1942, 1947, and 1949. He led the league in RBIs in 1939 (his rookie season!), 1942, 1947, and 1949. He was the batting leader in consecutive years three times: 1941–1942, 1947–1948, and 1957–1958.

Who was the oldest player to collect 3,000 hits?

Cap Anson. The Cubs star was 45 when he singled off Baltimore Orioles' pitcher Bill Hoffer on July 18, 1897.

The oldest player to get 3,000 hits in the twentieth century is Dave Winfield. He was 41 on September 16, 1993, when, as a Blue Jay, he singled off Dennis Eckersley of the Oakland A's.

Who was the youngest?

Ty Cobb. He was 34 when he got his 3,000th hit on August 19, 1921, off Elmer Myers of the Red Sox.

Only three players hit their 500th home runs before they were 35. Who are they?

Babe Ruth, 34 (August 11, 1929), Willie Mays, 34 (September 13, 1965), and Hank Aaron, 34 (July 14, 1968).

For four consecutive years, he had over 200 hits and 100 walks. No one else has ever done that. Who is he?

Wade Boggs of the Red Sox.

	HITS	WALKS
1986	207	105
1987	200	105
1988	214	125
1989	205	107

Lou Gehrig had at least 200 hits and 100 walks in a season eight times, but never four consecutively.

Who is the only batter to hit 50 home runs in a season before September?

Roger Maris, Yankees. He hit #50 off Angel Ken McBride on August 22, 1961. (Yet in April of that banner year, Maris hit only one home run, that one off Tiger Paul Foytack.)

He is the only Yankee to win two batting titles—and he did it in consecutive years. Who is he?

Joe DiMaggio, of course—in 1939, batting .381, and in 1940, batting .352.

Who won batting titles separated by the most years?

Ted Williams. He won in 1941 (.406) and in 1958 (.328).

Who are the only two hitters to lead their league in hits during their first three years?

Johnny Pesky and Tony Oliva.

Pesky, of the Red Sox, led the American League in hits in 1942, with 205, 1946, (his next year) with 208, and 1947, with 207.

Oliva, of the Twins, led the American League in hits in his three first full years—1964 (217), 1965 (185), and 1966 (191).

Who is the oldest man to win a batting title?

Ted Williams. At 40, he batted .328 to win the American League title in 1958.

Is that question too easy? Okay, who was the second oldest?

Ted Williams. The year before (1957), at age 39, he batted .388 to win the AL batting title.

In how many seasons did Hank Aaron hit exactly 44 home runs?

Aaron, who wore #44, did it four times, in 1957, 1963, 1966, and 1969.

In each of these years, two different players got their 3,000th hits. Here are the years: 1914, 1925, 1970, 1979, 1992. Who are the players?

1914	Honus Wagner, Nap Lajoie
1925	Tris Speaker, Eddie Collins
1970	Hank Aaron, Willie Mays
1979	Lou Brock, Carl Yastrzemski
1992	Robin Yount, George Brett

Only two American League third basemen (over 100 games at third base) have hit 40 or more home runs in a season. Who are they?

Al Rosen and Harmon Killebrew. In 1953, Al "Flip" Rosen (a member of the Jewish Sports Hall of Fame in Netanya, Israel) hit 43 homers for the Indians.

Killebrew did it three times, hitting 42 for the Senators in 1959, 49 for the Twins in 1969, and 41 in 1970.

Who are the only two National Leaguers to hit at least 40 home runs a year for five consecutive seasons?

Ralph Kiner (1947–51) and Duke Snider (1953–57).

Who is the youngest man to hit 100 major-league home runs?

Mel Ott. According to the Mel Ott 1949 Society, he hit his 100th career homer on July 12, 1931, when he was 22 years, four months old.

Who is the only batting champion to bat right-handed and throw left-handed?

Hal Chase, .339, for the 1916 Reds.

Thanks to Barry Halper for the previous question.

He is the only man to win batting titles in four successive odd-numbered years. Who is he?

Harry Heilmann, Tigers, in 1921, 1923, 1925, and 1927.

How many modern players have led the league in walks, stolen bases, RBIs, and hits in the same season?

None. This is an achievement waiting to be claimed.

What's the closest Joe DiMaggio ever came to hitting .400?

Sorry, this is a trick question. The operative word here is *ever*. In 1935, when he was with the San Francisco Seals in the Pacific Coast League, DiMaggio hit .398, but did not lead the league *or even the city*. Oscar "Ox" Eckhardt hit .399 for the San Francisco Missions.

Surprisingly, although he was considered a minor-league star, Eckhardt played only 24 games in the majors for the Braves and Dodgers in 1932 and 1936. He finished with a major-league career batting average of just .192.

How many home run titles did Carl Yastrzemski win?

One. In 1967, his Triple Crown year, he hit 44 to tie for the title with Harmon Killebrew.

Who is the only .400 hitter who never played in the minor leagues?

George Sisler. He hit .407 in 1920 and .420 in 1922 for the Browns.

Who is the only Mexican-born batting champion?

Bobby Avila of Veracruz, who hit .341 in 1954 for Cleveland.

He hit 30 or more home runs 12 years in a row—the only man to do so. Who was he?

Jimmie Foxx. His 30+-homer seasons were 1929–1940.

Who were the six Milwaukee Braves who, in 1965, hit at least 20 home runs?

Hank Aaron (32), Eddie Mathews (32), Mack Jones (31), Joe Torre (27), Felipe Alou (23), Gene Oliver (21).

Similarly, who were the six 1961 Yankees who hit over 20 homers?

Roger Maris (61), Mickey Mantle (54), Moose Skowron (28), Yogi Berra (22), Johnny Blanchard (the third-string catcher, 21), Elston Howard (21).

He hit 10 home runs in his first 77 at bats—the most home runs in the fewest at bats for a rookie. Who was he?

Yankee Kevin Maas, who hit #10 on August 2, 1990. He never again reached that level of success and finished his career in 1995 with 65 home runs.

Who is the first National Leaguer to hit 300 home runs?

Mel Ott, who reached that plateau with the New York Giants in 1937.

Who is the first pitcher to hit two home runs in a game twice in one season?

Wes Ferrell, Red Sox, on July 13 and August 22, 1934.

What's the highest batting average in the National League since Bill Terry hit .401 for the 1930 Giants?

Many will question its validity, but in the strike-shortened 1994 season, San Diego's Tony Gwynn hit .394.

Al Kaline of the Tigers finished his 22-year Hall of Fame career with 3,007 hits and 399 homers. In how many seasons did he hit 30 or more homers?

None. The most home runs he ever had in a season was 29, in 1962 and 1966.

In 1930, Chuck Klein of the Phillies belted 250 hits and drove in 170 runs. Did he lead the National League in either category?

No. Bill Terry had 254 hits, and Hack Wilson drove in a still-unmatched record of 190 RBIs. Klein's 170 RBIs in a single season still stands as the highest number of RBIs in a season that did not lead the league.

How many modern players have led their leagues in homers, triples, and doubles in the same season?

None. But James Edward "Tip" O'Neill of the old St. Louis Browns in the American Association (then a major league) accomplished this feat in 1887: 14 homers, 19 triples, 52 doubles.

Another record waiting to be claimed by a modern player.

Who hit the most career inside-the-park home runs?

Hall of Famer "Wahoo" Sam Crawford—50.

Stan Musial smacked 475 homers. How many home run titles did he win?

None. His 475 homers came at a rate of more than 21 per year for 22 years. He won the batting title seven times, and had over 30 homers in a season six times. The only time Musial hit more than 39 homers, however, was in 1948, one of his best years. Ralph Kiner of the Pirates and Johnny Mize of the Giants each hit 40 that year.

His 9 home runs were enough to lead the National League one year; yet during his entire career he hit only 10. Who was he?

Fred Odwell, Reds. In 1904 he had one homer; then he "erupted" for nine in 1905. He was with the Reds again in 1906 and 1907, but never connected for another home run in his 1,412 at bats.

Who is the only man to hit .400 with 20 or more home runs in each of three seasons?

Rogers Hornsby (1922, 1924, 1925).

Who was the first man to get two hits in one inning twice in the same game?

Max Carey, Pirates, June 22, 1925, first and eighth innings against the Cardinals in St. Louis. The Pirates won 24-6.

On July 23, 1957, off White Sox pitcher Bob Keegan, Mickey Mantle whacked a home run that hit a seat two rows from the top of the bleachers in Yankee Stadium. What else did Mantle do that day?

For the only time in his career, he hit for the cycle.

Who is the only American League shortstop to win two batting crowns?

Luke Appling of the White Sox, in 1936 (.388) and 1943 (.328).

When Hank Aaron got his 3,000th hit, on May 17, 1970, in Cincinnati, the only other living member of the 3,000-hit club was there. Who was he?

Stan Musial.

Long before his managerial career started, Davey Johnson was a power-hitting second baseman for the Braves and Orioles. In fact, he blasted 42 homers for Atlanta in 1973. How many triples did he have that year?

None.

Who is the only man to win a batting championship without hitting even a single triple?

Slow-footed Ernie Lombardi, Boston Braves, .330, 1942.

When was the first All-Star game with no extra-base hits?

In 1958. The teams combined for 13 singles as the American League triumphed 4-3.

Who is the first American Leaguer to drive in over 100 runs in his first two seasons?

Al Simmons. In fact, he drove in over 100 runs in each of his first 11 seasons.

Who hit the most home runs without being in a World Series?

Ernie Banks, 512.

Name the only men to have 100 RBIs, score 100 runs, hit 20 homers, walk 100 times, and bat .300—all for four years in a row.

Lou Gehrig (1934–37), Ted Williams (1941–42, 1946–49—his career interrupted by World War II service), and Frank Thomas (1991–96).

Who is the only man to play over 1,000 games as a DH and at least 1,000 games at a position?

Harold Baines. Through 1996, he played 1,060 games in the outfield, plus another 1,218 as DH.

Who was the first big leaguer since 1900 to smack 14 hits in three consecutive games?

Mike Benjamin of the Giants. June 11–14, 1995, he went 14-for-18 for the three games. But this hit barrage may have been a fluke. Benjamin finished the season with a .220 batting average.

In the history of the game, only two men have driven in at least 75 runs 19 years in a row. Who were they?

Hank Aaron and Eddie Murray.

Surprisingly for such a powerful RBI producer, the only season in which Murray led the league in RBIs was the strike-shortened 1981 campaign, when he drove in 78 with the Orioles.

Name the best-hitting outfield since 1900.

The 1925 Tigers, led by Hall of Famers Harry Heilmann in right field (.393, tops in the American League) and Ty Cobb (.378) in center field. Absalom "Al" Wingo (.370) played left field. Their combined batting average was

.382. Nevertheless, Detroit finished in fourth place (81-73) behind the Washington Senators (96-55).

Who is the only man to play at least 10 games at five different positions *in one season*?

Not Harmon Killebrew and not Pete Rose. The answer is Tony Phillips of the 1991 Detroit Tigers. He played 36 games at second base, 46 at third base, 13 at shortstop, 56 in the outfield, and 18 as the designated hitter.

Who are the only three players with at least 250 homers, 2,500 hits, and 250 stolen bases?

Andre Dawson, Willie Mays, and Vada Pinson.

	HOMERS	HITS	STOLEN BASES
Mays	660	3,283	338
Pinson	256	2,757	305
Dawson	438	2,774	314

Only one man has had more RBIs than games played in a full season since Joe DiMaggio did it in 1948 (155 RBIs, 153 games). Who was he?

Ted Williams, 1949: 155 games, 159 RBIs.

What was Mickey Mantle's salary in 1956, the year he won the Triple Crown with a .356 batting average, 52 homers, and 130 RBIs to go with his 132 runs, 376 total bases, and .705 slugging average?

$32,500–$86.40 per base, $625 per home run, and $246 per run scored.

Which players with at least 3,000 hits never had a 200-hit season?

Cap Anson, Dave Winfield, Carl Yastrzemski, and Eddie Murray.

Who is the first American Leaguer to hit five home runs in two consecutive games—*twice*?

Oakland's Mark McGwire. On June 17, 1987, he hit three homers, and the next day two more (against Cleveland). On June 10, 1995, he hit two and then smacked three more the next day (against Boston).

On July 28, 1994, Todd Haney of the Cubs hit his first major-league home run. When did he hit #2?

July 28, 1995.

Who hit the most home runs in one stadium?

Mel Ott—323 (of his 511) at the Giants' home, the Polo Grounds, where Ott played for his entire 22-year Hall of Fame career.

When Hack Wilson hit 56 home runs for the 1930 Cubs, whose National League record did he break?

Chuck Klein's. Klein hit 43 for the Phillies in 1929.

On August 26, 1930, when Wilson hit his 42nd, 43rd, and record 44th homers, he hit them in Philadelphia, all over the head of the right fielder—Chuck Klein!

Which player has broken up the most no-hitters with home runs?

Sorry, another trick question. Through the 1997 season, Rickey Henderson hit 72 leadoff home runs, more than anybody in history.

Name five Italian-Americans who have hit at least 40 home runs in a single season.

	TEAM	YEAR	HOME RUNS
Roy Campanella	Dodgers	1953	41
Rocky Colavito	Indians	1958	41
	Indians	1959	42
	Indians	1961	45
Joe DiMaggio	Yankees	1937	46
Jim Gentile	Orioles	1961	46
Rico Petrocelli	Red Sox	1969	40

How many home runs did the White Sox hit in 1908?

Three. Hall of Fame pitcher Big Ed Walsh, Frank Isbell, and Fielder Jones tied for the team home-run lead, with one each.

Nobody had more at bats as a pinch hitter. He had almost enough pinch hits to match his name. Who was he?

Greg Gross. During his 17 years with the Astros, Cubs, and Phillies (1973–89), he batted as a pinch hitter a record 588 times and amassed 143 pinch hits—one short of a gross.

During his illustrious career, Ted Williams clouted 521 home runs. How many were inside-the-parkers?

Just one, which occurred in Cleveland on Friday, September 13, 1946, in the first inning, with two outs and a 3-1 count. With the Indians in a "Boudreau shift," moving virtually all the fielders to the right side against the pulling Williams, Ted punched a Red Embree pitch through the left side. The run proved decisive not only in the game, which the Red Sox won 1-0, but also in clinching the American League pennant for Boston—their first since 1918. Tex Hughson was the winning pitcher, and Embree took the loss.

Which brothers had the highest combined career batting average?

Through the 1997 season, Tony and Chris Gwynn combined for a .331 lifetime average, six points ahead of the Waners and seven ahead of the Delahantys.

Only five position players in the Hall of Fame were switch-hitters. Which five?

Mickey Mantle, Frankie Frisch, Max Carey, Red Schoendienst, and Dave Bancroft. Eddie Murray and Pete Rose may join this list someday.

The first time it happened was on June 11, 1963, during a Boston-Detroit game. It didn't happen again until June 16, 1995, in a Mets-Astros game. What was it?

Batters hitting back-to-back home runs past the 14th inning. Boston's Frank Malzone and Dick Stuart did it in Detroit in 1963, and Houston's Brian Hunter and Craig Biggio did it at Shea Stadium 32 years later.

In 1995, Jay Buhner of the Mariners set an incredible single-season record by driving in 121 runs with just 123 hits—the highest ratio ever by a player with over 100 hits.

Only two other active players are among the top 25 in RBIs-per-hit ratio for a single season. Name them.

In 1990, Mark McGwire of the A's cracked the top 25 list with 108 RBIs and 123 hits (.88).

Joe Carter of the 1994 Blue Jays had 103 RBIs on 118 hits (.87).

In 1995, McGwire had a higher *ratio* (90 RBIs/87 hits), but less than 100 hits.

Would you want him on your team if in one game he hit into a triple play and two double plays and struck out—accounting for eight outs in four at bats?

Yes. His name is Stan Musial.

Who is the first man to hit home runs from both sides of the plate in a post-season game?

Mickey Mantle? No. Roy White? No. Not Eddie Murray, either. The answer is Bernie Williams of the Yankees. He hit solo shots off Randy Johnson and Bill Risley of Seattle on October 6, 1995, at the Kingdome, in Game 3 of the first American League Division Series. The Mariners won the game 7-4 and went on to win the Series.

Who was the last pitcher to smack five hits in a single game?

Mel Stottlemyre Sr., on September 26, 1964, when he had a double and four singles. And because he did it for the Yankees in the American League, where, with today's designated hitter, the pitcher rarely bats, even if a National Leaguer should surpass this record, Stottlemyre will probably remain the last American League pitcher with five hits in a game. In 1964, Stottlemyre hit .243, the highest in his 11-year career.

In contrast to modern sluggers like Mickey Mantle, Willie Stargell, and Reggie Jackson, who hit lots of home runs but paid for them with lots of strikeouts, this batter led the league in home runs and in *fewest* strikeouts *in the same season.* Who was he?

Tommy Holmes. In 1945 for the Boston Braves, in 636 at bats, he hit 28 home runs but struck out only nine times, ending the season with a .352 batting average and a league-leading .577 slugging average.

Only two men have hit at least 40 home runs in a single season while batting under .250. Who are they?

Hint: One of them—a Hall of Famer—did it twice.

Harmon Killebrew, Twins. In 1959, he had 42 homers to go with his .242 batting average. In 1962, he had 48 homers and hit .243.

In 1979, the Brewers' "Stormin'" Gorman Thomas hit 45 homers and batted just .244.

Who was the first man to hit at least 40 home runs while driving in fewer than 100 RBIs?

Duke Snider of the Brooklyn Dodgers, in 1957, with 40 homers and 92 RBIs.

Who was the first man to have 200 hits in a single season in each league?

George Sisler: 1920—257 hits with the Browns; 1929—205 hits with the Boston Braves. Sisler had 200+ hits in six different seasons.

Who is the first man to hit three homers in a game three times?

Lou Gehrig. He did it for the third time on May 4, 1929, with the Yankees.

Which players hit at least 250 home runs and stole at least 300 bases?

Barry Bonds, Bobby Bonds, Andre Dawson, Willie Mays, Joe Morgan, and Vada Pinson.

Which National Leaguer, appearing in at least 150 games, hit the fewest singles in one season?

Who cares? He can't hit, right?

Wrong. The answer is Mike Schmidt, who had only 63 singles in 1979, while smacking 25 doubles, 4 triples, and 45 homers. He also walked a league-leading 120 times and batted .253.

During his 11-year career (1974–1985) with the Indians and Giants, Duane Kuiper came to bat 3,379 times. His lifetime batting average was .270.
How many home runs did he hit?

Only one, off Steve Stone of the White Sox on August 29, 1977.

Only three switch-hitters besides Mickey Mantle have ever hit 35 home runs in a single season. (Mantle did it six times). Name the others.

Ripper Collins, Cardinals, 1934 (35); Ken Singleton, Orioles, 1979 (35); Howard Johnson, Mets, 1987 (36), 1989 (36), 1991 (38).

Of the 15 men who hit more than 500 career home runs, who hit the most career triples?

Willie Mays, with 140, with Babe Ruth a close second with 136. Willie also had the most triples in a single season—20 in 1957.

Who is the only man to win a batting title by bunting for a single in his last at bat of the season?

Pete Rose, Reds, September 29, 1968, at home against the Giants. His bunt came off Ray Sadecki. He finished at .335.

Rose edged Matty Alou (Pittsburgh), who finished the season at .332, and Matty's older brother Felipe (Atlanta), who finished at .317.

ONE OF THESE DAYS, POW DEPARTMENT

Johnny Cooney played in the majors from 1921 to 1944 with the Braves, Dodgers, and Yankees, first as a pitcher, then amassing 965 hits in 1,172 games (3,372 at bats) without hitting a home run.

Finally, *finally*, after 15 years in the big leagues, he hit one on September 24, 1939, while with the Braves, off Harry Gumbert of the Giants.
When did he hit his next homer?

The next day, in the third inning off Giants pitcher Bill Lohrman. The Giants won 6-5.

Although he played another five seasons, these were Cooney's only home runs in the big leagues.

Similarly, Mike LaCoss pitched for 14 years for the Reds, Astros, Royals, and Giants, appearing in 415 games with 481 at bats and a .125 batting average. He had 60 hits, but his only two home runs came in consecutive at bats. The first, while he was with the Giants, came on June 23, 1986, off Dane Iorg, pitching for the Padres in an 18-1 laugher. The next came on June 29 off Tom Browning of the Reds.

In the long history of the game, only three players have smacked at least 20 home runs a season for five different teams. Who were they?

Dave Winfield, Jack Clark, and Bobby Bonds.

Who hit the most home runs in Yankee Stadium?

Mickey Mantle—266. (He hit more—270—on the road. Go figure.) Were you going to say Babe Ruth? Ruth started out with the Red Sox, but even when he came to New York in 1920, the Yankees still played at the Polo Grounds. Ruth did not hit his first home run at Yankee Stadium until the day it opened, April 18, 1923—a three-run blast to help beat the Red Sox.

Ruth hit 259 homers at Yankee Stadium and 243 on the road during his Yankee career.

Name three men who have appeared as DH in at least 1,000 games.

Don Baylor: 1,289
Hal McRae: 1,428
Harold Baines: 1,352 (through 1997)

During his 10-year career as a DH 1982–91, Ron Kittle hit 176 home runs. How many were grand slams?

None.

This Hall of Famer hit over 500 home runs, including four in one game. Yet he hit only seven grand slams in his entire career. Who is he?

Mike Schmidt. Mel Ott also hit over 500 home runs, yet only seven were grand slams.

Only four men in the history of the game have hit at least 200 homers and stolen at least 450 bases. Who are they?

Paul Molitor*	(230, 495)
Rickey Henderson*	(252, 1,231)
Joe Morgan	(268, 689)
Bobby Bonds	(332, 461)

*Through the end of 1997.

Who is the only player in big-league history to drive in at least 100 runs in three consecutive seasons for three different teams?

Joe Carter (1989, Cleveland, 105; 1990, San Diego, 115; 1991, Toronto, 108).

Who hit the most doubles in a single season without stealing a base?

John Olerud, Blue Jays, 1993–54.

Who hit the most triples in a single season without stealing a base?

Big Johnny Mize, who had 16 triples for the 1938 Cardinals without a stolen base.

Who is #2 on that list?

Big Johnny Mize. The very next year, 1939, he hit 14 triples, again without a single stolen base.

Of the 15 men who have hit at least 500 career homers, only one hit #500 off a future Hall of Famer. Who was he?

On July 14, 1967, Eddie Mathews of the Astros hit career home run #500 off Giants pitcher Juan Marichal at Candlestick Park.

One year, this man accounted for 88% of his team's home runs. Who was he?

Babe Ruth. The Red Sox hit 33 homers in 1919, and Ruth had 29 of them.

He had more hits during his first 10 years in the big leagues than anybody else in the history of the game. Who is he?

Kirby Puckett of the Minnesota Twins, with 1,996 hits from 1984 to 1993.

Who is the only man to get his 3,000th hit in a season in which he had 200 hits?

Paul Molitor, who got #3,000 on September 16, 1996, for the Twins in Kansas City, off Jose Rosado. That hit was #211 of 225 hits for Molitor in 1996.

Who is the only member of the 3,000-hit club to triple for his 3,000th hit?

Paul Molitor, Twins, September 16, 1996.

He drove in nine runs in one game, which is the record for most RBIs in a game in which his RBIs were the only runs for his team. Who is he?

Mike Greenwell, Red Sox, September 2, 1996, in a game against the Mariners. He had four hits, including two home runs—one a grand slam—and a double.

Who hit the most triples in a year in which he hit at least 50 home runs?

Babe Ruth, Yankees. In 1921 he slugged 59 home runs and legged out 16 triples.

Which ballplayer used the most bats in his career?

No exact records have been kept, of course, but the answer is probably Orlando Cepeda. He is said to have believed that each bat had only one hit in it, so he discarded a bat after every hit. His 17-year career, with the Giants, Cardinals, Braves, A's, Red Sox, and Royals, included 2,351 hits. Add to that total perhaps a few dozen broken bats, plus bats discarded after fouling out, and the number of bats Cepeda used approaches 2,500.

Ozzie Smith, who retired after the 1996 season, played in the big leagues for 19 years with the Padres and the Cardinals. He was a switch-hitter with not much power.
How many at bats did he have in the big leagues before he hit a homer batting lefty?

Smith's first lefty homer came on October 14, 1985, in the National League Championship Series against the Dodgers—his first lefty home run in 3,009 at bats, including 2,967 as a lefty.

In 1937, only one National Leaguer homered in all eight National League parks. Who?

Big Johnny Mize. Playing for the Cardinals and the Giants in the National League and the Yankees in the American, he homered in each big-league park at least four times in his career.

This Hall of Fame pitcher hit home runs in 6 of his 56 shutouts—the big-league record. Who was he?

Bob Gibson.

Who has the most leadoff homers in a single season?

Brady Anderson, Baltimore Orioles, 12 in 1996.

Who are the only men to pinch-hit for Hank Aaron?

Lee May, Johnny Blanchard, Mike Lum, Johnny Briggs, Marty Pérez, and Mike Hegan.

May pinch-hit for Aaron in the seventh inning in a June 12, 1962, 15-2 drubbing of the Los Angeles Dodgers by the Milwaukee Braves. Aaron had already driven in three runs on three hits, and scored another two.

On September 11, 1965, the Mets were one-hit for the second consecutive game—the first team to reach that nadir in 48 years. The Milwaukee Braves beat them 9-0 at Shea Stadium. Aaron had two hits, stole a base, scored a run, and drove in another before Johnny Blanchard pinch-hit for him.

On May 29, 1969, in Atlanta, versus the Mets, the Braves were up 12-0 in the seventh. Lum was sent in for Aaron by another Lum—Braves manager Lum Harris. He doubled off Al Jackson and stayed in the game to play right field. Atlanta won 15-3.

On September 10, 1973, in the bottom of the third inning against the Giants, Aaron hit his 37th home run of the season, career home run #710. Second baseman Davey Johnson hit his 40th in that game, too.

Aaron did not feel well in the bottom of the fourth inning, and shortstop Marty Pérez (a career .246 hitter with 22 career home runs) was sent up to bat for him.

According to Pérez, "I was on a nine-game-hitting streak but I wasn't playing that day, and Henry was having muscle spasms, so Eddie Mathews [the manager] said 'Marty, get a bat.' P.S. I almost hit a home run to left!"

Thanks to Marty Pérez for this exclusive personal account of an unforgettable experience—pinch-hitting for Hank Aaron.

Johnny Briggs pinch-hit for Aaron on June 1, 1975, in the second game of a Milwaukee–Kansas City doubleheader. Kansas City won 11-5.

Finally, Mike Hegan pinch-hit for Aaron on July 8, 1975.

All of the men who had the distinction of pinch-hitting for Aaron batted lefty.

Thanks to SABR's David Smith and David Vincent (co-author of *SABR Presents the Home Run Encyclopedia*) for information on these unforgettable at bats.

On September 7, 1996, Scott Rolen of the Phillies came to bat in the bottom of the third inning against the Cubs. He was completing a so-so first season, batting only .254.

With 130 at bats, one more would be one at bat too many to qualify Rolen for Rookie of the Year consideration in 1997.

What happened in that last at bat?

Rolen's right arm was broken by a Steve Trachsel pitch. Thus his last plate appearance of the season was an HBP (hit by pitcher), *not* an official at bat. As it happened, Rolen recovered sufficiently to be named the National League's Rookie of the Year in 1997!

Name three Hanks who hit at least 40 homers in a single season. The first two are easy.

Hank Aaron, Hank Greenberg, and Hank Sauer (1954–41).

Although many others have done it, only one New York Yankee has ever hit a home run in his first big-league at bat. Who was he?

John Miller, September 11, 1966, off Lee "Stinger" Stange of the Red Sox. In fact, that was Miller's only homer for the Yankees. And in the American League. And for three years. His only other home run was in his last big-league at bat on September 23, 1969, for the Dodgers.

The 1927 Pittsburgh Pirates had three players (including two future Hall of Famers) who drove in over 100 runs on fewer than 10 home runs in one season. Who are they?

Pie Traynor (five home runs, 106 RBIs), Paul Waner (nine home runs, 131 RBIs), and Glenn Wright (nine home runs, 105 RBIs).

Name all the players who have hit 50 home runs and stolen at least 20 bases in a single season.

Willie Mays, Giants, 1955: 51 home runs, 24 stolen bases. Despite Mays's great season, the Giants finished third, 18½ games behind the Dodgers.

Brady Anderson, Orioles, 1996: 50 home runs, 21 stolen bases. Anderson just made it into the club. He hit #50 on September 29, 1996—the last day of the season.

List four players named Williams who have hit 40 homers in a single season.

Cy Williams, Phillies, 1923 (41)
Ted Williams, Red Sox, 1949 (43)
Billy Williams, Cubs, 1970 (42)
Matt Williams, Giants, 1994 (43)

Of the eight men who have hit at least .400 since 1901, how many led their teams to first-place finishes?

None.

Which Hall of Famer drove in the most runs in his first six big-league seasons?

Joe DiMaggio, with 816 (1936–1941).

Who is the only National Leaguer to drive in over 150 runs in a season *twice*?

Hint: He did it in consecutive years.

Hack Wilson, Cubs: in 1929, 159; in 1930, 190 (still the big-league record after 60+ years, and probably unassailable).

Who is the first man to hit 30 home runs in one season in both leagues?

Dick Stuart—"Dr. Strangeglove": Pirates, 1961, 35 homers; Red Sox, 1963, 42.

Who was the first man to play over 100 games in a single season and have more RBIs than games played?

Hint: He did it twice.

Ken Williams, Browns: 1922—153 games, 155 RBIs; 1925—102 games, 105 RBIs.

Babe Ruth, Jimmie Foxx, Lou Gehrig, and Joe DiMaggio have also accomplished this incredible show of power. When Hack Wilson drove in his record 190 runs in 1930, he played in 155 games—35 more RBIs than games played.

Who had the most big-league at bats in a career without a triple?

Craig Worthington—1,234 (1988–1996, Baltimore, Cleveland, Cincinnati, Texas). He did manage 50 doubles and 33 home runs.

Hall of Famers Gaylord Perry (1,076 at bats), Sandy Koufax (776), Whitey Ford (1,023), and Lefty Gomez (904) likewise never tripled. But they were all pitchers. Koufax never tripled? Not surprising: he had only 75 hits in 12 years.

Who had the most at bats without ever driving in even a single run?

Pitcher Rickey Clark (Angels, 1967–1972), who had 126 at bats and no RBIs.

Which position player had the most at bats without an RBI?

Gene Good, 119 at bats, 0 RBIs. An outfielder with the 1906 Boston Braves, he obviously did not live up to his name.

Who had the most at bats without ever hitting a double?

Pitcher Jim Deshaies—373 at bats (1985–1995, Yankees, Houston, San Diego, San Francisco, Philadelphia).

A number of players have hit over 40 homers in a single season, and many have had over 200 hits in a season. But only one man has hit 40 homers and had 200 hits in a season *five different times*. Who is he?

Lou Gehrig (1927, 1930, 1931, 1934, 1936).

In his march to 3,000 hits, Eddie Murray reached two unusual milestones: his very first hit and his 500th were both off pitchers born in the same European country. Which pitchers and which country?

First hit, April 7, 1977 off Bert Blyleven of the Rangers; 500th, September 9, 1979, off Wilhemus "Win" Remmerswaal of the Red Sox. Both are from the Netherlands (where it's not "baseball"—it's "honkball"). Remmerswaal is from The Hague, and Blyleven is from Zeist.

Who is the first man to lead his league in home runs, triples, and RBIs the same season?

Jim Rice (the pride of Anderson, South Carolina), Red Sox, 1978: 46 homers, 15 triples, and 139 RBIs. Rice also led the American League with 213 hits and a .600 slugging percentage.

Mike Tresh, father of 1962 American League Rookie of the Year Tom Tresh, holds a record nobody would envy. What is it?

Most years between home runs. He hit his first with the White Sox on May 19, 1940, off Dutch Leonard of the Washington Senators, in Chicago. Tresh's second—and final—homer came on Opening Day, April 20, 1948, in the seventh inning when he clubbed one into the left-field stands at Comiskey Park off Detroit's Hal Newhouser. The Tigers won 5-2, but Tresh's eight-year wait for his second home run had ended.

Mark Sagmoen's first hit in the big leagues (April 18, 1997, for the Rangers) was a home run—notable, but not really rare. What made this homer so unusual?

It was an inside-the-parker. Only three other big leaguers have hit inside-the-park home runs for their first hits:

Butch Henry, Astros, May 8, 1992, off Doug Drabek of the Pirates. It was the only home run of Henry's career.

Johnny LeMaster of the Giants, in his first big-league at bat, off Dodger Don Sutton September 2, 1975.

Brian Downing, White Sox, August 11, 1973, off Mickey Lolich of the Tigers.

Only one man in the history of baseball has accumulated 400 total bases in five different seasons. Who is he?

Lou Gehrig: 1927—447; 1930—419; 1931—410; 1934—409; 1936—403.

Who hit the most home runs in two consecutive months?

Albert Belle. During August and September 1995, he hit 31 homers for the Cleveland Indians.

Who hit the most career home runs in New York City?

Babe Ruth—334 at the Polo Grounds and Yankee Stadium.

Were you going to say Mickey Mantle? Sorry, he hit only 266 at home. What about Lou Gehrig? He hit only 251 at Yankee Stadium. And Mel Ott hit a mere 323 at the Polo Grounds.

Who is the only man to win the Triple Crown in his hometown?

Lou Gehrig, 1934 Yankees. The Manhattan native led the American League with a .363 batting average, 49 homers, and 165 RBIs.

FIRST OF ALL

Who had the first "Day" set aside in his honor?

Harry Wright, on "Harry Wright Day" held on April 13, 1896. Funds were raised at National League parks for a monument to the future Hall of Famer, who died of pneumonia on October 3, 1895. (Bad weather limited the total to $3,349.) The monument was dedicated on June 26, 1897, at Wright's gravesite in the West Laurel Hill Cemetery, Bala Cynwyd, Pennsylvania.*

Who is the first man to lead off four consecutive games with a home run?

Hint: It wasn't Rickey Henderson.

Brady Anderson of the Orioles. He did it against the Red Sox—his former team—at home on April 18, 1996, then at Texas on April 19, 20, and 21.

Who is the first rookie to start in an All-Star game?

Joe DiMaggio, 1936. His American League team lost 4-3 at Boston's Braves Field to the National Leaguers, in a game that saw 16 hits.

*For a fascinating article about the Harry Wright monument, see "A Monument for Harry Wright" by Jerrold Casway, in SABR's *The National Pastime, A Review of Baseball History*, #17, 1997, p. 35.

Which team has the dubious distinction of being the first to transport a relief pitcher from the bullpen to the mound by vehicle?

The Milwaukee Braves. On June 23, 1958, Don McMahon was transported by a chauffeur-driven motor scooter. He saved a 7-0 blanking of the Giants.

Who was the first foreign-born player in the World Series?

Olaf Henriksen. He played for the Red Sox in the 1912 Series and doubled in his only at bat. (Although he was born in Kirkerup, Denmark, his nickname was "Swede," in the same way, perhaps, that slow runners are called "Flash," big guys "Tiny," quiet guys "Gabby," or bald guys "Curly." For further research, visit Christy Mathewson's birthplace in Factoryville, Pennsylvania, which has no factories.)

When was the first All-Star game?

July 6, 1933, at Chicago's Comiskey Park? No! It actually took place on May 29, 1892, when the Hub Collins benefit game was played at Brooklyn's Eastern Park. Collins, a former ballplayer, had died of typhoid fever on May 21. The game was a contest between the St. Louis Browns of the American Association and the Brooklyn Bridegrooms (Collins' team). It featured future Hall of Famers John Montgomery Ward, Charlie Comiskey, and Dan Brouthers, among others, and raised $2,804.90 for Collins's widow.

The first true All-Star game (matching stars from different teams) was July 24, 1911. This was a fundraiser in Cleveland to help raise money for Addie Joss's widow. (Joss had died of tubercular meningitis on April 14, 1911, and although he played in the major leagues for only nine years—all with Cleveland—his spectacular pitching achievements led the Veterans Committee to waive the 10-year rule, voting him into the Hall of Fame in 1978.) The 15,281 fans contributed $12,931 to watch an American League All-Star team (including Hal Chase, Home Run Baker, Eddie Collins, Tris Speaker, Bobby Wallace, Walter Johnson, and Sam Crawford) defeat a Cleveland team featuring Joe Jackson, Nap Lajoie, and Ty Cobb. The All-Stars won 5-3.

Who was the first pitcher to be named Most Valuable Player and win the Cy Young Award in the same year?

Don Newcombe of the Dodgers, in 1956. That year there was only one Cy Young Award—given for both leagues combined.

Who was the first man to play on a team that was no-hit twice in a single season and then to manage a team that suffered the same fate?

Don Baylor. He was with the Angels in 1977 when they were no-hit by Dennis Eckersley of the Indians on May 30 and by Bert Blyleven of the Rangers on September 22.

With Baylor managing, the 1996 Rockies suffered no-hitters by Al Leiter of the Marlins in Florida on May 11 and by Hideo Nomo of the Dodgers at Coors Field on September 17.

Who was the first American Legion ballplayer to reach the Hall of Fame?

Bob Feller.

You're Jason Dickson. It's August 21, 1996. You're in Yankee Stadium—your very first time in a big-league ballpark. In fact, you're playing in the game—pitching for the Angels. The first batter you face in the bottom of the first inning is Derek Jeter. What happens?

You give up a homer to Jeter on the very first pitch of your major-league career. But you win the game.

Who was the first player to hit three home runs in a game twice in one season—*in two different seasons?*

Big Johnny Mize of the Cardinals, on July 13 and July 20, 1938, and on May 13 and September 8, 1940.

Who is the first player to win Gold Gloves at two different positions?

Al Kaline (Tigers), playing right field in 1957 and 1958 and center field in 1959.

Who was the first modern rookie to have 200 hits?

Chuck Klein, Phillies, in 1929, with 219. (In 1928, Klein played only 64 games, so he was still considered a rookie the next season.)

Who is the first man to manage a father and son at the same time?

Jim Lefebvre, Mariners, 1990. The players were Ken Griffey Sr. and Jr. (The younger Griffey has told the Yankees' public address announcer, the legendary Bob Shepherd, that he wishes to be known as "Ken Griffey Jr." for the remainder of his big-league career.)

Who was the oldest rookie manager?

Hans Lobert, 1942 Phillies, age 61. His team finished 42-109, dead last.

Who was the first pitcher to hit a grand slam?

Mike O'Neill of the Cardinals, off Braves' pitcher Togie Pittinger on June 3, 1902.

Who was the first Hispanic umpire in the big leagues?

Armando Rodriguez, American League, 1974. He was born in Veracruz, Mexico.

Who was the first Dominican in the major leagues?

The first Ozzie Virgil (Giants, 1956). He was born in Montecristi.

Who was the first Australian in the big leagues?

Joe Quinn, 1884–1901, who was born in Sydney.

Who was the first American Leaguer to hit at least 20 doubles, 20 triples, and 20 homers in one season?

Jeff Heath, Indians, 1941. The pride of Ft. William, Ontario, Canada, had 32 doubles, 20 triples, and 24 homers.

Even if this feat is duplicated, he'll always be the first Canadian in the 20-20-20 club.

Who gave up Hank Aaron's first home run?

Vic Raschi, the "Springfield Rifle," pitching for the Cardinals, April 23, 1954, at Sportsman's Park, St. Louis. (Bud Podbielan, the first pitcher Aaron faced, struck him out.)

Who is the first manager to win pennants with three different teams?

Bill McKechnie: 1925 Pirates, 1928 Cardinals, 1939–1940 Reds.

Who was the first American League manager to win pennants with two different teams?

Joe Cronin, in 1933 with the Senators and in 1946 with the Red Sox.

Who was the first man to smack two homers in one All-Star game?

Arky Vaughan, Pittsburgh, on July 8, 1941 at Briggs Stadium in Detroit.

Who was the first player to homer in three consecutive innings?

Hall of Famer George "Highpockets" Kelly, who homered for the New York Giants on September 17, 1923, in the third, fourth, and fifth innings. That year, he hit 16 home runs, finishing sixth in the league.

Who was the first man to play for both the Mets and the Yankees?

Marvin Eugene Throneberry, whose initials spell MET. Yankees: 1955, 1958, 1959. Mets: 1962, 1963. His first game for the Mets was on May 11, 1962, against the Milwaukee Braves at home. Gene Woodling, another former Yankee, joined the Mets the next month.

Who was the first Met All-Star?

Richie Ashburn, in 1962, his only year with the Mets. He retired at the end of the Mets' legendary 40-120 season.

Who was the first American League shortstop to win a batting title?

Luke Appling, who hit .388 for the 1936 White Sox. "Old Aches and Pains" had to go 4-for-4 on the final day of the season to beat Earl Averill of the Indians, who wound up batting .378.

When was the first curtain call in the big leagues?

May 28, 1956, in the fourth inning, when Dale Long of the Pirates hit his eighth homer (off Carl Erskine of the Phillies) in eight games—a record since tied (but only in the American League) by Don Mattingly and Ken Griffey Jr.

Responding to the fans' ovation, Long stepped out of the dugout and tipped his cap.

The shy Roger Maris literally had to be pushed out of the Yankee dugout on October 1, 1961, after hitting his 61st home run of the season.

When was the *first* time in big-league history that two batters went 6-for-6 in the same game?

September 3, 1897. Wee Willie Keeler and Jack Doyle, both of the National League's Baltimore Orioles, accomplished this awesome feat.

When was the *last* time two batters went 6-for-6 in the same game?

September 3, 1897.

> ## This is one of those unusual "you never know what you're going to see at the ballpark" events that has never happened in the modern era, but might tomorrow.

Who was the first manager to win three consecutive All-Star games?

Tony LaRussa, American League, 1989–91.

Who was the first Italian-American in the major leagues?

Lewis Pessano "Buttercup" Dickerson, who played from 1878 to 1885.

Who is considered the first Jewish big leaguer?

Lipman "Lip" Pike, who broke in with the St. Louis Brownstockings in 1876.

Who were the first umpires in the big leagues to wear glasses?

Frank Umont and Ed Rommel, April 18, 1956, Yankees versus Senators in Washington. Larry Goetz, a 21-year veteran, was the first in the National League.

Who was the first woman drafted by a big-league team in the amateur free-agent draft?

Carey Schueler, 18-year-old basketball standout at DePaul University, chosen by the White Sox in the 43rd round of the 1993 draft. Her father, Ron Schueler, former big-league pitcher and pitching coach, was the Sox' general manager at the time.

When was the first time an electric public-address system was used at a major-league stadium?

July 5, 1929, at the Giants' Polo Grounds.

Who was the first man to play in the big leagues for 20 years without being on a pennant winner?

Hall of Famer Jake Beckley, who played from 1888 to 1907 with the Pirates, Giants, Reds, and Cardinals in the National League and the Pittsburgh Burghers in the Players' League.

Who was the first National Leaguer to amass 2,000 RBIs?

Hank Aaron, on July 3, 1972, when he smacked a three-run homer—his 656th—against the Astros in Houston.

Who was the first pitcher ejected—and then suspended for 10 days—for throwing a spitball? Who ejected him?

Nels Potter of the Browns, ejected by future Hall of Fame umpire Cal Hubbard on July 20, 1944.

American League umpire Dave Phillips ejected Gaylord Perry (then of the Mariners) on August 23, 1982, for throwing a ball that did things no legal pitch could do. Though he was frequently accused of throwing a spitter, that was Perry's only spitball ejection.

Who was the first rookie pitcher to lead the league in strikeouts?

Dazzy Vance. He struck out 134 for Brooklyn in 1922.

Who were the first players to hit back-to-back home runs in an All-Star game?

Ray Boone and Al Rosen, American League, July 13, 1954, at Cleveland's Municipal Stadium. The American League won 11-9.

Who is the first American to manage a big-league ball club in Japan?

Bobby Valentine, who skippered the Chiba Lotte Marines, 1995. The team finished with a 69-58 record, second best in the Pacific League, their best finish in a decade.

Don Blasingame, "The Blazer," was a bench coach for the Nankai Hawks in 1973 when they won the Pacific League pennant.

Who was the first player on an expansion team to win a batting title in the team's first year in the league?

Andres Galarraga. In 1993, he led the National League with a .370 batting average in the Colorado Rockies' first year.

Who was the first South American to play regularly in the big leagues?

Alex Carrasquel, of Caracas, Venezuela. He played for the Senators (1939–1945) and White Sox (1949). His nephew, Chico Carrasquel, was the White Sox shortstop from 1950 to 1955 and is the longtime play-by-play announcer on the White Sox' Spanish-language radio broadcasts.

Who was the first shortstop to hit 30 home runs and steal 30 bases in a single season?

Barry Larkin, Cincinnati Reds, 1996. In a September 22, 1996, game against the Cardinals, he hit home run #30 to go with his 36 stolen bases.

Name the only other infielder with at least 30 homers and 30 stolen bases in a single season.

Howard Johnson, New York Mets, third base, 1987 (36 homers, 32 stolen bases), 1989 (36 and 41), and 1991 (38 and 30).

When was the first night game in the American League?

May 16, 1939. Johnny Humphreys of the Cleveland Indians beat Roy Parmalee of the Philadelphia A's 8-3 in Philadelphia.

Who was the first player to steal second, third, and home in one game?

The appropriately named "Flying Dutchman," Honus Wagner (Pirates), June 15, 1902.

Who is the first modern rookie to smack five hits in his first game?

Cecil Travis, on May 16, 1933, for the Senators—five singles, as Washington beat Cleveland 11-10. (He also reached base on an error.) The game saw 34 players and 43 hits—including 5 by Joe Kuhel of the Senators.

Travis finished a distant second to Ted Williams in 1941, hitting .359 to Williams's .406. But unlike Williams, who was five years younger, Travis's wartime service cost him his baseball skills. He was never the same after returning to the Senators in 1945, hitting just .241, .252, and .216 in his final three seasons.

Who was the first man to play big-league baseball and pro football in the same year?

Bert Kuczynski. In 1943, he pitched for the Philadelphia A's and played football for the Detroit Lions.

Who were the first three teammates to steal at least 50 bases each in a single season?

Hint: One is a future Hall of Famer.

1980 Padres teammates Ozzie Smith (57), Jerry Mumphrey (52), and Gene Richards (61). The three hit a total of eight homers that year.

Who was the first Jewish pitcher to win at least 20 games in back-to-back seasons?

Hint: not Sandy Koufax.

Erskine Mayer: 1914 Phillies, 21; 1915 Phillies, 21. He finished his career in 1919 with a respectable 91-70 record.

Who was the first black player to play for two different major-league teams?

Hank Thompson. A utility player, he joined the Browns in 1947. In 1949, along with Monte Irvin, he joined the Giants.

Thompson hit three inside-the-park home runs on August 16, 1950, and hit three homers in one game again on June 3, 1954. He finished his career in 1956 with a .267 batting average and 129 home runs.

Name the first team in the big leagues to have three native-born Canadians in its starting lineup.

The Montreal Expos, September 6, 1993. Catcher Joe Siddall (Windsor, Ontario), outfielder Larry Walker (Maple Ridge, British Columbia), and pitcher Denis Boucher (Montreal).

Siddall and Boucher became the first all-Canadian starting battery in big-league history.

Who gave up Joe DiMaggio's first home run?

George Turbeville of the Philadelphia A's, on May 10, 1936, at Yankee Stadium. Joe's homer came in the first inning with Red Rolfe aboard. The Yankees won 7-2.

What did Ty Cobb do in his first at bat?

He doubled off Yankee Jack Chesbro, another future Hall of Famer, on August 30, 1905.

Who was the first American Leaguer to walk six times in a nine-inning game?

Jimmie Foxx, Red Sox, June 16, 1938.

"Good eye!"

Who was the first American Leaguer to hit three home runs in a nine-inning game?

Ken Williams, Browns, April 22, 1922, in a 10-7 win over the White Sox—the first big leaguer to do so since 1884.

Who was the first American Leaguer to hit two home runs in the same inning?

Ken Williams, Browns, on August 7, 1922—the first man in the big leagues to do so since 1880! His blasts came in the sixth inning of a 16-1 rout of the Senators.

Who was the first man to hit 30 homers, bat .300, and steal 30 bases in the same season?

Ken Williams, 1922 Browns, homered 39 times, batted .332, and stole 37 bases. Talk about a career year—he played in 153 games and led the league with 155 RBIs.

No other American Leaguer accomplished this feat until, 66 years later, in 1988, Oakland's José Canseco hit 42 home runs, stole 40 bases, and hit .307.

Ken Williams was also the first man to hit home runs in six consecutive games. He still holds part of the arcane American League record for most home runs in a season at home by a left-hander (32) set with the Browns in 1922. (He tied Babe Ruth's 1921 record.)

Virtually unknown today, Williams, a native of Grant's Pass, Oregon, was a terrific player who had the misfortune to spend most of his career (1915–1929) with the dreadful Browns. A career .319 hitter, he has been enshrined in the Oregon Sports Hall of Fame in Portland.

Who was the first switch-hitter to lead the National League in RBIs?

Howard Johnson, Mets, 117 RBIs in 1991.

What did Will Clark do in his first major-league at bat?

As a Giant on April 8, 1986, he hit a home run off Houston's Nolan Ryan.

What did Casey Stengel do in his first game as a player?

With the Dodgers versus Pittsburgh, on September 17, 1912, in Brooklyn, he smacked four hits, stole a base, and walked.

Who is the first member of a first-year expansion club to start in an All-Star game?

Gary Sheffield, Marlins, 1993. He homered in his first All-Star at bat.

Who was the first pinch hitter to homer on his first pitch in the big leagues?

Chuck Tanner, Milwaukee Braves, April 12, 1955, off Gerry Staley of the Reds in Milwaukee.

What was Joe DiMaggio's first number with the Yankees?

He wore #9 in 1936 before becoming the immortal #5 in 1937. Hank Bauer later wore #9 for the Yankees, as did Roger Maris, for whom it was retired.

Who was the first pitcher to have at least 20 wins in his first four full years in the big leagues?

Wes Ferrell, Indians, in 1929 (21), 1930 (25), 1931 (22), and 1932 (23).

Who was the first rookie to lead the American League in RBIs?

Ted Williams, in 1939, with 145. He exceeded that number only once, in 1949, when he had 159.

Who was the first big leaguer with 200 home runs and 500 stolen bases?

Joe Morgan, who smacked his 200th home run on August 28, 1978.

Who was the first manager of a New York American League team?

Clark Griffith, New York Highlanders, 1903. The name was changed to "Yankees" in 1913.

Who was the first batting champion to wear glasses?

Chick Hafey, who hit .349 as a Cardinal outfielder in 1931 and, thanks to his improved vision, became a Hall of Famer, retiring with a .317 lifetime batting average.

Connie Mack managed in the big leagues for 53 years—a record that will never be approached. During his later years, Mack owned the team! New rules prohibit owners from managing.

Name the first team Mr. Mack managed.

The Pittsburgh Pirates, from 1894 to 1896. He managed the Philadelphia A's from 1901 to 1950.

Three years after he led the National League in triples, he led the American League—the first man to lead both leagues in triples. Who is he?

Brett Butler: Atlanta Braves, 1983, 13 triples. Cleveland Indians, 1986, 14 triples.

When was the first major-league game in which both managers were black?

June 27, 1989. Frank Robinson managed the Orioles against Clarence "Cito" Gaston's Blue Jays.

Who was the first black coach in the big leagues?

Buck O'Neil, 1962 Cubs.

Who was the first pitcher to be named MVP *twice?*

Carl Hubbell, Giants, 1933 and 1936. In fact, he is the only National League pitcher with two MVP awards.

In the American League, Hal Newhouser of the Tigers won back-to-back MVP awards in 1944 and 1945—the only AL pitcher with two MVPs.

Who is considered the first Native American to play in the big leagues?

Louis M. Sockalexis, of the Penobscot tribe, an outfielder with the Cleveland Spiders of the National League, 1897–1899. In 1914, a Cleveland newspaper held a contest to rename the "Naps" (for Nap Lajoie), and the winner was "Indians"—in honor of Sockalexis.

Who was the first major-league manager to win a pennant who was *not* a big-league player?

Joe McCarthy, 1929 Cubs.

Who was the first manager to win pennants in both leagues?

Joe McCarthy, with the Cubs in 1929 and the Yankees in 1932.

What did Hank Aaron do in his first major-league game?

He went 0-5 against the Reds, April 13, 1954.

Who was the first rookie to win a Gold Glove?

Cubs' second baseman Ken Hubbs, 1962.

Who was the first man to hit pinch-hit home runs in consecutive games?

Ray Caldwell, Yankees, at home (at the Polo Grounds) against the White Sox, June 10 (in the ninth inning) and June 11 (in the sixth inning), 1915.

Who was the first National Leaguer to hit at least 50 home runs in a season _twice?_

Ralph Kiner, Pirates, 51 homers in 1947 and 54 in 1949.

Who was the first broadcaster to use the phrase "Going, going, gone!" in calling a home run?

Cincinnati's Harry Hartman, in 1929. It later became the trademark call of Mel Allen, "The Voice of the Yankees" from 1939 to 1964. How 'bout that!

Who led the National League in triples in his first two years in the league?

Ival Goodman of the Reds, who had 18 triples in 1935 and 14 in 1936.

Who was the first National Leaguer to play all nine positions in one season?

José Oquendo, Cardinals, 1988.

Who was the first National Leaguer to hit 500 home runs?

Mel Ott.

What was the first all-Irish brother battery in the majors?

Catcher Jack and pitcher Mike O'Neill, Cardinals, 1902–1903. Both were born in Galway.

Who was the first Canadian-born player in the big leagues?

Bill Phillips, from St. John, New Brunswick. Primarily a first baseman, he played from 1879 to 1888 for Cleveland in the National League and for both Brooklyn and Kansas City in the American Association. He is a member of the Canadian Baseball Hall of Fame.

Deion Sanders played for both the Atlanta Braves and Falcons and later for the San Francisco 49ers, the Yankees, the Giants, and the Reds. He was the first man to play in both the World Series (Atlanta, 1992, 1993) and the Super Bowl (49ers, 1995)—though he has never been on a World Series winner.

Who was the first to play for three professional teams in two different sports in the same city?

Gene Conley: Boston Celtics (1962–1964), Boston Braves (1952) and Red Sox (1961–1963).

Name the first club to win a total of 9,000 games.

The Chicago Cubs. Win #9,000 came on May 21, 1995, a 2-1 victory over the Dodgers.

Who was the first Yankee rookie to have at least 200 hits?

Earle Combs, 1925—203.

Who was the first rookie to hit 30 home runs in a season?

Wally Berger of the Braves hit 38 homers in 1930.

Who was the first man to hit two grand slams in the same game?

Tony Lazzeri, Yankees, May 24, 1936, against the Philadelphia A's at Shibe Park.

Who was the first rookie pitcher to win 20 games?

Roscoe Miller of the Tigers in 1901, 23-13.

In 1930, Hack Wilson became the first National Leaguer to hit 50 homers in one season, when he had 56 for the Cubs. That's still the National League record.

Who was the *second* National Leaguer to hit 50 home runs in a season?

Ralph Kiner of the Pirates hit 51 homers in 1947. Johnny Mize of the Giants also hit 51 that year, but he hit his 50th two days *after* Kiner did!

Who was the first man to get more walks than hits in a full season?

Max Bishop of the 1926 Athletics, with 400 at bats, 116 walks, and 106 hits.

Who was the first modern pitcher to throw shutouts in his first two major-league starts?

"Slow" Joe Doyle, New York Highlanders (later Yankees). He beat Cleveland 2-0 on August 25, 1906, and Washington 5-0 five days later.

Who was the first rookie to pitch 300 innings?

Irv Young, Braves, 1905. He pitched 378 innings and completed 41 games—a rookie record. He won 20 but lost 21.

Name the first pitcher to throw a shutout in his first major-league game.

Alex Hardy, Cubs over Brooklyn, 1-0, September 4, 1902.

Who was the first designated hitter to hit a home run?

Tony Oliva: April 6, 1973, Twins versus Oakland.

Before interleague play began in mid-1997, who was the last American League pitcher to hit a grand slam?

Steve Dunning, Cleveland, May 11, 1971.

Who is the first modern player to score nine runs in a doubleheader?

Baldomero "Mel" Almada, Washington Senators, July 25, 1937. Batting leadoff and playing center field against the Browns, he had two doubles, a homer, a single, and two stolen bases (in nine at bats). He scored four runs in the first game and five in the second.

Who was the first Latin American player in the big leagues?

Armando Marsans, Cincinnati Reds, 1911. Born October 3, 1887, in Matanzas, Cuba, he hit .269 in an eight-year career for the Reds, the Browns, the Yankees, and the St. Louis Terriers of the Federal League.

Who was the first Latin American to play in an All-Star Game?

The White Sox' Chico Carrasquel, of Caracas, Venezuela, July 10, 1951, at Briggs Stadium in Detroit.

Thanks to Chico Carrasquel himself for this question.

Who was the first modern player to homer in his first major-league at bat?

Johnny Bates, Boston Braves, April 12, 1906, off Harry McIntire in Brooklyn.

What was the first year that both leagues' batting champions hit under .330?

1960. Boston's Pete Runnels was the AL champ, batting .320, while Dick Groat of the Pirates led the National League with .325.

Who was the first man to pinch-hit home runs in *both* games of a doubleheader?

Hall of Famer Joe Cronin, June 17, 1943. In the first game, the Red Sox player-manager pinch-hit for the pitcher, Lou Lucier, and smacked a three-run homer (with Babe Barna and Skeeter Newsome aboard) off Russ Christopher of the Philadelphia A's in the seventh inning. The Red Sox won 5-4.

In the second game, Cronin had another pinch-hit three-run homer off Don Black, with Bobby Doerr and Skeeter Newsome on base in the eighth.

Who was the first modern outfielder to play a full season without committing any errors?

Danny Litwhiler, Phillies, 1942. He played in 151 games.

Who was the first shortstop to lead his league in total bases and slugging in the same season?

Robin Yount, Milwaukee, 1982. He had 367 bases and a .578 slugging average.

Who was the first player to hit 300 home runs and steal 300 bases?

Willie Mays.

Who was the first infielder to wear glasses?

George "Specs" Toporcer, 1921. The Cardinals' first baseman was perhaps the only big leaguer who never played baseball in the minors, college, or even high school.

Who was the first National Leaguer to hit at least 50 home runs in a season for two consecutive seasons?

This has never been accomplished in the National League.

Who was the first—and surely the only—man to lead his league in home runs by hitting only inside-the-park home runs?

Tommy Leach, who hit six for Pittsburgh in 1902.

Who appears on the first baseball bubblegum card, a 1933 Goudey?

Catcher Benny Bengough of the 1932 Browns.

Who was the first White Sox player to homer in an All-Star game?

Frank "The Big Hurt" Thomas, July 11, 1995—the 66th All-Star Game.

Who was the first man to play for both 1993 expansion teams, the Florida Marlins and the Colorado Rockies?

Shortstop Walt Weiss—Marlins, 1993; Rockies, 1994–1997.

Perhaps he dressed up for the occasion. After all, he's from Tuxedo, New York.

When was the first playoff game?

October 8, 1908, between the Giants and the Cubs, for the National League flag. The Cubs won 4-2.

Who was the first rookie to homer in every National League ballpark?

Johnny Rizzo. He hit 23 home runs for the 1938 Pirates, and a total of 61 dingers in his five-year career.

Who got the first hit off Walter Johnson?

Ty Cobb—a bunt single on August 2, 1907.

Who was the first pitcher to record 300 career saves?

Hall of Famer Rollie Fingers, August 21, 1982 (Brewers vs. Mariners). He finished his career in 1985 with 341 saves, the record at the time. This record has since been eclipsed by Jeff Reardon (367), Lee Smith (478 through 1997), and Dennis Eckersley (389 through 1997).

Who was the first rookie to hit three home runs in one game?

Eddie Mathews, Boston Braves, September 27, 1952, at Ebbets Field, off Brooklyn Dodger pitchers Joe Black and Ben Wade.

Who was the first shortstop in the American League to hit at least 30 homers, bat .300, and drive in 100 runs in one season?

Cal Ripken Jr., Orioles, 1991, who hit 34 homers, batted .323, and had 114 RBIs.

Who was the first player to strike out 1,000 times in his career?

Babe Ruth, in 1930. He went on to whiff a total of 1,330 times.

Who was the first player to strike out 1,500 times in a career?

Mickey Mantle, who reached this milestone in 1966. He retired after the 1968 season with 1,710 strikeouts. Surprisingly for such a prodigious slugger and whiffer, he also amassed more walks (1,734) than strikeouts!

When was the first time an American League batter came to bat three times in one inning?

July 4, 1948.

Who was the batter?

Ted Williams. In the seventh inning, against Charlie Harris of the visiting Philadelphia A's, he walked and scored, walked and scored again, and then grounded out to the shortstop for the third out of a six-hit, five-walk, 12-run inning. The Sox won 19-5.

Who was the first full-time coach in the big leagues?

Arlie Latham, for the 1909 Giants.

Who was the first former big leaguer to become a team physician—and for his hometown team?

Ron Taylor, M.D., team physician for the Blue Jays. A native of Toronto, Taylor compiled a 45-43 record while pitching for the Indians, Cardinals, Astros, Mets, and Padres from 1962 to 1972.

He hit a leadoff homer in consecutive games—the first modern player to do so. Who was he?

Sam Mertes, Cubs, June 8, 1900, versus the Braves. During his 10-year, 1,190-game career between 1896 and 1906, Mertes played all nine positions. Total homers: 40.

Two future Hall of Famers played in the first game to feature an all-minority lineup. Name the teams and the lineup.

On September 1, 1971, the Pirates beat the Phillies at Three Rivers Stadium. The Pirates' lineup:

P	Dock Ellis
C	Manny Sanguillen
1B	Al Oliver
2B	Rennie Stennett
3B	Dave Cash
SS	Jackie Hernandez
LF	Willie Stargell
CF	Gene Clines
RF	Roberto Clemente

Name the first team to sport players' last names on their backs.

Bill Veeck's 1960 Chicago White Sox.

Who was the first president of the United States to see a big-league baseball game?

Benjamin Harrison, who watched the National League Washington Senators lose 7-4 to Charlie Comiskey's Cincinnati Reds on June 2, 1892.

Who was the first player to notch at least 500 hits for four different teams?

Rusty Staub, who had 500+ hits each with the Astros, Expos, Mets and Tigers.

Who were the first teammates to hit 30 home runs and steal 30 bases in the same year?

The 1987 Mets' Darryl Strawberry (39 homers, 36 stolen bases) and Howard Johnson (36 and 32).

The first American Leaguer to hit a home run in his first major-league at bat (as a pinch hitter) is in the Hall of Fame in Cooperstown. The second one is also in a Hall of Fame—but not in Cooperstown. Who are they?

The first is Baseball Hall of Famer Earl Averill of the Indians, who homered in his first at bat on April 16, 1929—Opening Day!—against the Tigers' Earl Whitehill.

Clarence "Ace" Parker homered in his first big-league at bat, too, on April 30, 1937. His baseball career consisted of parts of two seasons (1937–1938) with the Philadelphia Athletics. He was better on the gridiron, where his exploits with the Brooklyn Dodgers, Boston Yanks, and New York Yankees (all football teams) from 1937 to 1946 earned him enshrinement in the Pro Football Hall of Fame in Canton, Ohio, in 1972.

Who was the first man inducted into the Hall of Fame for Distinguished Little League Graduates, in Williamsport, Pennsylvania, in 1968?

> *Hint: He's also in the National Baseball Hall of Fame in Cooperstown.*

Tom Seaver.

Who is the first big-league pitcher to have two sons pitch in the big leagues?

While a number of other players have had two sons *play* in the big leagues, on July 17, 1990—16 years after his career ended—Mel Stottlemyre Sr. became the first pitcher with two sons *pitching* in the majors. On that date, Mel Jr. made his pitching debut for the Kansas City Royals. His younger brother Todd has been pitching in the big leagues since 1988.

Who is the first black player in the big leagues whose father was also a major leaguer?

Johnny Hairston. His first game was on September 6, 1969, for the Cubs. (He played only two more.) His father Sam played four games for the White Sox in 1951.

Johnny's younger brother Jerry later played for the White Sox and Pirates (1973–1989), thus making Sam the first black big leaguer to have two sons play in the big leagues.

Who was the first Canadian-born umpire to work in a World Series?

It's a tie! In the 1979 Pirates-Orioles series, American League umpire Jim McKean of Montreal worked with the National League's Paul Runge of St. Catharines, Ontario.

McKean was the quarterback and punter for the Montreal Alouettes in the Canadian Football League in 1964. He was the Montreal punter in 1966, then joined the Saskatchewan Roughriders and played in the Grey Cup Championship Game, where his Roughriders beat the Ottawa Rough Riders 29-14 on November 26 in Vancouver, British Columbia.

Thanks to Karen Smedley of the CFL for the previous information on the only man to play in the Grey Cup and umpire in a World Series!

On July 20, 1947, Hank Thompson (2B) teamed with this man on the Browns as they opposed the Red Sox. It was the first game in which a team fielded two black players. Who was Thompson's teammate?

Center fielder Willard Brown. His big-league career lasted just 21 games at the end of the 1947 season.

Who was the first drafted player to go right to the big leagues—without any time in the minors?

Dave Winfield, San Diego Padres, 1973.

Who was the first man to be named to the All-Star team at three different positions?

Harmon Killebrew.

In 1961, he played third base in the second All-Star Game. (He did so again in 1970.)

In 1964, he was a left fielder.

In 1965, 1967, 1968, and 1971, Killebrew played first base.

He pinch hit in 1963, 1965, 1966, and 1969.

Who was the first Filipino to play in the big leagues?

Bobby Chouinard, a native of Manila, who pitched five innings for the Oakland A's against the Orioles on May 26, 1996.

Who was the first player with 6,000 total bases?

Stan Musial. His record-setting hit, a single, came on April 13, 1963, at home off Elroy Face of the Pirates. Gary Kolb then pinch-ran for Musial. Musial's record for most total bases in a career (6,134) was subsequently eclipsed by Hank Aaron (6,856). Willie Mays is a distant third with 6,066—an interesting number to go with his 660 home runs. Aaron, Musial, and Mays are the only players with over 6,000 total bases.

Who was the first man to catch no-hitters in both leagues?

Gus Triandos. First was Hoyt Wilhelm's gem for the Orioles over the Yankees on September 20, 1958. Second was Jim Bunning's perfect game for the Phillies against the Mets on June 21, 1964.

Who was the first Jewish batting champion?

George Stone, American League, who batted .358 for the 1906 St. Louis Browns.

Who is the first National Leaguer to hit home runs from both sides of the plate in a single game *twice* in one season?

Kevin Bass, Astros. He accomplished this for the second time on September 2, 1987, in a 10-1 drubbing of the Cubs.

Who is the first Canadian-born player named to the American League All-Star team?

Oscar Judd, a native of London, Ontario, who played for the 1943 Red Sox.

Who was the first man to bat on television?

Billy Werber, the Reds third baseman, who led off against the Dodgers at Ebbets Field on August 26, 1939 in the first televised big-league game, which was broadcast by Red Barber.

Which was the first American League team to beat another team 1,000 times?

The New York Yankees. Their defeat of the Cleveland Indians on June 27, 1997, was the 1,000th time they had beaten the Tribe.

Who is the first big-league manager to lose over 1,000 games before winning 1,000?

Joe Torre. During his managerial career (Mets, Braves, Cardinals, Yankees, 1977–1996), he lost 1,073 games but won only 986. But in 1997, Torre guided the Yankees to a 96-66 record, putting his career W-L record at 1,082-1,139.

LAST OF ALL

——

It happened on August 10, 1952, and has probably not happened since in a regular season game. What is it?

The same man pinch-hit for two players.

In the sixth inning of a Cubs-Pirates game in Pittsburgh, Ed Fitz Gerald pinch-hit for pitcher Howie Pollet and flied out. But in the ninth, when catcher Clyde McCullough of the Pirates had to leave the game with an injury, Fitz Gerald—with the approval of Cub manager Phil Cavaretta—was permitted to pinch-hit for McCullough, too. Ralph Kiner and Joe Garagiola also played in that game, the second of a doubleheader, which the Cubs won 4-3.

Who was the last player from the old Negro leagues to play in the big leagues?

Hank Aaron. He played for the Indianapolis Clowns in 1952 before starting his major-league career with the Milwaukee Braves in 1954. Aaron played in the majors through 1976.

Who was the last player to bat in the big leagues without a batting helmet?

Bob Montgomery, Boston Red Sox catcher, 1970–1979. When helmets became mandatory, he was permitted to finish his career with only a protective wafer inside his cap.

Who was the last Washington Senator to play in the big leagues?

Hint: He later became the only palindromic manager in history.

Colbert Dale "Toby" Harrah. He was with the second Senators team in 1969 and 1971, then moved with the team when they became the Texas Rangers in 1972. He was with the Indians from 1979 to 1983 and the Yankees in 1984, and finished his career with Texas again in 1986. Harrah managed the Rangers in 1992.

Name the last remaining ballpark used by teams in the "outlaw" Federal League.

Chicago's Wrigley Field. The Chicago Whales played there in 1915. In fact, Wrigley was built for the Federal League and taken over in 1916 by the team eventually known as the Cubs.

Who was the last legal spitballer in the American League?

Hall of Fame White Sox pitcher Urban "Red" Faber, who retired in 1933 after a 20-year career.

Who was the last active member of the Philadelphia Athletics?

Slick-fielding Vic Power, whose career ended with the 1965 Angels. He played for the A's just one year in Philadelphia (1954), then moved with the team to Kansas City (1955–1958).

Who was the last active St. Louis Brown?

Don Larsen. He was with the Browns in 1953, then the Orioles, Yankees, Kansas City A's, White Sox, Giants, Astros, and Orioles again, and finished his career with the Cubs in 1967.

Who was the last man to lead the league in homers and stolen bases in the same year?

Chuck Klein of the 1932 Phillies: 38 homers, 20 stolen bases. He also led in runs scored (152) and hits (226).

Who was the last New York Giant to play in the big leagues?

Willie Mays. His last year was 1973, with the Mets.

Who was the last active Boston Brave?

Eddie Mathews. He finished his career with the Tigers in 1968.

Who was the last active player for the original Washington Senators?

Pitcher Jim "Kitty" Kaat (a member of the "inevitable nickname" club). He broke in with the Senators in 1959, had some very good years with the Twins, and finished his incredible 25-year career (which included a record 16 Gold Gloves) with the Cardinals in 1983 (with stops on the White Sox, Phillies, and Yankees), becoming one of only a handful of players to pitch during four decades.

Who was the last player to lead the league in homers and triples the same year?

Boston's Jim Rice, in 1978: 46 homers, 15 triples. In 1978, he amassed 406 total bases, the most in the American League since Lou Gehrig's 409 in 1934.

Who was the last player to steal home in an All-Star Game?

Pie Traynor of the National League, on July 10, 1934, in the second modern All-Star Game.

Which was the last team to bring on a black player among its regulars?

The Detroit Tigers. Although Ozzie Virgil was the first black on the team in 1958, followed by Larry Doby in 1959, not until 1961 did Jake Wood become a regular.

Who was the last American League pitcher (before interleague play started in June 1997) to steal home?

Harry Dorish of the Browns, on June 2, 1950, against the Senators.

Who was the last pitcher to steal home in the National League?

Rick Sutcliffe of the Cubs, against the Phillies, on July 29, 1988.

Who was the last active Seattle Pilot?

Fred "Chicken" Stanley, who finished his career with the Oakland A's in 1982.

Stanley is a member of the all-avian team, which includes Ducky Medwick, Pete LaCock, Frank "Crane" Reberger, Frank "Crow" Crosetti, George "Dodo" Armstrong, Ralph "The Road Runner" Garr, Alan Cockrell, Phil "The Vulture" Regan, Johnny Peacock, Jay Partridge, Don Crow, Cuckoo Christensen, Andre Dawson ("The Hawk"), Tom "Little Hawk" Long, George Crowe, Jayhawk Owens, Gene "Blue Goose" Moore, Charles "The Golden Goose" Finley, "Turkey" Mike Donlin, Goose Goslin, Chick Hafey, Byrd Lynn, Jim "Emu" Kern, Tom Parrott, Mark "The Bird" Fidrych, Chick Gandil, Nelson "Chicken" Hawks (a double qualifier), Craig and Russ Swan, Gene "Blue Goose" Moore,

Birdie Cree, Robin Ventura, Sammy Drake, Turkey Tyson (also a double quali-
fier), Doug Griffin, Hawk Taylor, Doug Bird, Ed Crane, Sparrow Morton, Tris
"The Grey Eagle" Speaker, Sammy Strang ("The Dixie Thrush"), Turkey Gross,
The Boston Doves, Ed Hawk, George "The Stork" Theodore, José Cardenal,
Robin Yount, Ken "Hawk" Harrelson, Doug "The Red Rooster" Rader, Ron
"The Penguin" Cey, Don "Gooneybird" Larsen, Joe "Tweet" Walsh, Rick "The
Rooster" Burleson, Goose Gossage, Birdie Tebbetts. Coach: Bob Cluck. Um-
pire: Lon "The Arkansas Hummingbird" Warneke (also a fine pitcher). After
the game, they can all visit Al Cabrera, from the Canary Islands.

Who hit the last home run in Ebbets Field?

Duke Snider, on September 22, 1957.

Who was the last pitcher (before interleague play began) to hit a home run in the American League?

Roric Harrison, on October 3, 1972, for the Orioles, off Ray Lamb of the
Indians in the sixth inning at Cleveland. Harrison was the winning pitcher, as
Baltimore won 4-3. It was Harrison's only homer that season.

The last time it happened was September 8, 1957. It has never happened again and never will. What is it?

The New York Giants played the Brooklyn Dodgers. In all, the teams met
1,256 times (starting on April 19, 1900, when Brooklyn beat New York 3-2
at the Polo Grounds). The Giants won 650 of those games, and the Dodgers
won 606.

The Giants won the final game of this fabled New York City rivalry 3-2 on
a Hank Sauer homer.

The *San Francisco* Giants first played the *Los Angeles* Dodgers on April 15,
1958, at San Francisco's Seals Stadium, beating them 8-0.

Future Hall of Famers who appeared in the final New York game were Don Drysdale, Pee Wee Reese, Duke Snider, and Willie Mays. But one other man, who was still in uniform in 1997, appeared in the game. Who was he?

Don Zimmer of the Dodgers, who pinch-ran for Elmer Valo in the seventh inning. The former manager of the Cubs, Red Sox, Rangers, and
Padres, he has been the Yankee bench coach since 1996.

Who was the last veteran of World War II to play in the major leagues?

Hoyt Wilhelm. His last season was 1972, when he was 49.

Wilhelm survived the Battle of the Bulge, where he suffered a wound that
led to a permanently crooked neck.

What did Mets catcher Joe Pignatano do in his last major-league at bat?

On September 30, 1962, with Richie Ashburn on first (in the last game of his Hall of Fame career), Sammy Drake at second, and no outs, Pignatano broke his bat hitting into a triple play at Wrigley Field during the last game of a disastrous (yet storied) season for the Mets.

Ken Hubbs, at second base for the Cubs, caught the ball and flipped it to first baseman Ernie Banks, who threw to Andre Rodgers, covering second base, for the third out.

The Mets' 5-1 defeat was loss #120. They finished 60½ games out of first place.

Who was the last active player in the big leagues to have been managed by Casey Stengel?

Frank Edwin "Tug" McGraw. His first year in the big leagues—with the 1965 Mets—was Stengel's last year as manager. McGraw pitched through the 1984 season.

ONLY WHO?

Who was the only man to catch two perfect games?

Ron Hassey, who caught Indian's pitcher Len Barker's perfect game on May 15, 1981, against Toronto and Expo Dennis Martinez's perfect game against the Dodgers on July 28, 1991. Hassey is a member of the University of Arizona Sports Hall of Fame in Tucson.

Who was the only man to play in a regular season perfect game *and* a post-season perfect game?

Jim "Junior" Gilliam. He was with the Dodgers for Yankee Don Larsen's perfect World Series game on October 8, 1956, and for Sandy Koufax's September 9, 1965 perfect win over the Cubs.

Since 1923, when Yankee Stadium opened, who is the only Yankee manager who never lost a game there?

Bill Virdon (a member of the Missouri Sports Hall of Fame). He never won one, either. During Virdon's tenure as Yankee manager (1974–1975), the Yankees played their home games at the Mets' Shea Stadium while Yankee Stadium was being refurbished.

Name the only member of the 200-100 club (200 hits and 100 stolen bases in a single season).

Maury Wills of the Los Angeles Dodgers, who had 104 stolen bases and 208 hits in 1962.

The 30-30-200 club (30 homers, 30 stolen bases, and 200 hits in the same season) has only two members. Name them.

Hank Aaron of the Milwaukee Braves, 1963, with 44 homers, 31 stolen bases, and 201 hits.

Ellis Burks of the Colorado Rockies, 1996, with 40 home runs, 32 stolen bases, and 211 hits.

Who was the only man to wear the uniform of all four New York teams: Yankees, Dodgers, Giants, and Mets?

Casey Stengel. He played for the Dodgers from 1912 to 1917 and the Giants from 1921 to 1923. From 1949 to 1960, he managed the Yankees, and he was the first Met manager, from 1962 to 1965.

Darryl Strawberry played for the New York Mets and Yankees, the *Los Angeles* Dodgers, and the *San Francisco* Giants.

Who was the only player ever to hit a home run from both sides of the plate *in the same inning*?

Cleveland's Carlos Baerga, against the Yankees on April 8, 1993–Opening Day. The first homer was from the right side off Steve Howe, and the second was hit lefty off Steve Farr.

Who are the only men to manage the Cubs, the Yankees, and the Red Sox?

Frank Chance and Joe McCarthy.

	CUBS	YANKEES	RED SOX
Chance	1905–1912	1913–1914	1923
McCarthy	1926–1930	1931–1946	1949–1950

Only one man has hit home runs in three consecutive All-Star games. Who was he?

Ralph Kiner (1949–51).

Who was the only man to both pitch and catch in the same game *twice*?

Rick Cerone. He did it on July 19 and again on August 9, 1987, when he was with the Yankees.

Name the only man who led his league in triples for four consecutive years.

Lance Johnson of the White Sox. He tied for the lead with 13 in 1991, had 12 in 1992, 14 in 1993, and 14 again in 1994. In 1996, Johnson was inducted into the South Alabama Sports Hall of Fame. He had attended college in Alabama from 1983 to 1984.

Who was the only catcher to win two batting titles?

Hall of Famer Ernie Lombardi—probably the slowest player of his era. In 1938, while with the Reds, he hit .342. In 1942, with the Braves, he hit .330.

Who was the only player to wear his birthday on his back?

Carlos May. While he was with the White Sox from 1968 to 1976, his number, 17, appeared below his name. Thus his back read *MAY 17*—his birthday.

Who is the only big leaguer to appear in an Alfred Hitchcock movie?

Johnny Berardino, who played the New York City police officer who gave Cary Grant a ticket for drunk driving in *North by Northwest*. By the way, Grant's character was drugged, not drunk.

Who was the only man to win batting titles in both leagues?

Big Ed Delahanty: National League, 1899, batting .410; American League, 1902, batting .376.

Name the only major single-season offensive title Willie Mays never won.

The RBI title. Although Mays ranks seventh on the all-time RBI list with 1,903 in his magnificent 22-year career, he never led the National League in RBIs. In 1962, the year he knocked in 141 runs—a career best—Tommy Davis of the Dodgers had 153. (Harmon Killebrew won the American League RBI title that year with only 126.)

TRICK QUESTION DEPARTMENT

Who was the only batting champion named Gladys?

Gladys Davis, who—although she was from Toronto, Canada—led the All-American Girls' Pro Baseball League in 1943 with a .332 average for the Rockford (Illinois) Peaches.

Who is the only man to have played pro football (Boston Shamrocks, 1936; New York Giants, 1937–1946), coached pro basketball (Providence Steam Roller, Basketball Association of America, 1947), and umpired in a World Series (1953, 1956, 1962, 1964, and 1969)?

Hank Soar, American League umpire (1950–1972).

Who was the only man to play, coach, and manage in both the American and National Leagues—and umpire in the big leagues, too?

Johnny Cooney. He pitched for the Boston Braves from 1921 to 1930 (going 34-44), played in Brooklyn from 1935 to 1937, then returned to Boston from 1938 to 1942, and went back to Brooklyn again from 1943 to 1944. Cooney finished his playing career with the Yankees in 1944, compiling a .286 average and hitting two home runs.

Cooney coached for the Braves from 1946 to 1949 and was manager for 46 games in 1949. He coached for the Braves again from 1950 to 1955. From 1957 to 1964, he was a White Sox coach, occasionally managing when Al Lopez was unavailable.

Although still on the Braves' roster, he umpired in one game in 1941 when the National League umpiring crew did not arrive in time for the game.

When was the only game in which there were two triple steals?

July 25, 1930, by the Philadelphia A's, in the first and fourth innings against the Indians. The A's won 14-1.

In the first inning, Al Simmons, Bing Miller, and Dib Williams were on base, and they all advanced. Simmons scored.

In the fourth, Mickey Cochrane, Simmons, and Jimmie Foxx (a Hall of Fame threesome!) were on base when manager Connie Mack flashed the triple steal sign. The runners all stole, and Cochrane scored.

Who was the only ex-pharmacist to have a big-league stadium named after him?

A 1933 graduate of the Capitol City College of Pharmacy in Denver, Colorado, Hubert Horatio Humphrey was a pharmacist at his father's drugstore, Humphrey Drug Company in Huron, South Dakota, from 1933 to 1937 before he became mayor of Minneapolis, United States senator from Minnesota, vice president of the United States, and then United States senator again.

The Hubert H. Humphrey Metrodome, home of the Minnesota Twins, made its debut on April 6, 1982.

Thanks to Jo Anne McCormick Quatannens, assistant historian in the Office of the Secretary of the United States Senate, for this information on Humphrey.

———————————

Abner Doubleday is buried at the Arlington National Cemetery. Although his connection with baseball is apocryphal, he was a real general.

Who is the only major leaguer buried at Arlington?

Luzerne A. "Lu" Blue, who entered the United States Army on September 2, 1918 and was discharged three months later as a sergeant.

He was a first baseman for 13 years (1921–1933) with the Tigers, Browns, White Sox, and Dodgers.

On his death on July 28, 1958, Blue was buried in section 15, grave 272, at Arlington. His widow was buried there 10 years later.

Also buried at Arlington is Spotswood "Spot" Poles, a Negro League star from 1906 to 1923. Poles, nicknamed "The Black Ty Cobb," interrupted his baseball career when he enlisted in the Army in 1917. His service as a sergeant in France during World War I earned him five medals, including a Purple Heart. He went back to baseball after his 1919 discharge.

Upon his death on September 12, 1962, Pole was buried in section 42, grave 2324. His wife is also buried there.

Thanks to Arlington Cemetery Administrator Donald C. Snyder for this information.

Who was the only batter to lead the league in hits and strikeouts in the same season?

Andres Galarraga of the Expos, with 184 hits and 153 strikeouts in 1988.

Who was the only man to hit for the cycle on Opening Day?

Gee Walker did it for the Tigers on April 20, 1937 against the Indians. In fact, his hits came in reverse order: homer, triple, double, and single.

"Gee, Gee, nice game."

THEY DON'T HAVE NICKNAMES LIKE
THEY USED TO DEPARTMENT

Who was the only batting champion nicknamed "Bubbles"?

Eugene Franklin "Bubbles" Hargrave, who led the National League with a .353 batting average in 1926—the first catcher to do so. His brother, William McKinley Hargrave—also a big leaguer—was known as "Pinky."

Name the only two Norwegian-born Yankees.

"Honest" John Anderson and Arndt Jorgens.

Anderson (born in Sasbourg)—the first Norwegian to play in the big leagues—played outfield and first base for the Yankees from 1904 to 1905.

Jorgens (known as Art) was born in Modum. As Bill Dickey's backup behind the plate between 1929 and 1939, he appeared in only 306 games. In 1931, when Dickey was suspended for fighting, Jorgens played 40 games behind the plate. But during the World Series of 1932, 1936, 1937, 1938, and 1939, Dickey caught every inning of every game, so Jorgens, though eligible, warmed the bench—for 23 World Series games. The Yankees won each of those World Series, beating the Cubs, the Giants, the Giants, the Cubs, and the Reds. Jorgens never appeared in a World Series, but collected lots of bonus checks.

Put me in! Put me in!

Hal Trosky, from Norway, Iowa, did not play for the Yankees.

What did the Giants' Bobby Bonds do on June 25, 1968, that no American Leaguer has ever done?

He hit a grand slam in his first major-league game!

"Frosty" Bill Duggleby did this for the Phillies in his first major-league *at bat*—on April 21, 1898—still the only man to accomplish *that* feat.

Who was the only player with 50 home runs in a season but fewer than 50 strikeouts?

Johnny "The Big Cat" Mize, 1947 Giants. Mize played in all 154 games, had 586 at bats, and led the league with 51 homers, but struck out only 42 times! He batted .302.

Who was the only man to hit at least 40 home runs in one season in both leagues?

Darrell Evans. In 1973 he hit 41 for the Atlanta Braves, and in 1985 he belted 40 for the Tigers.

Name the only men who led both leagues in home runs.

Hall of Famer Wahoo Sam Crawford, Buck Freeman, and Fred McGriff.

In 1901, while playing for the Cincinnati Reds, Crawford led the National League with 16 homers. In 1908, as a Tiger, he led the American League with 7.

Buck Freeman led the National League (with the Washington Nationals) in 1899 with 25 homers (this record was shattered in 1922 when Rogers Hornsby hit 42). In 1903, while playing for Boston, Freeman led the American League with 13 home runs (a record that stood until Babe Ruth bettered it by hitting 29 in 1919).

Fred McGriff hit 36 homers for Toronto in 1989 and 35 for San Diego in 1992.

Ty Cobb led the American League in batting and stolen bases in a single season five times (1907, 1909, 1911, 1915, 1917). Only one National Leaguer has ever done this, and he did it only once. Who is he?

Jackie Robinson. In 1949, he hit .342 and stole 37 bases—both career bests.

He played in more games, had more at bats, and had more hits than any other eligible player *not* in the Hall of Fame. Who is he?

Vada Pinson, who played in 2,469 games, with 9,645 at bats and 2,757 hits.

Did you say Pete Rose? Sorry. As of this writing, he is on the "ineligible" list for Cooperstown consideration.

TRICK QUESTION DEPARTMENT

Who were the only men to be present both at St. Louis's Busch Stadium on May 2, 1954, when Stan Musial had five homers in a doubleheader, and in Atlanta on August 1, 1972, when San Diego's Nate Colbert also had five homers in a doubleheader?

Nate Colbert and Milo Hamilton. Colbert, a St. Louis native, was an 8-year-old fan in the stands on Musial's big day.

Also, working both games was Hall of Fame broadcaster Milo Hamilton. He was the Cardinals' broadcaster in 1954 and the "Voice of the Braves" in 1972.

It happened on October 2, 1920, and has not happened—and probably will not happen—ever again. What was it?

The last tripleheader in the big leagues, and the only one this century—Pirates versus Reds. Peter Harrison was the plate umpire for all three games.

Who was the only man to get a hit in all three of those games?

Clyde Barnhart, Pirates. He doubled in the first game, which the Reds won 13-4; doubled again in the second, which the Reds won 7-3; and singled in the final contest, which the Pirates won 6-0.

Who was the only man in major-league history to hit the first pitch on Opening Day for a home run?

Dwight Evans, Red Sox, April 7, 1986, off Jack Morris of the Tigers. Morris won the game for Detroit 6-5.

Who was the only man to hit 500 homers in a career without having a single 40-home-run season?

Eddie Murray. The most he ever hit in a single season was 33, with the 1983 Orioles.

Who was the only man to play in the Washington Senators' last game—twice?

Ron Hansen. As an Oriole, he played in the original Senators' last game in Washington on October 2, 1960, before the team moved to Bloomington, Minnesota to become the Twins. Hansen was back in Washington as a Yankee on September 3, 1971 for the final game of the second Senators team, which moved to Texas to become the Rangers.

Perhaps Hansen would like to meet Diego Segui, the only man who played for both the Seattle Pilots (1969) and the Seattle Mariners (1977). In fact, Segui pitched in the very first game for each Seattle team.

It wasn't a tripleheader, but the Braves, the Cardinals, and the Reds were all at Braves Field in Boston on September 24, 1954. Why?

Two days earlier, a Braves-Reds game ended with an appeal by the Reds of a double-play call. When the appeal was upheld, the game had to be resumed from the point of the disputed play. After that game (which the Braves won 4-3), the Reds went on to beat the Cardinals 4-2.

Who was the only player to lead his league in home runs and errors in the same season?

> *Hint: He's a Hall of Famer.*

Ernie Banks. In 1958, the Cub shortstop hit 47 homers and committed 32 errors.

Who was the only player to lead his league in home runs and fielding average *in the same year*?

Ernie Banks again. In 1960, "Mr. Cub" hit 41 home runs, and as a shortstop had a fielding average of .977.

Who are the only switch-hitters with at least 100 home runs in each league?

Chili Davis: National, 101; American, 227 (through 1997).
Reggie Smith: National, 165; American, 149.
Eddie Murray: American, 396; National, 108.

Who was the only man to hit three home runs in a game six times?

Johnny Mize. He did it twice in 1938 and 1940, plus once in 1947 and 1950.

George Brett won batting championships in three decades: 1976 (.333), 1980 (.390), and 1990 (.329). Who was the only pitcher to win World Series games in three different decades?

Jim Palmer of the Orioles: 1966 (Game 2) versus the Dodgers, 1971 (Game 1) versus the Pirates, 1983 (Game 3) versus the Phillies.

Who was the only player to drive in at least 100 runs but score fewer than 50 runs in the same season?

Vic Wertz, Red Sox, 1960. He drove in 103, but scored only 45.

What was the best battery in baseball?

AlKaline. Between 1953 and 1974, he just kept going, and going, and going: 399 homers, 3,007 hits.

Who was the only man to hit over .400 and swat over 40 homers in the same season?

Rogers Hornsby, in 1922, his Triple Crown year. As a Cardinal, he hit .401 with 42 homers.

Who was the only man to win the stolen base crown in both leagues?

Ron LeFlore, with 68 (1978 Tigers) and 97 (1980 Expos).

Twelve men have hit four homers in a single game, but only one has also had a game in which he hit four doubles. Who is he?

Big Ed Delahanty. His four homers came on July 13, 1896, for the Phillies versus Chicago. On May 13, 1899, he hit four doubles for the Phillies over the Giants.

Who was the only man to start two triple plays in the same game?

Twins' third baseman Gary Gaetti, July 17, 1990, versus Boston. Boston won anyway 1-0.

Who was the only third baseman to hit at least .300 and swat 40 or more home runs in a season *twice*?

Eddie Mathews, Milwaukee Braves. 1953: .302, 47; 1959: .306, 46.

Who was the only man in the history of the game to drive in *and score* more than 170 runs in a single season?

Who else? Babe Ruth! In 1921, his second season with the Yankees, he scored 177, and his then-record 59 homers helped drive in 171—the seventh-highest season total ever. He led the American League in both categories.

Who was the only player to have over 10 homers, triples, doubles, and stolen bases four years in a row?

Juan Samuel, Phillies, 1984–1987. Samuel also led the National League in strikeouts in each of those seasons.

Who was the only man to play for and manage pro baseball and basketball teams?

Lou Boudreau. He played and managed in the big leagues from 1942 to 1950 and in 1952. He continued to manage from 1953 to 1957 and in 1960.

In 1939 and 1940, Boudreau also played for and managed the Hammond, Indiana team in the National Basketball League, a predecessor of the NBA. His managerial record was 38-39.

One of Boudreau's basketball teammates went on to a Basketball Hall of Fame career. Who was he?

Future UCLA coach John Wooden, "The Wizard of Westwood."

Only two modern catchers have led their leagues in triples in one season. Who were they?

James Timothy "Tim" McCarver, Cardinals, 1966 (13), and Carlton Fisk, Red Sox, 1972 (9).

Who was the only man to walk eight times in a doubleheader—twice?

Max Bishop, on May 21, 1930 with the Philadelphia A's, and July 8, 1934 with the Red Sox.

Who was the only man to play for the Boston, Milwaukee, and Atlanta Braves?

Eddie Mathews. And, because nobody played for the Philadelphia, Kansas City, and Oakland A's, Mathews is the only man to play for the same major-league franchise in three cities.

Who was the only man to play in a baseball All-Star game, a World Series, and the National Basketball League, predecessor of the National Basketball Association?

Irv Noren. An All-Star in 1954 with the Yankees, he also played in the 1952, 1953, and 1955 World Series for the Yankees.

He was a forward for the Chicago Gears of the NBL, 1946–1947.

Who was the only American Leaguer to get at least 200 hits in each of his first three seasons?

Johnny Pesky (1942, 1946, 1947), perhaps the greatest Red Sox shortstop of all time. He led the league in hits those years, too.

Pesky was in the service during World War II (1943–1945). Thus, after 1942, 1946 was his next season.

Although Pesky recently told us "this kid is far better than me," it remains to be seen whether Nomar Garciaparra can match Pesky's record.

Who was the only designated hitter ever to score more than 100 runs in one season?

Paul Molitor of the World Champion 1993 Toronto Blue Jays—he had 121 runs for the season, 107 as a DH.

Who was the first pitcher—and the only Hall of Fame pitcher—to surrender a World Series grand slam?

Dodger Burleigh Grimes, to Cleveland's Elmer Smith on October 10, 1920 (Game 5). Cleveland won the game 8-1 and went on to take the best-of-eight Series 5-2.

I'LL HAVE WHAT HE'S HAVING DEPARTMENT

Who were the only two players to homer three times in an Opening Day game?

George Bell, Blue Jays, April 4, 1988 (three dingers off Bret Saberhagen of the Royals) and Karl "Tuffy" Rhodes, Cubs, April 4, 1994. In fact, Rhodes' three homers (off the Mets' Dwight Gooden at Wrigley Field) were in his first three at bats of 1994. (He later walked, then singled off John Franco.)

Who was the only modern pitcher to hit three homers in one game?

Jim Tobin, Boston Braves, May 13, 1942. He won the game, too, 6-5 over the Cubs in Boston. His homers came in the fifth, seventh, and eighth innings. These three hits, combined with another homer in the previous game, raised Tobin's batting average to .407—the best on the team!

Only two shortstops in the history of the game stole at least 20 bases a season for 16 consecutive seasons. Who were they?

No, not Luis Aparicio. It was Honus Wagner and Ozzie Smith. Wagner did it between 1898 and 1915 for Louisville and Pittsburgh in the National League. Smith also accomplished this amazing feat of consistency for the Padres and Cardinals between 1978 and 1993.

Who was the only man to play for the New York football Giants *and* the New York baseball Giants?

Steve "Flip" Filipowicz. He was an outfielder with the baseball Giants (.223) in 1944–1945, and a running back with the football Giants in 1945–1946.

Who was the only major leaguer to homer in his first *two* at bats?

Bob Nieman, Browns, September 14, 1951, off Maurice "Mickey" McDermott of the Red Sox.

Nieman had reported to the visiting Browns in Boston only that morning. His first blast came with none on in the second. His second homer was with one on in the third. The Browns lost 9-6.

Those were the only homers Nieman hit in 1951. In his 12-year career, the journeyman outfielder for the Browns, Tigers, White Sox, Orioles, Cardinals, Indians, and Giants hit a total of 125.

Who were the only men to play in a World Series and a Rose Bowl?

Jackie Jensen and Chuck Essegian.

While a college football star at the University of California at Berkeley, Jensen appeared in the 1949 Rose Bowl with his undefeated team. But Northwestern beat Cal 20-14.

Jensen appeared in the World Series with the Yankees in 1950.

In 1958 and 1959, Jensen achieved an unusual feat: he led the American League in RBIs without a single triple. (1958: 122 RBIs. 1959: 112.) Jensen is the only man to play in a Rose Bowl, a World Series, a baseball All-Star Game, and an East-West All-Star Game.

Essegian was a Stanford linebacker in the 1952 Rose Bowl, and pinch-hit two home runs for the Los Angeles Dodgers in the 1959 World Series—their first championship in Los Angeles.

Who was the only man to hit at least 30 home runs in each of his first four seasons?

Mark McGwire hit 49 in 1987 (the rookie record, which might have been greater had McGwire not missed some games to be with his wife at the birth of their child), 32 in 1988, 33 in 1989, and 39 in 1990.

Who is the only man to hold the team record for most stolen bases in a season for two different teams?

Rickey Henderson, with 130 for the 1982 Oakland A's and 93 for the 1988 Yankees.

Who was the only big-league player hit by lightning during a game?

Red Murray, New York Giants. He was hit in the 21st inning in a 3-1 win over the Pirates on July 17, 1914.

Who were the only Twins with at least 1,000 RBIs?

Kent Hrbek, who retired after the 1994 season, with 1,086, and Harmon Killebrew, who had 1,325.

TRICK QUESTION DEPARTMENT

Who was the only man to bat behind both #1 and #2 on the all-time home run list?

Davey Johnson. With the Atlanta Braves in 1973, he smacked 43 homers batting behind Hank Aaron—who hit 40 of his own. Johnson later batted behind Sadaharu Oh, for the Yomiuri Giants, and hit 26 home runs in 1976.

Who was the only man to retire from the big leagues in the middle of a game—with exactly 100 career home runs and a batting average of exactly .300?

John Kruk of the White Sox (and Phillies and Padres), who retired on July 30, 1995 after singling in the first inning.

Only two second basemen have played in 2,000 games, stroked 2,000 hits, and had at least 200 home runs. Who were they?

Hall of Famer Joe Morgan and "Sweet" Lou Whitaker.

Who was the only modern player to walk at least 100 times in his first five full seasons?

Frank Thomas of the White Sox. In fact, he did it in his first seven seasons.

Only Roy Thomas of the Phillies had accomplished this amazing show of patience at the plate before Frank Thomas. Roy did it with the Phillies from 1899 to 1904. Roy Thomas also led the National League in on-base percentage in 1902 (.415) and 1903 (.453). While batting .290 over his 13-year career, he hit seven home runs in an era that disdained the home run as vulgar.

What a coincidence that the only two men to accomplish this feat, albeit almost a century apart, had the same last name!

Who was the only man to steal at least 100 bases in his first three years in the big leagues?

Vince Coleman, St. Louis Cardinals—1985: 110; 1986: 107; 1987: 109. He led the National League in each of those years.

Who was the only man to play in every World Series game ever played by the Washington Senators?

Hall of Famer Leon "Goose" Goslin (1924, 1925, 1933).

YEAR	NUMBER OF GAMES	HOW DID SENATORS DO?
1924	7	Beat Giants, 4-3
1925	7	Lost to Pirates, 4-3
1933	5	Lost to Giants, 4-1

Who was the only player who had more than 1,500 walks, yet fewer than 2,000 hits?

Eddie Yost—"The Walking Man." He had 1,614 walks and 1,863 hits while playing for the Senators, Tigers, and Dodgers (1944–1962).

Who was the only man to pitch in four decades and win 300 games?

Early Wynn of the Senators, Indians, and White Sox: 1939–1963, exactly 300 wins.

Who was the only manager to win over 800 games in each league?

Sparky Anderson.

Reds (1970–1977): 863 wins.
Tigers (1979–1995): 1,331 wins.

Who was the only player with at least 100 hits in each of his first 20 seasons in the majors?

Carl Yastrzemski, Red Sox, 1961–1980. He had only 83 hits in 1981, but that season was shortened by a players' strike, so he played in only 91 games. In 1982, the next full season, Yaz was at it again, with 126 hits, followed by 101 in 1983, his final season. Thus he had over 100 hits in every full season he played—all 22.

Who was the only player to hit .300, score 100 runs, drive in 100 runs, and steal 50 bases in a single season?

Barry Bonds, Pirates, 1990—.301, 104 runs, 114 RBIs, 52 stolen bases, 33 home runs. Bonds also won a Gold Glove and led the league with a .565 slugging percentage.

Only one catcher has hit three home runs in a single game *three different times*. Who was he?

Johnny Bench, Reds—July 26, 1970; May 9, 1973; May 29, 1980.

Who was the only man to hit two inside-the-park home runs in a single game in each league?

Hall of Famer Roger Bresnahan, who did it on May 30, 1902 for the American League Orioles, and June 6, 1904 for the National League Giants.

Since the turn of the century, only one man has completed a full season in which he had more runs scored than hits. Who was he?

Max Bishop, 1930 Philadelphia A's: 117 runs, 111 hits.

Only two men in the history of baseball have had 3,000 hits, 300 home runs, 600 doubles, and 100 triples. Who were they?

Stan Musial and George Brett.

Who was the only Hall of Famer to have two major-league ballparks named after him?

Charles A. Comiskey.

Only two men have 500 home runs, 3,000 hits, and a lifetime batting average over .300. Who were they?

Hank Aaron (755; 3,771; .305) and Willie Mays (660; 3,283; .302).

Who were the only men to smack 50 homers in a single season and not hit .300?

Cecil Fielder, 1990 Tigers: 51 homers, .277.
Roger Maris, 1961 Yankees: 61 homers, .269.
Brady Anderson, 1996 Orioles: 50 homers, .297.
Mark McGwire, 1997 A's and Cardinals: 58 homers, .274.

Who was the only Olympian to hit 50 homers in a single season?

Mark McGwire of the Oakland A's, in 1996 (52). He was on the gold-medal-winning 1984 U.S. Olympic Team in Los Angeles. In 1997, splitting his season between Oakland and St. Louis, he hit 58.

Who was the only Olympian to be named Most Valuable Player?

Barry Larkin, Reds, 1995. He too was on the 1984 U.S. Olympic Team.

Who is the only man to be *Time* Magazine's Man of the Year and to have a baseball stadium named for him?

Ted Turner, owner of the Atlanta Braves, *Time*'s Man of the Year in 1991. Turner Stadium, which hosted the 1996 Atlanta Olympics, was converted for use as the Braves' home field and is named for Turner, although many thought "Hank Aaron Stadium" had a nice ring to it.

Who are the only big leaguers with stars on the Hollywood Walk of Fame?

Johnny Berardino and Chuck Connors.

For over 30 years Berardino appeared as Dr. Steve Hardy on *General Hospital*; he was awarded his star on April 1, 1993. It's at 6801 Hollywood Boulevard.

Connors' star is at 6836 Hollywood Boulevard.

Who is the only man to have a star on the Walk of Fame and to have had his number retired by a big-league team?

Gene Autry. In fact, he's the only man to have *five* stars, in recognition of his career in films, on radio, on television, as a recording artist, and as a live performer. The Angels retired a number (26) in his honor.

Only two shortstops have ever hit over .300, stolen at least 30 bases, and had at least 200 hits in a single season. The first was Honus Wagner, who did it in 1908 with the Pirates (.354, 53, 201). Who was the second?

Mark Grudzielanek, 1996 Montreal Expos. In his first full big-league season, he hit .306, stole 34 bases, and had 201 hits.

Who was the only man to strike out at least 1,000 times in the minor leagues and another 1,000 times in the majors?

Rob Deer. During his minor-league career, he struck out 1,129 times. In the majors (1984 through 1996), he whiffed 1,409 times.

HIGHS AND LOWS

————

Who hit the most home runs in a single season without even one triple?

Mark McGwire of the 1997 Oakland A's and St. Louis Cardinals—58.

Who hit the most home runs for his hometown team?

Lou Gehrig, born in New York City. During his 17-year career, he hit 493 home runs for the New York Yankees, including 251 at Yankee Stadium.

Who hit the most home runs in a season in which he had no stolen bases?

Roger Maris, 1961 Yankees: 61 homers, no stolen bases.

When Babe Ruth hit 60 home runs for the Yankees in 1927, he stole seven bases.

Who had the most stolen bases in a season in which he hit no home runs?

Vince Coleman. In 1986, he stole 107 bases for the Cardinals without a homer.

Who drove in the most runs in a single season without any triples?

Jay Buhner of the Seattle Mariners: 138 in 1996.

Who hit the most home runs in a career with one team?

Hank Aaron of the Milwaukee and Atlanta Braves (1954–1974), with 733. Babe Ruth hit 714 homers in his career, but "only" 659 as a Yankee.

Sorry, Babe—you miss by 74!

Who hit the most home runs in a season in which he won a batting championship?

Mickey Mantle. In 1956, his Triple Crown year, Mantle hit .353 to lead the majors. The 52 homers he walloped that year were also tops in the major leagues, as were his 130 RBIs.

Who appeared in the most games without batting, pitching, or playing in the field?

Herb Washington, a world-class sprinter, signed by Oakland as a "designated runner". In 1974 and 1975, he appeared in 105 games—scoring 33 runs and stealing 31 bases—but never played a position and never came to bat. In his biggest game, Game 2 of the 1974 World Series, on October 13, he pinch-ran for Joe Rudi in the ninth inning, only to be picked off by Mike Marshall of the Dodgers! Oakland won the Series anyway, 4-1.

Which designated hitter has had the highest single-season batting average?

Paul Molitor, 1994 Blue Jays, .339 in 110 games as DH. He also played five games at first base, and his overall average for the season was .341. He hit .339 again as a DH for the Twins in 1996 in 144 games.

Who drove in the most runs in a single post-1900 season without hitting any home runs?

Lave Cross. With the Philadelphia A's in 1902, he drove in 108 runs without a homer. In fact, he's the only man ever to drive in 100 runs without a homer. Talk about dead ball!

Who scored the most runs in a single season without an at bat?

Herb Washington, Oakland's "designated runner". In 1974, he scored 29 runs—all as a pinch runner—without ever batting. He also holds the career mark for runs scored without an at bat, with 33. He did not come to bat in 1975 either.

At the time of his death, on December 7, 1969, this pitcher-turned-everyday-player had the highest career batting average of any living former big leaguer—.349. Who was he?

Lefty O'Doul.

Of the ballplayers who have homered in their first big-league at bats, which one hit the most homers in his entire career?

Gary Gaetti–332 through the end of the 1997 season. He hit his first homer on September 20, 1981 as a Twin, off Charlie Hough of the Texas Rangers.

Who had the most career at bats without a stolen base?

Cecil Fielder. As of the end of the 1995 season, Fielder had 3,789 consecutive at bats with no stolen bases. On June 10, 1995, in a game at Minnesota, he became the first man to play 1,000 consecutive games without a stolen base. But his streak (1,097 games and 3,794 at bats without a stolen base) came to an end on April 3, 1996, when, as a Tiger, he walked in the ninth inning in a game against the Twins, then stole second as teammate Melvin Nieves swung and missed on a 3-2 count. Twins' catcher Greg Meyers's throw was off-line to Pat Meares at second base, and Meares dropped the ball. SB! Fielder later scored, and the Tigers won.

By the end of the 1997 season, Fielder had 4,741 at bats with just two stolen bases.

Russ Nixon (Indians, Red Sox, Twins, 1957–1968) completed his career with 2,504 at bats without ever stealing a base.

Who stole the most bases in a single season without hitting a triple?

Miguel Dilone, Oakland A's, 1978 (50). This is surprising, because during his career Dilone hit 25 triples.

Who stole the most bases in a single season without hitting any doubles?

Larry Lintz of the 1976 A's–31. He had no homers or triples that year either, or singles, or even hits. In fact, he had only one at bat.

Who played the most games for just one team?

Carl Yastrzemski: 3,308 for the Boston Red Sox (1961–1983).

Who hit the most home runs in a career without ever leading the league in homers?

Stan Musial–475. Although he set more batting records than any player of his time, the league home run crown eluded him.

Which native of Mexico hit the most home runs in a single season in the big leagues?

Vinny Castilla of the Colorado Rockies hit 40 in 1996.

Which native of Canada hit the most home runs in a single season?

Larry Walker of Maple Ridge, British Columbia, hit 49 for the Colorado Rockies in 1997.

Who hit the fewest home runs to lead a league in one season?

Tommy Leach of Pittsburgh led the National League in 1902 with 6 homers.

Which team amassed the fewest hits in an extra-inning game?

The Milwaukee Braves, who had just one hit (a double by Joe Adcock) against the Pirates' Harvey Haddix on May 26, 1959, when Haddix pitched 12 perfect innings, then lost the game.

TRICK QUESTION DEPARTMENT

What was the furthest distance ever traveled by a baseball?

Were you going to say Mickey Mantle's drive at Griffith Stadium on April 17, 1953? Or his monster blast on September 10, 1960 at Detroit? His shot off the Yankee Stadium facade on May 22, 1963? What about Reggie Jackson's titanic home run off the light tower in Detroit during the 1971 All-Star Game? Perhaps you were thinking of one of Babe Ruth's legendary blasts, such as the one he hit onto the roof at the old Comiskey Park on August 16, 1927? Or were you thinking of a humongous smash by Jimmie Foxx on June 16, 1936?

None of the above. The Space Shuttle *Columbia* carried a baseball into Earth orbit—in fact, 255 orbits—on STS (Space Transportation System) 73. During its 15 days, 21 hours, 53 minutes, and 16 seconds in space (at an orbit of 172 statute miles), the ball traveled approximately 6,600,000 miles. On October 26, 1995, Commander Ken Bowersox and his colleagues on *Columbia* threw the ball to each other while the television shots of this event were beamed to Jacobs Field in Cleveland—the first extraterrestrial throwing out of the first pitch in a World Series game (Game 5). One of the balls from *Columbia* is the in Hall of Fame in Cooperstown. Another is at NASA's Lewis Research Center in Cleveland.

The *softball* that traveled the furthest was carried aloft on the space shuttle *Atlantis* when it blasted into space on October 18, 1989. The shuttle and the ball returned to Earth after approximately 2 million miles (79 orbits, 185 nautical miles up) on October 23. The flight, STS 34, was commanded by astronaut Don Williams, an umpire with the American Softball Association. (He took his ASA umpire patch with him, too.) According to Bill Plummer III of the Softball Hall of Fame in Oklahoma City, the ball was sealed in a special plastic prior to liftoff to prevent the escape of gases from the softball into the shuttle cabin.

A secondary mission of the flight was the launching of the Galileo/Jupiter spacecraft.

On March 1, 1990, Don Williams presented the ball to the Softball Hall of Fame where it is on exhibit.

Thanks to Mark Kahn, Archivist of history for the National Aeronautics and Space Administration, for details on STS 34. Thanks too to David M. DeFelice of NASA's Lewis Research Center for information on STS 73.

Who hit the most home runs in his career without a stolen base?

Cecil Fielder, who had hit 250 homers before he stole his first base for the Tigers on April 3, 1996. This astounding record seems unassailable because the man closest to Fielder's record is Sam Horn, who had hit only 62 homers without ever stealing a base.

Who hit the most home runs in the 1930s?

Jimmie Foxx—415.

Would you want a player on your team if he hit into 328 double plays—more than anybody else in history?

Yes, you would. His name is Hank Aaron.

Who has played in the most no-hitters?

Bert Campaneris—10.

PITCHER	TEAM	OPPONENT	DATE
Catfish Hunter*	*Oakland*	Twins	May 8, 1968
Jim Palmer	Orioles	*Oakland*	August 13, 1969
Clyde Wright	Angels	*Oakland*	July 3, 1970
Vida Blue	*Oakland*	Twins	September 21, 1970
Jim Bibby	Rangers	*Oakland*	July 30, 1973
Dick Bosman	Indians	*Oakland*	July 19, 1974
Vida Blue, Glen Abbott, Paul Linblad, Rollie Fingers, Blue Moon Odom	*Oakland*	Angels	September 28, 1975

Jim Colburn	Royals	*Rangers*	May 14, 1977
Bert Blyleven	*Rangers*	Angels	September 22, 1977
Dave Righetti	*Yankees*	Red Sox	July 4, 1983

*: Perfect game.

Campaneris's teams appear in italics.

Who had the most hits in the 1950s?

Hall of Famer Richie Ashburn of the Phillies—1,875. Only 19 were home runs.

Which 17-year-old pitcher had the most wins?

Bob Feller, Indians—five in 1936.

Juniors and Seniors

Who was the youngest person ever to throw out a ceremonial first pitch in a postseason game—and probably in any big league game?

Travis John, son of Yankee pitcher Tommy John, on October 9, 1981 before Game 3 of the Yankees-Brewers American League East Championship Series (created in the wake of the 1981 strike.)

Travis, recovering from critical injuries and a coma after a fall from a third-floor window of the Johns' summer home in New Jersey eight weeks earlier, was just 2½ when afforded the honor. Tommy John started and lost the game 5-3 to Rollie Fingers.

Who is the oldest player to get a hit?

Minnie Minoso, a 1996 inductee into the Mexican Baseball Hall of Fame. The Cuban native was 53 on September 12, 1976, when he hit safely for the White Sox against Sid Monge of the Angels. Minoso also had two at bats in 1980, without a hit.

Who is the oldest man to throw a legal spitball?

Jack Quinn. He was 50 when he finished his career in 1933 with the Reds. When he was 49, he became the oldest man to win a game. In 1931, when he was 48, he led the National League in saves with 15. In 1932, at age 49, he again led the league in saves with eight.

Who is the youngest National Leaguer to win a batting title?

Pistol Pete Reiser, 1941 Dodgers—.343. He was 22 years, 6 months, and 8 days old when the season ended on September 25th.

Who was the youngest big leaguer to die?

Jay Dahl. His entire major-league career consisted of one game with the Houston Colt .45s (later the Astros) on September 27, 1963, when he was 17—part of the youngest team ever to take the field in a big-league game. Also on that team were 20-year-old Joe Morgan and 19-year-old Rusty Staub. Dahl pitched 2.2 innings and lost, giving up seven hits, no strikeouts, and no walks.

Two years later, on June 20, 1965, Dahl was killed in a car crash in Salisbury, North Carolina. He was 19.

Who is the youngest player to hit at least 40 home runs in one season?

Eddie Mathews. In 1953, he walloped 47 for the Braves. The future Hall of Famer was just 21.

Who was the oldest rookie in the American League?

Satchel Paige. After a lifetime of dominating the Negro Leagues—he estimated that he had won 2,000 and lost 500 games—he made his big-league debut with Cleveland on July 9, 1948, when he was reputed to be 42. He won six games for the pennant-bound Indians.

Who was the oldest rookie in the National League?

Diomedes Olivo, a relief pitcher who debuted with the Pirates on September 5, 1960. He was 41.

Who is the oldest man to appear in his first All-Star Game?

Dennis Martinez. He was 35 when he made his first All-Star appearance as an Expo in 1990, his 14th year in the majors.

Who was the oldest player to hit a grand slam?

Carlton Fisk of the White Sox, on October 3, 1991, at age 42. The White Sox beat the Twins 13-12 in Game 2 to sweep a doubleheader.

The oldest and youngest pitchers in the American League in 1965 were teammates. Both were elected to the Hall of Fame. Who were they?

The oldest was Satchel Paige, 59, who was added to the Kansas City Athletics' roster by owner Charlie Finley as a publicity stunt. As Paige sat in a rocking chair provided for the occasion—"Satchel Paige Night," September 25—Jim "Catfish" Hunter, all of 19, posed on his lap.

Who was the oldest rookie to hit a home run?

"Sweet" Lou Johnson of the Dodgers, in 1965. He was 31. Although he appeared in 34 games in 1960, 1 game in 1961, and 61 games in 1962 (when he hit two homers), he was still considered a rookie in 1965.

Who was the oldest home run champion?

Darrell Evans, Tigers, 1985. He hit 40 when he was 38.

Who was the youngest player to hit a home run?

Tommy Brown, Dodgers, August 20, 1945, off Preacher Roe of the Pirates. Brown was 17. He hit only 30 more homers.

Who is the oldest man to drive in at least 100 runs in a season?

Dave Winfield, 1992 Blue Jays. He was 40 when he drove in 108.

Who is the youngest pitcher to strike out 1,500 batters?

Bert Blyleven of the Rangers, who was 25 when he struck out right fielder Sixto Lezcano of the Brewers at Arlington Stadium on August 25, 1976.

Who is the youngest umpire in the modern history of the major leagues?

Bill Evans. He was 22 in 1906, when he began his 21-year Hall of Fame career as an American League umpire.

Who was the oldest pitcher to throw a complete-game shutout?

Phil Niekro. He was 46 when, on October 6, 1985, he notched win #300, an 8-0 shutout, for the Yankees over the Blue Jays.

Who was the oldest pitcher to lead the American League in innings pitched and starts in the same season?

Charlie Hough. In 1987, when he was 39, the knuckleballer had 40 starts and pitched 285.1 innings with the Texas Rangers.

Who is the oldest player to steal a base?

Arlie Latham, age 50, did it for the Giants in 1909.

Where is the oldest professional ballpark still standing?

Rickwood Field in Birmingham, Alabama. The 9,600-seat stadium, built in 1910, was modeled after Forbes Field in Pittsburgh.

It was the home of the Birmingham Barons through 1988, and for many years the home of the Birmingham Black Barons. A $6,000,000 renovation project is under way.

DREAM TEAMS

━━━━━━━

The All-Equine Team

Del Paddock, Moses "Chief" Yellowhorse, Lerton Pinto, Ewell Blackwell ("The Whip"), Jimmy "Pony" Ryan, Trot Nixon, Lou Gehrig ("The Iron Horse"), Pony Sager, Harry "The Horse" Danning, Hanson Horsey, Ray "Jockey" Kolp, Cowboy Jones, Tim "Crazy Horse" Foli, Bill Kelso, Vince Horsman, Pepper Martin ("The Wild Horse of the Osage").

The All-Weather Team

Dave Weathers, Ernie Gust, Roy Weatherly, J. T. Snow, Bob "Hurricane" Hazle, Jamie Easterly, Mark Clear, Clint Hartung ("The Hondo Hurricane"), "Tornado" Jack Weimer, Jake Freeze, Cyclone Ryan, Sunny Jim Bottomley, Tim Flood, George Winter, Dusty Baker, Nippy Jones, Sammy Hale, Rich Gale, Frosty Bill Duggleby, Frosty Thomas, Dave Frost, Harry Bright, Tim Raines, Windy McCall, Storm Davis, Alvin Dark. Manager: Mike Hargrove ("The Human Rain Delay"). Umpires: Bill Summers, Jim Summer.

The All-"Time" Team

Billy Sunday, August Bergamo, June Greene, Rudy May, Leon Day, Sunset Jimmy Burke, Maurice Morning Wills, Rick Monday, Johnny Weekly, Skipper

Friday, Ray Knight, Fred Fussell ("The Moonlight Ace"), Jack Spring, Reggie Jackson ("Mr. October").

The All-Cartoon Team

Don Mueller ("Mandrake the Magician"), Moon Mullen, Don Slaught ("Sluggo"), Peanuts Lowery, Charlie Brown, Linus Frey, Bob Schroder, Joe Lucey, Don Mossi ("Dumbo"), Felix Millan, Minnie Minoso, Sylvester Simon, Daffy Dean, Chip Hale and Dale Berra, Casper Asbjornson, Flash Gordon, Mickey Mantle, Goofy Gomez, Hughie Jennings, Dewey Evans, Looie Aparicio, Donald Mattingly, John "Daisy" Davis, Alvin Davis, Mike Simon, George Theodore, Beauty Bancroft, "The Beast"—Jimmie Foxx, Albert Belle, Doc Cramer, Happy Felsh, Prince Oana, Bugs Raymond.

The All-Law-Firm Team

Sterling Hitchcock, Webster Garrison, Spencer Armstrong Pumpelly, Logan Drake, Burgess Whitehead, Jennings Poindexter, Overton Tremper, Thaddeus Inglehart Wilborn, Broderick Perkins, Skelton Napier, Decatur Poindexter Jones, Pembroke Finlayson, Cadwallader Coles, Quinton McCracken, Salomon Torres, Bristol Robotham Lord, Oliver Dinwiddie Tucker, Reid Cornelius, Donovan Osborne, and Heathcliff Slocumb. Senior partner: Craig Counsell. And what if Scott Jacoby and Chief Meyers got together to practice law?

The All-Vegetarian Team

Bob Sprout, Frank "Squash" Wilson, Pee Wee Reese, Nick "Tomato Face" Cullop, Camilo ("Little Potato") Pascual, José Lima, Hub Perdue ("The Gallatin Squash"), Herb Cobb (twice), Harry "Beans" Keener, Beany Jacobson, Spud Chandler, Walker Cress, Yam Yaryan, Bibb Falk, "Pea Soup" Dumont, Clyde "Pea Ridge" Day, Luke "Hot Potato" Hamlin, Lerton Pinto, Harry Colliflower, Russ Heman (from Olive, California), Oscar "Spinach" Melillo. Captain: Turkey Gross. Starter: Bob Seeds. Manager: Joe Crisp. Umpire: Beans Reardon.

Do not invite Ham Wade, Bull Durham, Chicken Wolf, Herb Hash, Laymon Lamb, Coot Veal, Ox Miller, Chuck Finley, Ox Eckhardt, Charlie Gassaway, or Sweetbreads Bailey to eat with this group.

The All-Travel Team

Nolan "The Express" Ryan, Johnny Hudson, Ty Pickup, Cy Ferry, Harry Craft, John Dodge, Cotton Nash, Choo Choo Coleman, Lerton Pinto, Mac Suzuki, Ray Mack, Ed Charles ("The Glider"), Steamboat Struss, "Hot" Rod Kanehl, Henry Mercedes, Willis Hudlin, Skyrocket Smith, Scooter Tucker (twice!), Phil "Scooter" Rizzuto, Joe DiMaggio ("The Yankee Clipper"), Van Fletcher, Joe Benz, Carr Smith, Lew Carr, Pat Deisel, Steamboat Williams, Bill "Steamboat" Otey, Ed "Battleship" Gremminger, Showboat Fisher, Frenchy Uhalt, Virgil Trucks, Whitey Ford, Jack Bentley, Walter Johnson ("The Big Train"), Jim "Pud" Galvin ("The Little Steam Engine"), Pat Rockett, Gunboat Gumbert, Roger "Rocket" Clemens. Make sure to ask Walt Cruise to play with this team. Umpire: Dale Ford. Do not sign: Crash Davis.

The All-Bar Team

John Boozer, Ed Stein, Rod Beck, Punch Knoll, Miller Huggins, Dan Tipple, Pedro Borbon, Pinch Thomas, Jim Brewer, Jerry Remy, Bobby Wine, Danny Schaeffer, James Mouton, Jimmy Ripple, Wedo Martini, Ed Pabst, Pete Rose, Bill White, Red Schoendienst, Frank Reisling, Bud Harrelson, Johnny Lush, Chief Bender, Bock Baker, Johnny Walker, Brewery Jack Taylor, George "Three Star" Hennessey, "Half-Pint" Rye, Highball Wilson, Ed Busch, Bill Knickerbocker, Chris Sabo ("Spuds MacKenzie"), the Milwaukee Brewers, Jack Daniels ("Sour Mash"), and Big Jeff Pfeffer (from Champaign, Illinois). Owners: Jacob Ruppert, August Busch. General Manager: Branch Rickey.

The All-Condiment Team

Salty Parker, Harry Sage, Brad Gulden, Pepper Martin, Frank "Jelly" Jelinich, Mayo Smith, Tony Hellman, Pat Caraway, Tom Butters, Jim Curry, Curry Foley, Chili Davis, Wayne Kirby, Steve Gerkin, Vinegar Bend Mizell, Ginger Beaumont, Kirby Puckett, Kid Elberfeld ("The Tabasco Kid"), John "Honey" Romano, Pickles Dillhoefer.

The All-Game Team

Sport McAllister, Steve Bowling, Emmett Bowles, Harry Billiard, Dave Rowan, Jumping Joe Dugan, Ches Crist, Ace Parker, Ski Melillo, Harlan Pool, Elwood "Bingo" Demoss (of the Negro Leagues), Lonnie "Skates" Smith, Walt Ockey, Kick Kelly, Bibb "Jockey" Falk, Leaping Mike Menosky, and Mack Wheat (from Polo, Missouri). Also to be considered are Buddy Blattner, 1936 and 1937 World Doubles Ping-Pong Champion, and Johnny Kling, 1908 World Pool Champion.

The All-Bug Team

Bugs Morris, Buzz Stephen, Buzzy Wares, Tony "Mosquito" Ordenana, Willard "Grasshopper" Mains, Lee "Stinger" Stange, Miller Huggins ("The Mighty Mite"), Spider Jorgensen, Lenn Sakata, Skeeter Webb, Flea Clifton, Loren

"Bee Bee" Babe, Mike Roach, Freddy Patek ("The Flea"), "Grasshopper" Jim Whitney, Bill Rigney ("The Cricket"), Frank Bonner ("The Human Flea"), Bug Holliday, Carson Bigbee, and Curt "Honey" Walker (from Beeville, Texas).

Their archrivals: Swat McCabe, Jack Chapman and Robert Ferguson (both known as "Death to Flying Things"), Roger Cramer ("Flit"), and Harry "Swats" Swacina.

Wonder if any of them ever played for the Lubbock Crickets of the Texas-Louisiana League?

The Gender-Bender Team

Barbara Chrisley (played as Neil), Liz Funk, Bill "Mary" Calhoun, Lou "Lena" Kretlow, Judy Johnson, John "Liz" Malarkey, Tim "Bridget" Donahue, Tillie Shafer, Anna Compton (played as Pete), Paul "Molly" Meloan, Sargent "Sadie" Houk, Charles "She" Donahue, William "Beverly" Bayne, Clair Johnson (played as Bart), Molly Moore, Grayson "Gracie" Pierce, Carlos Paula, Gail Hopkins, Nick Polly, John "Bonnie" Hollingsworth, Ulysses "Lil" Stoner, Bill Lange—"Little Eva," Roy "Polly" Wolfe, Lena Blackburne, Paul "Polly" Speraw, Dolly Gray, Monroe "Dolly" Stark, Sadie McMahon, Maurice "Molly" Craft, Carmen "Bunker" Hill, Tilly Walker.

The All-College Team

Roe Skidmore, Ken Williams, Yale Murphy, Schoolboy Rowe, Cal Ripken, Jim Converse, Bob Tufts (a Princeton graduate), Jim Creighton, Brian Hunter, Jeff Cornell, Jim Ball, Jack Clark, Joel Finch, Denver Lemaster, Dallas Green, Don Baylor, Wayne Terwilliger, Elston Howard, Emory Helfrich, Duke Snider, Bobby Brown, Jeff Kent, Junior Gilliam, Roy Smalley Senior, Rip Radcliff, Darryl Boston, George Washington, Frankie Frisch ("The Fordham Flash"), Pat Rice. Proctor: Red Proctor. Manager: Dean Palmer.

The All-Dog Team

Jack Russell, Lew "Old Dog" Ritter, Darryl Boston, Irish Meusel, Aaron Pointer, "Benji" Gil, Bill "Mad Dog" Madlock, Jim "Bulldog" Bouton, George "Doggie" Miller, Harry "Collie" Colliflower, Butch Huskey, Russ Springer, Charley Bassett, Poodles Hutcheson, Pug Bennett, Fido Baldwin, Bow Wow Arft, Mutt Wilson, George "Pooch" Puccinelli, Mario Mendoza (from Chihuahua, Mexico), Fred McGriff ("The Crime Dog"), Tony "Doggie" Pérez, Keith Shepherd, Orel "Bulldog" Hershiser, Rex "The Wonder Dog" Hudler, Dane Iorg, the St. Louis

Terriers (of the Federal League), Brian Bark, Ed Sicking (from St. Bernard, Ohio). Umpire: Frank Pulli.

The All-Sweet-Tooth Team

David Cone, Ed Mars, Candy Cummings, Peach Pie O'Connor, Mike Heath, Sweet Lou Piniella, Merritt "Sugar" Cain, Taft "Taffy" Wright, Duke Carmel, Mark Lemongello, Mickey Mantle and Roger Maris ("The M&M Boys"), Billy Sunday, Rick Sweet, all the Brownies, Pie Traynor, Cookie Lavagetto, and Dots Miller, followed by Norm Sherry.

The All-Toy Team

Jim Toy, Art Doll, Scooter Rizzuto, Scooter Tucker, Kewpie Pennington, Yo-yo Davalillo, Bunt Frisbee, Baby Doll Jacobson.

The All-Breakfast Team

Sam Rice, Zack Wheat, Skinny Graham, George Creamer, Johnny Oates, Joe Crisp, Sugar Cain, Terry Cornutt, Honey Romano, Wally Post, Samuel Ralston, Al Kellogg, Johnny "Bananas" Mostil, Scoops Carey, Joe Berry, Darryl Strawberry, Karl Spooner.

The Valentine's Day Team

Slim Love, Paul Dear, Frank Bliss, Ernie Kish, Cuddles Marshall, Eros "Cy" Barger, Cupid Childs, Bobby Bonds, Candy Cummings, Ben Flowers, Honey Barnes, Beau Bell, Ellis Valentine, Diamond Jim Gentile, Jimmy Ring, Bill Hart, Ron Darling, Sugar Cain, Steve Sparks, Rick Sweet, Vincente Amor. Captain: Paul Casanova. Managers: Bobby Valentine and Miller Huggins ("Hug"). Umpire: Gary Darling.

The All-Initial Team

C. B. White, El Tappe, Sadaharu Oh, Bill Kay, Johnnie Gee, U. L. Washington, A. J. Sager, Elzie "Clise" Dudley, B. J. Surhoff, Frank Ellerbee, J T Mooty, Dwight "Dr. K" Gooden, Elbie Fletcher, J. B. Young, Eric Owens, J. T. Snow, T. R. Bryden, C. B. Burns, J. R. Richard, Jeff Dee McMurry, J C Hartman, C. J. Nitkowski, D. C. "Dee" Moore, Esty Chaney, De Wayne Vaughn, J. T. Bruett, Larry See, Xavier "Mr. X" Rescigno, Don "Big D" Drysdale, Casey Stengel, G. Bryant, Spike Owen, Tommy Agee, Emerit "Em" Lindbeck, Artie Dede (twice!), Chad Ogea (pronounced "O. J."), Jimmie "Double X" Foxx, Jim Beattie, Ewell Blackwell,

Gee Walker, Alpha Brazle, F. P. Santangelo, R. L. Stevens, O. F. Baldwin, Tommy John—"T. J.", Elston "Ellie" Howard, T. J. Mathews, J. J. Thobe, Fred Beebe, Jay Johnstone, Dee Fondy. Commissioner: A. B. "Happy" Chandler.

The All-Floral Team

Bud Harrelson, Cactus Keck, Ivy Olson, Pete Rose, Daisy Davis, Guy Morton ("The Alabama Blossom"), Hoe Schultz, Lefty Grove, Kevin Flora, Mike Gardiner, Wes Gardner, Ben Flowers, Buttercup Dickerson, and Thorny Hawkes. Captains: Bob Spade and Tom Dowse. Manager: Garland Braxton. Broadcaster: ESPN's Gary Thorne.

The All-Cheese Team

John Romano, Al "Cheese" Schweitzer, Clarence Kraft, "Colby" Jack Coombs.

The All-Court Team

Tom Lawless, Willie Miranda, Henry Lynch, Law Daniels, Vern Law (wife: VaNita; sons: Varlin, Vaughn, Vance, Verl, and Veldon; but no Victor), Harmon "Killer" Killebrew, George Case, Norm Cash (from Justiceburg, Texas), Joe Judge, Dave Justice, Eddie Solomon, Rob Dibble, Cuddles Marshall, Frank Howard ("Capital Punishment," when he was with the Washington Senators), Anthony "Bunny" Brief, Al Heist, Josh Booty, Frank Lary ("The Yankee Killer"), Jack Crooks, Jim Constable, Johnny Bench, Harry "Judge" Lumley, Craig Counsell, Con Dempsey, Wayne Nordhagen (from Thief River Falls, Minnesota), Jeff Leonard, a.k.a. "Penitentiary Face".

The All-Irish Team

Irish Meusel, Mayo Smith, "Irish" Mike Shannon, Danny Claire, Claire Patterson, Kerry Taylor, Irish McIlveen, Mike Kilkenny, Hal Irelan.

The All-Investment Team

Ernie Banks, Don Money, Hal Chase, Silver Flint, Norm Cash, Felipe Lira, Sterling Hitchcock, Troy Neel, Wes Stock, John Kroner, Curt Schilling, Herman Franks, Goldie Rapp, Derek Aucoin, Matt Ruebel, Bobby Bonds, Reid Nichols, Bill Pounds, Mark Koenig, Bill Madlock. Do not invite to play on this team: Oscar Gamble. These players can do their banking at the Guaranty Bank of Brown Deer, Wisconsin, which offers certificates of deposit tied to the success (or failure) of the Milwaukee Brewers.

The All-Job Team

Charlie Shoemaker, Bill Plummer, Dave Parker, Farmer Vaughn, Clyde King, Mel Queen, Lance Painter, Prince Oana, John Miller, Duffy Dyer, Max Butcher, Earl Weaver, Bob Usher, Darrell Porter, Bob Skinner, Cecil Cooper, Jimmy Sexton, Johnnie Priest, Jim Mason, Cuddles Marshall, Mike Cook, Lee Smith, Preacher Roe, Dusty Baker, Brett Butler, Ed "Junkman" Lopat, Hick Carpenter, Jim Brewer, Chuck Tanner, Arlas Taylor, Catfish Hunter, Joe Carter, Red Dorman. Part-timer: Glen Hobbie. Broadcaster: Red Barber. Commissioner: Happy Chandler.

The All-Fish Team

George Gill, Dizzy Trout, Bobby Sturgeon, Lu Blue, Rod Carew, Catfish Hunter, "Wahoo" Sam Crawford, Thornton Kipper, Jack "Crab" Warhop, George Haddock, Snapper Kennedy, Ed Whiting, Bobby Sturgeon, Al "Cod" Myers, Brian Fisher, Clay Roe, Chub Collins, William Bass, Shad Barry, Jess Pike, Tim and Chico Salmon (Salmon for two!), Roy Crabb, Lefty Herring, Thomas "Oyster" Burns, the Chicago Whales (even though whales are mammals, not fish). Manager: Jack Creel. Umpire: Rocky Roe.

The All-Terrain Team

Mickey Rivers, William Land, Mike Heath, Marsh Williams, José Mesa, Bucky Waters, Fred Glade, Chan Ho Park, Doug Creek, Forest "Greg" Swindell, Ruben Sierra, Cliff "Mountain Music" Melton (twice), Jake Wood, Gary Woods, Floyd Caves "Babe" Herman, Charlie Lea, Brook Jacoby, Lee Tunnell, Arlie Pond, Al Platte, Brooks Robinson, Glen Gorbous, Hector Valle, Punch Knoll, Terry Burrows, Muddy Ruel, Luis Arroyo, Trench Davis, Ted Firth, Matt Beech, Joe Lake, Dale Berra, Ken Hill, Gabby Street, Dick Lane, Frank Mountain, Dusty Rhodes, Sandy Amoros, Louie Meadows, John Wetteland. Umpire: Rocky Roe.

Do not invite Wildfire Schulte to play on this team.

The "Are You Sure That's How You Spell It?" Team

Jacke Davis, Jeoff (not Jeff, not Geoff) Long, Loyd Colson, Dennis Konuszewski, Verdo Elmore, Rheal Cormier (a lumberjack in the off-season), Brian Maxcy, Art Hoelskoetter (who, during his three-year career—1905–1908—with the Cardinals, played at least 15 games at each position), Johnny Welaj, Kirt Manwaring, Dax Xenos Jones, Scot Thompson, Joe Kmak, Astyanax Douglass, Ryan Hawblitzel, Mark Grudzielanek, Jouett Meekin (his record of three triples in one game by a pitcher has stood for over 100 years!), Joe Zdeb, Rob Lukachyk, Myrl

Brown, Paul Spoljaric, Ricky Trlicek, Jack Kubiszyn, Wid Matthews, Eli Grba, Jimy Williams, Dale Sveum, Steve Wojciechowski, Greg Pirkl, Emerit Lindbeck, Joe Oeschger, Hawatha Terrell Wade, Ron Mrozinski, Jeromy Burnitz, Midre Almeric Cummings, Dave Mlicki, Ken Szotkiewicz (2 *Z*s and a *K*–38 points in Scrabble!), Jim Czajkowski, Shawn Kealoha ("loved one" in Hawaiian) Boskie, Jerry Dybzinski, Emil Yde, Chet Hajduk, the Krsnich boys—Mike and Rocky— Gus Mcginnis, Doug Konieczny, Al Hrabosky, Mike Rogodzinski, Jimmy Uchrin-scko, Doug "Eye Chart" Gwosdz, Jerry Ujdur, Monte Pfyl, John Pyecha, Kimothy Batiste, Phil Todt, Hal Janvrin, Ed Zmich, Johnny Wyrostek, Walt Hriniak, Joe Grzenda, Sal Yvars, Tim Pyznarski, Mike Cvengros, Ed Fitz Gerald, George Pik-tuzis, Bugs Reisigl, Johnny Podgajny, Dennis Paepke, Johnny Grodzicki, John Wockenfuss, John Tsitouris, Graig Nettles, Ed Walczak, Howdie Groskloss (later Howard Groskloss, M.D.), Jonathan Trumpbour Matlack, Ike Samuls (real first name: Samuel), Frankie Pytlak. And don't forget these: Ray Krawczyk, Mike Blyzka, Jerry Schypinski, Rick Herrscher (D.D.S.), Craig Smajstrla, Pop Burtschy, Bert Kuczynski. Umpire: Charles "Cy" Pfirman.

The "Double" Team

Robb Nen, Edd Roush, Dann Bilardello, Benn Karr, Dann Howitt, Gregg Jef-feries, Donn Clendenon, Ronn Reynolds, Lenn Sakata.

   Want more? How about "Double" Joe Dwyer (12 career games, *no dou-bles!*), Morrie Steevens, Tim Harikkala, Larry Biittner ("two *i*s, two *t*s, no hits"), Herb Juul, Pete Mikkelsen, Rikkert Faneyte, Clyde Kluttz, Claude Gouzzie, Dick Errickson, Harry Pettee, Robert Eenhoorn, Slim Harriss, Jay Faatz, Jimmie Foxx, Kevin Mmahat, Chet Laabs, Homer Ezzell, Kid Willson, Mickey Klutts, Ossee (that *is* his true name) Schreckengost, Harry Eells, Bill Wambsganss, Jule Mal-lonee, Jim Kaat, Dave Nilsson, and George Cappuzzello—a triple double!

The "Dressed for Baseball" Team

Cap Anson, Jim Bluejacket, Harry "The Hat" Walker, Socks Seibold and Socks Seybold (a pair of Socks), Pants Rowland, George Derby, Ty Cobb, Jersey Bakely, Felix Mantilla, Gary Buckels, Don Hood, Zip Collins, Jimmy "Loafer" McAleer, Stan Jok, Tex Jeanes, Joe Haynes, "Long" Levi Meyerle, Ron Gant, John "Tight Pants" Titus, Cotton Nash, Buttons Briggs, Dave "Rags" Righetti, R. J. "Shoes" Reynolds, Boots Poffenberger, Rube Oldring, Charlie Spikes, Jim Converse, Clete Boyer, Jim Coates, Jesse Levis, George "Highpockets" Kelly, Spike Owen (real name Spike), Bill Dickey, Spec Shea, Jock Menafee, Sam Frock, the White Sox, the Red Sox, the Red Legs. Manager: Charlie Dressen. Umpire: Silk O'Laughlin. You might invite Earle Combs to play with this team, but don't invite Emmett "Snags" Heidrick, Rip Williams, or Fuzz White.

The "Name Sounds Familiar" Team

Michael Jordan, Kenny Rogers, Zachary Taylor, John Kennedy, Kaiser Wilhelm, Mike Myers, Ed Sullivan, Mathew Broderick, Ed Begley, R. J. Reynolds, James Baldwin, George Washington, Terry Bradshaw, Jimmy Dorsey, George Burns, Bill James, Davey Crockett, Jim Bowie, King Cole, Al Smith, Albert Schweitzer, Kit Carson, Red Smith (all four of them!), Bobby Jones, Johnny Walker, Al Unser, Mike Tyson, Eddie Fisher, Bill Bradley, Trader Horne, Nick Carter, Jack Horner, Gary Cooper, Ethan Allen.

The All-Baseball Team

Sport McAllister, Enos Slaughter, Buddy Lively, Champ Summers, Pete Center, Boo Ferris, Phil Roof, Rick Camp, Aaron Clapp, Andy High, Gene Alley, Hugh East, David West, Joe Wood, Johnny Bench, Trot Nixon, Early Wynn (twice!), Bob Blewitt, Fielder Jones, Jim Command, Herb Score, Willie "Stretch" McCovey, Fleet Walker, Win Kellum, Union Man Holke, Charlie Pickett, Speed Walker, Rip Collins, Pop Swett, Charlie Root, Home Run Baker, Charlie Chant, Bill Crouch, George Fair, Bruce Fields, Bunt Frisbee, Joe Wall, Lively Everett, Herman Franks, Tony Suck, Randy Ready, George Upp, Jeff Tabaka (today he might be nicknamed "Chewin' "), Joe Start, Roy Hitt, Bob Swift, Gene "Rubber" Krapp, Eric Plunk, Curtis Pride, Ralph Houk ("The Major"), Blas Minor, Ty Pickup, Press Cruthers, Phenomenal Smith, Jim Ball, Jim Greengrass, Matt Batts, Eddie Quick, Tom Seats, Billy Bean, Homer Sumner, Warren Hacker, Rowland Office, Bob Walk, Jim Park, Darcy Fast, Archie Yell, Johnny "Hippity" Hopp, John "The Count" Montefusco, Hack Wilson, Cot Deal, Bob Locker, Vic Power, Shag Thompson, Homer Bush, Charley Pick, Horace Speed, Johnny Rawlings. Closer: Nap Kloza. (For Wrigley Field only: Ivy Griffin.) Manager: Skipper Friday. Broadcaster: DeWayne Staats. Commissioner: Spike Eckert.

The All-Body Team

Russ Heman, Floyd "Three-Finger" Newkirk, Josh Booty, Ribs Raney, Bump Hadley, Don Gullett, Roscoe "Rubberlegs" Miller, Bartolo Colon, Barney Mussill, Mike Overy, George Brunet, Runt Walsh, Archie "Lumbago" Stimmel, Bob Pate, George "Grin" Bradley, Eddie Eayrs, Bob "Crooked Arm" Cremens, Bun Troy and Bunn Hearn (a set of Buns), Dave Beard, Butch Huskey, Half-Pint Rye, Marv "Babyface" Breuer, Bris Lord ("The Human Eyeball"), Zeke (for his physique) "Banana Nose" Bonura, Harry Boyles, Wee Willie Keeler, Len Dykstra ("Nails"), Joe Dobson and Ferris Fain (both known as "Burrhead"), Baldy Louden, Dick "Twitches" Porter, Pop "Dimples" Tate, Hank Small, Hickey Hoffman, Fred "Bootnose" Hoffman, Slim McGrew, Red Cox, Jug Thesenga, Tom

"The Arm" Hafey, Scott Brow, Footer Johnson, Crazy Schmit, Carey Selph, "Glass Arm" Eddie Brown, Davy "Tom Thumb" Force (5'4", 130 pounds), Ray Bare, Pudgy Gould, Elroy Face, Rollie "Bunions" Zeider, Butts Wagner, Lorin Grow, Ross "Crazy Eyes" Grimsley, Dave Short, Mike Palm, Tom Hart, George Burpo, Bones Ely, Ricky Bones, Sammy Byrd ("Babe Ruth's Legs"), Shorty Howe, Heinie Manush, Rich Hand, Phil Knuckles, Bill Hands, Buck Marrow, Pinky Higgins, Footsie Blair, Leo "The Lip" Durocher, George "Twinkletoes" Selkirk, Harry Cheek, Sixto Lezcano, Fats Fothergill, Fatty Briody, Bill Keister, Jumbo Brown, Chubby Dean, Walt "No-Neck" Williams, "Voiceless" Tim O'Rourke (his nickname distinguished him from "Orator" Jim O'Rourke), Joe "Muscles" Gallagher, Marvin "Baby Face" Breuer, Bob "Bigfoot" Stanley, Dave Brain (who had three triples in a game twice in one season), Lip Pike, Ed Head, Rollie Fingers, Clyde "Foots" Barfoot, Benny "Earache" Meyer, Puddin' Head Jones, Yale "Midget" Murphy (5'3", 125 pounds, also known as "Tot"), Barry Foote, Piano Legs Hickman, Blondy Ryan, Ben Van Dyke, Luke Appling ("Old Aches and Pains").

The Interplanetary Team

Ed Mars, Bill "Spaceman" Lee, Wally Moon, George "Mercury" Myatt, Mickey Mantle ("The Commerce Comet"), Danny Wallin (from Neptune, New Jersey). Broadcaster: Bob Starr.

The International Team

Steve Nicosia, George Pipgras ("The Danish Viking"), Israel Sanchez, Dolf Luque ("The Pride of Havana"), Moe Solomon, Ray Scarborough, Steve Gibralter, Osman France, Paul Sorrento, Parisian Bob Cruthers, Frank Brazill, Trenidad Hubbard, Germany Schaefer, Pat Capri, Mike Kilkenny, Paul Florence, Harry "Doc" Tonkin, Al Madrid, Klondike Douglass, Babe Danzig, Bill Salisbury, Jeff Kent, Bob Natal, Arthur Rhodes, Weldon Henley, John "Egyptian" Healy (from Cairo, Illinois), Miguel Cairo, Johnny Vander Meer ("The Dutch Master"), José Lima, Allan Lewis ("The Panamanian Express"), Kelly Paris, Luzerne (Lu) Blue, Andrew Lorraine, Jersey Bakely, Chad Kimsey, Dave Altizer ("Filipino"), Lefty Gomez ("The Gay Castilian"), Johnny Miljus ("The Big Serb" whose wild pitch ended the 1927 World Series), Red Shannon, Germany Long, Mark Portugal, Larry French, German Gonzalez (from Venezuela!), German Barranca (from Mexico!) Olaf "Swede" Henriksen (from Kirkerup, Denmark), Juan Marichal ("The Dominican Dandy"), Flame Delhi, Steve Parris, Tim Ireland, Troy Neel, Bobby Thomson ("The Flying Scot"), Charles Comiskey ("The Old Roman"), Bill Bergen, Joe Hague, Rafael Santo Domingo, Blas Monaco, Charles "Greek" George, Roger Bresnahan ("The Duke of Tralee," born in Toledo, Ohio), Chile

"Jose" Gomez, Dutch Leonard, Gus Brittain, Clyde Milan, Bill Roman, Hugh Poland, Irish Meusel, Dutch Jordan (twice!), Lou "The Mad Russian" Novikoff, Turk Lown, Tom Oran, Paul Moskau, Joe Malay, Al "The Mad Hungarian" Hrabosky, "Turkey" Mike Donlin, Harry "The Golden Greek" Agganis, Lou Skizas ("The Nervous Greek"), Bill Wight, Rudy York, Heinie Meine ("The Count of Luxembourg"), Al Naples, Charlie Nice, Evar Swanson ("The Swift Swede"), Woody English, Pat Borders. Umpire: Dutch Rennert. Broadcasters: France Laux and Dutch Reagan.

God's Baseball Team

Jim Devine, Moses Solomon ("The Rabbi of Swat"),* Max Bishop, Jim Abbott, Tony Mullane—"The Apollo of the Box," Angel Mangual, Sabath "Sam" Mele, Emmett "Parson" Perryman, Deacon Philippe, Wally Moses, Jesus Alou, Lance Parrish, Maurice Archdeacon, Bris Lord, John Calvin Klippstein, Jimmy Sexton, Dave Pope, Luke Easter, Charlie Abbey, John Parsons, José Cardenal, Ebba St. Claire, Henry Easterday, Jake Virtue, Pryor McElveen, Russ Morman, The Angels, Cupid Childs, Bob Christian, Gregory Pryor, Johnny Priest, Howie Nunn, Jiggs Parson, Billy Sunday, Vernon "The Deacon" Law, Jim Gentile, Preacher Roe, Larry See, Pius Schwert, Ivan DeJesus, Deacon White, Russ "The Mad Monk" Meyer, Monk Sherlock, Adonis Terry, The Padres, Conrad Cardinal, Bubba Church, Johnny Temple, Mark Christman, Lem Cross, Hi Church, Billy Scripture (a college star at Wake Forest). Managers: Tiny Chaplin, Tony Faeth, George "The Miracle Man" Stallings. Umpire: Doug Harvey, nicknamed "God." They can hold a prayer meeting at the home of George Lyons, from Bible Grove, Illinois, Pepper Martin (Temple, Oklahoma), Ray Jarvis (Providence, Rhode Island), or Tex Hughson (Buda, Texas.)

Not on this list: José Pagan.

The All-Royal Team

King Kelly, Noble Dukes (twice), John Tudor, Clyde King, Queenie O'Rourke, Old Hoss Radbourn ("The King of Pitchers"), Al Schacht ("The Clown Prince of Baseball"), Ray Knight, King Lehr, Bris Lord, Earl Torgeson ("The Earl of Snohomish"), Bob Marquis, Prince Oana, Mel Queen, Fred Lear, Babe Ruth

*Two games, no home runs. Hoping to attract New York City's many Jewish fans back to the Polo Grounds—and away from Babe Ruth at the new Yankee Stadium—Giants' manager John McGraw signed Solomon in 1923. But Solomon could neither field nor hit big-league pitching. He left baseball to play pro football.

("The Sultan of Swat"), Irvin "Kaiser" Wilhelm, Don Kaiser, Marquis Grissom, "Prince" Hal Schumacher, Danny Napoleon, The Royals, John McGraw ("The Little Napoleon"), Squire Potter, Cesar Geronimo, Sir Timothy Keefe, Tom Prince, Duke Carmel, Red Barron, Roger Bresnahan ("The Duke of Tralee"), Rogers "Rajah" Hornsby, Chief Bender, "Prince" Hal Chase, John "The Count" Montefusco. Umpire: Tom Lynch ("King of the Umpires").

The Typesetter's Dream Team

Ed Ott, Ron Cey, Lee May, Al Tate, Joe Lis, Ed Gill, Hi Ladd, Ed Bahr, Ed Kent, Ed Cole, Al Aber, Bob Way, Al Weis, Hi West, Al Maul, Mel Ott, Ty Cobb, Jim Ray, Don (and Tom, Roy, and Bob) Lee, Gus Gil, Ed Hug, Hi Bell, Ed Hawk, Ed Head, Bob Uhl, Joe Foy, Lon Ury, Joe Ohl, Ad Yale, Lu Blue, Ted Cox, Lou Say, Jay Fry.

The All-Leader Team

George Washington, John Kennedy, Bob Kennedy, Ted Kennedy, Art Garibaldi, Otis Nixon, Sheriff Blake, Admiral Schlei (not necessarily better than Ensign Cottrell), Abraham Lincoln Wolstenholme, Calvin Coolidge Julius Caesar Tuskahoma McLish, Joe Judge, Geronimo Peña, Von Joshua, Grover Cleveland Alexander, Grover Cleveland Lowdermilk, Taft Wright, Tito Fuentes, Ulysses Simpson Grant "Lil" Stoner, Mark Clark, General Stafford, General Crowder, Colonel Alex Ferson, the Washington Senators, Zack Taylor, Al Smith, Dave Justice, Colonel Mills, Colonel (real name "Colonel") Snover, Sarge Connally, Frank Chance ("The Peerless Leader"). Commissioner: General William D. Eckert.

The All-Family Team

Freddy Parent, Dad Clarkson, Kid Elberfeld, Babe Ruth, Johnny Mann, Henry "Father" Chadwick, John "Grandma" Murphy, Herman Son Winningham, Tot Pressnell, Bob Daughters, Laddie Renfroe, Hi Ladd, Coaker Triplett, Guy Lacy, Father Kelly, Philip "Grandmother" Powers, Rick "Big Daddy" Reuschel, Howard "Old Man" Ehmke, Elder White, Lady Baldwin, Cool Papa Bell, Papa Williams, John Papa, "Cousin" Ed Barrow, Bill Popp, Walter "Mother" Watson, Dan Brouthers, Hank Grampp, Sherm Lollar ("Dad"), Pop Lloyd, Alexis Infante, Sis Hopkins, Dawson Grama, Jimmy Bannon ("Foxy Grandpa"), Uncle Wilbert Robinson, Harry Child, Stan "The Man" Musial, Uncle Al Pratt, Kid Nichols, Pete Childs, Ellis Kinder ("Old Folks"), Baby Ortiz, Charles "Baby" Jones, Sonny Jackson, Granny Hamner, Cy Neighbors, Bob Friend. Babysitter: Nanny Fernandez. Umpire: Darryl Cousins. Do not invite: Richard Batchelor.

The Typesetter's Nightmare Team

Bob Giallombardo, Nick Strincevich, Al Hollingsworth, Vito Valentinetti, Leo Christopher Magee (born Leopold Christopher Hoernschmeyer), Constantine Keriazakos, Roger Peckenpaugh, Riggs Stephenson, William "Don't Call Me Bill" Van Landingham, Charlie Reipschlager, Lou Schiappacasse, Cliff Pastornicky, John Eichelberger, Dave Wehrmeister, Tim Griesenbeck, Lee DeMontreville, Stanwood Partenheimer, Wayne Terwilliger, Ray Ripplemeyer, Count Sensenderfer, Alan Hargesheimer, Stan Perzanowski, Warren Shannabrook, Fritz Ostermueller, Ken Raffensberger, Carl Yastrzemski (when he came up to the big leagues, one writer quipped: "You don't say his name—you sneeze it!"), Billy Grabarkewitz, Denny Riddleberger, Austin Knickerbocker, Kirk Dressendorfer, Arnold Portorcarrero, Steve Lombardozzi, Red Schoendienst, Dan Quisenberry, José Valdevielso, Andy Messersmith, Bill Monbouquette, Joey Amalfitano, Gene Vadboncoeur, Nino Bongiovanni. Manager: Cornelius McGillicuddy.

The "Team" Team

Rocky Colavito, Houston Jiminez, Brownie Foreman, Stuart Marlin, Yank Terry, Conrad Cardinal, Denver Grigsby, Bobby Brown, Socks Seibold, the Brewers—Jim, Rod, Mike, Tom, and Jack—Red Bird, Angel Mangual, Red Schoendienst, José Cardenal, Red Leg Snyder, Dave Philley, Tyler Houston, Elmer Cleveland, Reggie Cleveland, Grover Cleveland Alexander, Johnny Podres, Roy Cleveland Johnson, Cub Stricker, Daryl Boston. Manager: Buck Showalter.

The All-Echo Team

Coco Laboy, Choo Choo Coleman, Bobo Newsom, Zaza Harvey, Cuckoo Christensen, Pepe Frias, Bam-Bam Meulens, Bye-Bye Balboni, Yo-yo Davalillo, Boom-Boom Beck, Artie Dede, Chi Chi Olivo, Jo-Jo Moore, Cuckoo Jamieson, Pepe Mangual, Ty-Ty Tyler, the Go-Go White Sox of 1959, Kiki Cuyler, Jo-Jo White.

Minor Leaguers We Hope Make It to the Big Leagues, so We Can Include Them in This Chapter in the Next Edition of This Book

Eric Christopherson (Giants), Wonderful Terrific Monds (Braves), Andy Zwirchwitz (Mets), John Dillinger (Pittsburgh).

WHAT'S IN A NAME?

Who is Jack Norworth and why is his name in this book?

In 1908, he wrote "Take Me Out to the Ballgame," although he had never seen a baseball game! His other big hit was "Shine on Harvest Moon."

By what names were these players known?

Roy Wolfe, Monroe Stark, Smead, Solomon Hemus, Moore, Moon, Fingers, Oliver Johns.

Polly, Dolly, Jolley, Solly, Molly, Wally, Rollie, Ollie.

Besides the same parents, what did Joe, Vince, and Dom DiMaggio have in common?

The same middle name—Paul. Their father was Guiseppe Paolo.

Name the first four-Smith team.

The 1994 Baltimore Orioles' roster included Dwight, Lee, Lonnie, and Mark Smith.

Did players ever wear their nicknames on the backs of their jerseys?

Yes. Shortly after Ted Turner bought the Braves in 1976, nicknames were featured—albeit briefly—on their backs. Andy Messersmith, who wore #17, decided that his nickname would be "*Channel*," so his uniform back read *CHAN-*

NEL 17–not coincidentally, the station that broadcast Braves games. Turner owned the station, too.

When was the last time the word *Brooklyn* appeared on the Dodgers' uniforms?

On their 1945 road jerseys.

Who is career minor-leaguer Roger Alexander, and what is his name doing in this book?

On November 2, 1974, Alexander and Dave May were traded by the Milwaukee Brewers to the Atlanta Braves for Hank Aaron.

INEVITABLE NICKNAMES DEPARTMENT

Bob "Ach" Duliba, William "Pol" Perritt, Rip Vowinkel, Leaky Fausett, Pickles Dillhoefer, Soup Campbell, Molly Meloan, Rocky Stone, Virgil "Fire" Trucks, Carmen "Bunker" Hill, Dutch Holland, Hank "Bow Wow" Arft.

What did Junior Felix name his son?

Junior Felix Jr.

What did Juan Samuel name his son?

Samuel Samuel.

Who was 1962 Met Bob Miller's roommate?

Bob Miller (Robert Gerald Miller and Robert Lane Miller).

Cy Barger pitched for the Yankees and Dodgers, and for Pittsburgh in the Federal League, for seven years from 1906 to 1915. While his 46-63 record was run-of-the-mill, his real first name was definitely not. What was it?

Eros. His middle name was Bolivar.

What is the worst nickname in all of baseball, and perhaps in all of sports?

During his nine-year career with the Phillies and the Pirates, Hugh "Losing Pitcher" Mulcahy had a 45-89 W-L record—a .336 winning percentage, or, viewed another way, a .664 losing percentage. In 1937 Mulcahy led the National League with 56 appearances, but also led the league by surrendering 97 walks. In 1938, he was 10-20 and led the league in losses, a feat he accomplished again in 1940 with 22. That year he also led the league by giving up 283 hits.

Runner-up in the worst nickname of all time list: James Cato "Bad News" Galloway. Indeed. In his 21 games with the Cardinals of 1912 (his only season) Galloway went 10-for-54–a .185 batting average.

Honorable mention: Pitcher Lynn "Line Drive" Nelson, Pearce "What's the Use?" Chiles, Goat Anderson, Goat Cochran.

What is the best nickname in baseball?

Because of his mastery of the rules, Doug Harvey, who umpired in the National League from 1962 to 1992, was reverentially known as "God"!

What are the real names of these stars?

Bo Jackson	Vincent
Lew Burdette	Selva Lewis
Roger Clemens	William Roger
Babe Dahlgren	Ellsworth Tenney
Boo Ferris	David Meadow
Nolan Ryan	Lynn
Cookie Lavagetto	Harry Arthur
Butch Hobson	Clell Lavern
Babe Herman	Floyd Caves
Rusty Staub	Daniel
Jim Konstanty	Casimir James
Dean Chance	Wilmer

What is Chris Chambliss's real first name?

Carroll.

What is Ken Griffey Jr.'s real first name?

George. Sr. too.

Who was the only big leaguer in the history of the game whose initials were U. U.?

Expos pitcher Ugueth Urbina. Even if another U. U. comes along, Urbina will probably always be the only U. U. U. in the history of the game: his middle name is Urtain. His brothers are Ulises Utah Urbina and Ulmer Ulses Urbina.

Perhaps his boyhood heroes were Frank Francis Frisch, Carroll Christopher Chambliss, Homer Hiller Henry Hillebrand—if he had a fan club, would it be the 4-H club?—and Woodrow Wilson Williams. Is his Web site www.uuu?

Who is the only player whose name, when announced, told you what he was about to do?

Matt Batts, a catcher for the Red Sox, Browns, Tigers, White Sox, and Reds (1947–1956).

Who is the only big leaguer whose first name is Dudley?

Dudley "Mike" Hargrove.

Name the three Yankee Babes.

Babe Ruth, Ellsworth "Babe" Dahlgren, and Loren Babe.

Neil Chrisley (Senators, Tigers, Braves, 1957–1961) had an unusual first name for a big leaguer. What was it?

Barbra.

Why was All-Star first baseman Bill Skowron (Yankees, Dodgers, Senators, White Sox, Angels, 1954–1967) nicknamed "Moose"?

Though Skowron was a Chicago-born Polish American, his grandfather called him "Mussolini," which was mercifully shortened to "Moose."

WACKY NAMES IN A TRADE DEPARTMENT

Who were Whammy and Smoky?

On January 30, 1959, Charles William "Whammy" Douglas was traded by the Reds to the Pirates for Forrest "Smoky" Burgess.

Were Dick Stuart's nicknames, "Dr. Strangeglove" and "Old Stonefingers," well earned?

You decide: In 1958, he played only 64 games at first base but led the league with 16 errors.

What is the most common nickname in the major leagues?

"Lefty." To date, there have been over 175 "Lefty's." Research reveals no player nicknamed "Righty." The 1962 Mets had two players with identical first and last names—the only time this has happened in big-league history. Their names? Bob Miller. Both were pitchers. One hit right-handed and threw righty, too. To distinguish him from the other Bob Miller, who hit righty but threw lefty, he was referred to as "Righty Bob Miller," although that was not really a nickname.

The first "Lefty" was one Charles W. "Lefty" Marr. who hit .284 batting for Columbus and Cincinnati in the American Association and National League (1896, 1889–1891).

What was Pete Compton's first name?

Anna—the only big leaguer with that name. Compton was an outfielder for the Browns, Braves, Pirates, and Giants during a six-year career (1911–1918).

Who were the Doves?

The future Boston Braves, when the team was still owned by the Dovey brothers, 1907–10.

Who are the only big leaguers named after *two* different presidents?

Hall of Famer Zachary Davis Wheat (Dodgers, A's, 1909–1927), named for Zachary Taylor and Jefferson Davis; and Thomas Jefferson Davis Bridges (Tigers, 1930–1946).

Honorable mention: Tyler Sam Houston, William Jennings Bryan Herman—known as Billy.

Cal (Calvin Coolidge Julius Caesar Tuskahoma) McLish (Dodgers, Pirates, Cubs, Indians, Reds, White Sox, Phillies, 1944–1964) was probably named after more people than any other ballplayer.

Where was Estel Crabtree (Reds and Cardinals, eight seasons between 1929 and 1941) from?

Crabtree, Ohio.

What do these players have in common? Percival Rising, William Schriver, Edward Tate, Frank Dillon, John Henry Lloyd, Charles Smith, Charles Snyder, Clarence Foster, John Corkhill, Walter Williams.

They were all known as "Pop." And don't forget Bill Popp and Willie Stargell ("Pops").

Which players have the longest names to both start *and* end with the letter *K*?

Scott Klingenbeck (Orioles, Twins, 1995) and Will Koenigsmark (Cardinals, 1919).

What's the connection? John Thompson, Arthur Conlon, John Milligan, William Halligan, John Fields, John Conlan, John Flynn.

All are members of the all-"Jocko" team.

GUYS WHOSE NICKNAME SHOULD BE "PHIL" DEPARTMENT

Del Bissonette (full first name Adelphia).

GUYS WHOSE NICKNAME SHOULD BE "SANTA" DEPARTMENT

Billy and Bobby Klaus.

GUYS WHOSE NICKNAME SHOULD BE "O" DEPARTMENT

Hugh Bedient.

In 1944 and 1945, the Philadelphia Phillies were known by another name, thanks to a fan contest conceived by new owners—perhaps as a distraction from consistently bad teams. They went back to "Phillies" in 1946. That other name was subsequently adopted by a new major-league team. What was it?

The Blue Jays. It didn't help, either: the erstwhile Phillies finished last in both those years.

The name "Blue Jays" was revived in 1977 when Toronto entered the American League.

What is Eddie Murray's real first name?

Eddie. Similarly, Mickey Mantle's real first name was Mickey.

Who was baseball's first Babe?

The first Babe in the big leagues was Babe Adams, a pitcher who debuted on April 18, 1906 with the Cardinals. After losing his only game with the Cardinals, he went on to pitch for the Pirates from 1907 to 1926, compiling a 194-140 won-lost record and an ERA of 2.76.

Match these old team names with the current names.

OLD	NEW
A. Broncos	1. Cubs
B. Blue Jays	2. Phillies
C. Spiders	3. Indians
D. White Stockings	4. Giants
E. Molly Maguires	
F. Greenstockings	
G. Mutuals	
H. Colts	
I. Cowboys	
J. Superbas	

A-1; B-2; C-3; D-1; E-3; F-4; G-4; H-1; I-1; J-3.

INTRODUCTIONS WE'D LIKE TO HAVE MADE DEPARTMENT

Mel Stottlemyre, meet Merle Settlemire!

Tom Lynch, "King of the Umpires," meet Old Hoss Radbourn, "King of
Pitchers"!

Bill Grief, meet Jack Bliss.

Don Mueller, do you know Dan Moeller?

Bo Belinski, this is Bob Polinsky.

John Smiley, say hello to Vida Blue.

Smead Jolley? May I present Charlie Grimm.

U. L. Washington, I'd like you to meet Uel Eubanks and his friend Euel
Moore. And over there, that's Ewell Blackwell.

Sad Sam Jones, this is Happy Chandler.

Abba Dabba Tobin, meet Eppa Jeptha Rixey.

Jimmy Key, say hi to Chuck Locke!

Vince Molyneaux, meet Rance Mullinix.

Ken Caminiti, say hello to Scott Kaminiecki.

If General Crowder (Senators, Browns, Tigers, 1926–1936) married Jack
Mills (Indians, 1911) would he be General Mills?

Here's a well-spoken team: Ron Cey, Lou Say, Bob Speak, Tris Speaker,
Spoke Emery, Orator Jim O'Rourke, and Orator Schaffer.

Which ballplayer had the longest name—first, middle(s), and last?

Possibilities:

Christian Frederick Albert John Henry David Betzel, who went by "Bruno."

Calvin Coolidge Julius Caesar Tuskahoma McLish, who went by "Cal" or
"Buster."

Alan Mitchell Edward George Patrick Henry Gallagher.

Who were the most egotistical players in the history of the game?

Tommy Mee, Curtis Pride, and Carey Selph.

**Name two owners of big-league teams whose last name, spelled backwards,
is the last name of the other.**

Warren Giles, Cincinnati Reds 1946–1951, who served as President of the
National League 1951–1969, and Acting Commissioner of Baseball Bud Selig,
owner of the Milwaukee Brewers since they entered the American League in
1970.

**Thanks to baseball historian Daniel Okrent
for this oddity.**

This player had his *entire* name on his back for one season. Who was he?

Jay Howell. In 1988, he and Ken Howell were both with the Dodgers, so the back of Jay's uniform read *J. HOWELL*.

# # #

In the list below, we have tried to match U.S. presidents and major leaguers.

PRESIDENT	BIG LEAGUER
George Washington	George Washington (Sloan Vernon Washington)
John Adams	John Adams
Thomas Jefferson	Thomas Jefferson Davis Bridges
James Madison	James Madison Toy
James Monroe	Monroe Mitchell

They were probably all friends of Paul Revere Radford, Lafayette Henlon, and Ethan Allen.

John Quincy Adams	Quincy Trouppe, John Adams
Andrew Jackson	Andrew Jackson Knox
Martin Van Buren	Martin Van Buren Walker
William Henry Harrison	William Harrison Pepper
John Tyler	John Tyler
James Knox Polk	John Knox
Zachary Taylor	Zachary Davis Wheat (named for both Zachary Taylor and Jefferson Davis)
	Zack (James Wren) Taylor
Millard Fillmore	Millard Howell
Franklin Pierce	Monty Franklin Pierce Stratton
James Buchanan	James Buchanan
Abraham Lincoln	Abraham Lincoln Wolstenholme, Abraham Lincoln Bailey
Andrew Johnson	A. (Alex) Johnson
Ulysses Simpson Grant	Ulysses Simpson Grant Stoner
Rutherford Hayes	Johnny Rutherford, Von Hayes
James Garfield	Bill Garfield
Chester A. Arthur	Chester Arthur Spencer

PRESIDENT	BIG LEAGUER
Grover Cleveland	Grover Cleveland Alexander, Grover Cleveland Lowdermilk, Grover Cleveland Land, Grover Cleveland Baichley
Benjamin Harrison	Ben Harrison
William McKinley	William McKinley "Max" Venable, William McKinley "Pinky" Hargrave
Theodore Roosevelt	Jack Roosevelt Robinson
William Howard Taft	Taft Wright
Woodrow Wilson	Woodrow Wilson Williams
Warren Gamaliel Harding	Charlie Harding, Harding Peterson
Calvin Coolidge	Calvin Coolidge Julius Caesar Tuskahoma McLish, Calvin Coolidge Ermer
Herbert Hoover	John Hoover
Franklin D. Roosevelt	Franklin Delano Roosevelt Wieand
Harry Truman	Truman (Tex) Clevinger
Dwight Eisenhower	Ike Delock, Dwight Evans
John F. Kennedy	John Kennedy
Lyndon B. Johnson	L. B. Johnson (Louis Brown)
Richard Nixon	Russ Nixon
Gerald Ford (born Leslie King)	Wenty Ford, Leslie (Charlie) Spikes
Jimmy Carter	Gary Carter
Ronald Reagan	Rip Reagan
George Bush	Randy Bush
Bill Clinton	Clinton (Dan) Gladden

Two of the players named above (Jackie Robinson and Grover Cleveland Alexander) wound up in the Hall of Fame. Yet another Hall of Famer was named for a man who ran for president (and lost) three times. Who was he?

No, not William Jennings Bryan "Slim" Harriss. He is not a Hall of Famer. The correct answer is William Jennings Bryan "Billy" Herman.

What's the best poker hand in baseball?

Ace Adams, Robert "Ace" Williams, Clarence "Ace" Parker, and Asa "Ace" Stewart.

Who is the only person named in Dave Hirshberg's haunting song, "Van Lingle Mungo," who was not a baseball player?

Art Passarella, an American League umpire (1941–1942, 1945–1953). The rest of the lyrics consist entirely of ballplayers' names.

Thanks to Stuart Klein of FOX-TV for this question.

Name three players who called their bats "Black Betsy."

Joe Sewell, Joe Jackson, and Babe Ruth. In 1927, when Ruth hit 60 homers, his "Black Betsy" was joined by "Big Bertha" and "Beautiful Bella."

Who were the first modern teammates whose last names were reversals of each other?

Rob Deer and Jody Reed of the 1996 Padres.

Herman Iburg, Abraham Wade, Hamilton Patterson, Robert Hyatt, Herman Schulte.

The all-"Ham" team. Honorable mention: Piggy Ward, Ed Linke.

Jeff Pfeffer, Johnny Mize, Ed Delahanty, Frank Howard, Eddie Waitkus, Sam Thompson, Bill Lee, Edd Roush, Cecil Fielder.

The all-"Big" team. Fielder was called "Big Daddy." Randy Johnson, at 6'10″ the tallest man in the history of the game, is known as "The Big Unit."

Name the fastest team ever.

Bob Swift, Horace Speed, Sudden Sam McDowell, Eddie Quick, Bob Hasty, Fleet Walker, Speed Walker, Darcy Fast. Do not invite to play for this team: Bob Walk. And whatever you do, do not invite Tripp Cromer even to work out with these guys! Rapid Robert Feller could've fanned every one of them!

WHERE ARE YOU FROM?

Country Natives

PLAYER	HOMETOWN
Ollie Fuhrman	Jordan, Minnesota
Pius Schwert	Angola, New York
Hal Trosky	Norway, Iowa
Sam Rice	Morocco, Indiana
Jim Miles	Grenada, Mississippi
Joe Bowman	Argentine, Kansas
Tom Lynch	Peru, Illinois
Dick Thoenen	Mexico, Missouri
Wally Schang	South Wales, New York
Mike Brohert	Jamaica, New York
Doug Jones	Lebanon, Indiana
John Grim	Lebanon, Kentucky
Dave Roberts	Lebanon, Oregon
Paul Fittery	Lebanon, Pennsylvania
Ed Busch	Lebanon, Illinois
Red Ostergard	Denmark, Wisconsin
Walt Bond	Denmark, Tennessee
Curt Simmons	Egypt, Pennsylvania

| Oscar Dugey | Palestine, Texas |
| Wynn Hawkins | East Palestine, Ohio |

Name two big-league managers from Bastrop, Louisiana.

Bill Dickey and Mel McGaha. Dickey, a Hall of Famer, managed the Yankees in 1946. McGaha was the skipper for Cleveland in 1962, and for the Kansas City Athletics in 1964 and part of 1965.

American Dream Hometowns

PLAYER	HOMETOWN
Pete Standridge	Black Diamond, Washington
Art Jacobs	Luckey, Ohio
Byron Houck	Prosper, Minnesota
Howard Ehmke	Silver Creek, New York
Tom Grubbs	Mt. Sterling, Kentucky
Orval Grove	Mineral, Kansas
John Buzhard	Prosperity, South Carolina
Slim Love	Love, Mississippi
Frank Buttery	Silvermine, Connecticut

This player could never go back to his birthplace. There is no such place, never was, and never will be. Who was he and where was he born?

> *Hint: He is not Hall of Famer Rod Carew, born in a train near Gatun, in the Panama Canal Zone, on October 1, 1945.*

Ed Porray, who pitched three games for Buffalo in the Federal League in 1914. He was born on a ship in the Atlantic on December 5, 1888—the only player born at sea.

"My hometown recently changed its name—again. It has a population of 5,000,000. What city is it? And who am I?"

Victor Cole, from Leningrad, Russia (formerly Petrograd), which changed its name back to St. Petersburg in September, 1991.

When Jake Livingstone was born there, on New Year's Day, 1880, it was St. Petersburg.

BASEBALL IS A NATIVE AMERICAN GAME DEPARTMENT

PLAYER	HOMETOWN
Sheldon "Available" Jones	Tecumseh, Nebraska
Larry Biittner	Pocahontas, Iowa

PLAYER	HOMETOWN
Paul Zahniser	Sac City, Iowa
Joe Wilhoit	Hiawatha, Kansas
Steve Melter	Cherokee, Iowa
Lou Kretlow	Apache, Oklahoma
Moses "Chief" Yellowhorse	Pawnee, Oklahoma
Tom Thomas	Shawnee, Ohio
Steve Howe	Pontiac, Michigan
Alvin Dark	Comanche, Oklahoma
Bruce Hitt	Comanche, Texas
Cot Deal	Arapaho, Oklahoma
Dennis DeBarr	Cheyenne, Wyoming
Jesse Duryea	Osage, Iowa
Terry Forster	Sioux Falls, South Dakota
Dave Bancroft*	Sioux City, Iowa

*Hall of Famer.

He came from Ulm and died in Stuttgart. Who was he?

Bill Kerksieck, an 0-2 pitcher with the 1939 Phillies. He was Born December 6, 1913 in Ulm, Arkansas and died March 11, 1970 in Stuttgart, Arkansas.

If You're Going to Play in the Big Leagues, Why Not Be From a Town with a Name Like:

HOMETOWN	PLAYER
Catchings, Mississippi	George Gill
Greybull, Wyoming	Bill Wilkinson
Humble, Texas	Paul Kardow
Friendship, New York	Rube Kroh
Bible Grove, Illinois	George Lyons
Knob Knoster, Missouri	Charlie Kerfeld
Sleepy Eye, Minnesota	Dana Kiecker
Birthright, Texas	Tex Shirley
Shade, Ohio	Clyde Goodwin
Globe, Arizona	Don Lee
Speed, Indiana	Wayne LaMaster
Wawawai, Washington	Speed Martin
Lost Nation, Iowa	George Stone
Lyons, Georgia	Don Collins
Lyons, New York	Mel Hall
Ben Hur, Virginia	Walker Cress

Victor, Iowa

Waterproof, Louisiana

Shiner, Texas

Acadia, Maryland

Big Beaver, Michigan

Twenty-Nine Palms, California

William Penn, Pennsylvania

Paw Paw, Michigan

Rural Retreat, Virginia

Fancy Gap, Virginia

Big Cabin, Oklahoma

Pleasant Village, Pennsylvania

Sweet Home, Oregon

San Quentin, California

Utopia, Texas

Pillow, Pennsylvania

Liberal, Missouri

Metropolis, Illinois

Pewee Valley, Kentucky

Swift Current, Saskatchewan, Canada

Homer, Nebraska

Homer, Louisiana

Homer, Georgia

Nuuyli, American Samoa

Thief River Falls, Minnesota

Island, Kentucky

Hollidaysburg, Virginia

Napoleon, Ohio

Napoleonville, Louisiana

Sunset, Texas

Jackie Collum

Johnny Weekly

Ross Youngs

Otis Stocksdale

Jimmy Peoples

Jack O'Connor

Marty O'Toole

Pat Paige

Deacon Philippe

Doc Ayers

Ralph Terry

Walter Bernhardt

Lyle Bigbee

Duster Mails

Gordon Maltzberger

Fred Stiely

Bob Harmon

Moxie Manuel

John Haldeman

Reggie Cleveland

Irv Higginbotham

Mule Watson

Lucas Turk

Tony Solaita

Wayne Nordhagen

Bobby Veach

Silent Joe Martin

John Parsons

Roland Howell

Max West

YOU CAN'T GET THERE FROM HERE DEPARTMENT

PLAYER	HOMETOWN
Bob Ewing	New Hampshire, Ohio
Eddie Higgins	Nevada, Illinois
Bill James	Iowa Hill, California
Bruce Dal Canton	California, Pennsylvania
Doc Gessler	Indiana, Pennsylvania
Buck Rodgers	Delaware, Ohio

PLAYER	HOMETOWN
Tommie Reynolds	Arizona, Louisiana
John Peters	Louisiana, Missouri
Fred Osborn	Nevada, Ohio
Clyde Sukeforth	Washington, Maine
Fred Andrus	Washington, Michigan
Joe Verbane	Washington, Pennsylvania
Darren Daulton	Arkansas City, Kansas
Hal Jones	Louisiana, Missouri
Emil Levsen	Wyoming, Iowa
Don Larsen	Michigan City, Indiana
Bob McHale	Michigan Bluff, California

This man—the first from his country to play in the big leagues—wound up in Cooperstown. Who is he?

Harry Wright, born in Sheffield, England. His first game was on May 5, 1876, with Boston, in the old National League.

Who is the best ballplayer to come out of Prague?

Jim Thorpe, born May 28, 1888 in Prague, Oklahoma. (He was actually born in Keokuk Falls, a Sauk and Fox Indian town that no longer exists. The nearest existing town is Prague.) In December, 1995, the Committee for the 1996 Olympic Games revised the route of the Atlanta-bound Olympic torch to pass through Prague, in Thorpe's honor.

Out-of-Place Hometowns

PLAYER	HOMETOWN
Darcy Fast	Dallas, Oregon
Mike Regan	Phoenix, New York
Luis Salazar	Barcelona, Venezuela
Jock Somerlott	Flint, Indiana
Dave Stapleton	Miami, Arizona
Ken Crosby	New Denver, British Columbia Canada
Tom Niedenfuer	St. Louis Park, Minnesota
Billy Southworth	Harvard, Nebraska
Red Lanning	Harvard, Illinois
Lefty Leifield	Trenton, Illinois
Bert Niehoff	Louisville, Colorado
Hub Northen	Atlanta, Texas

Jimmy and Doc Johnston	Cleveland, Tennessee
Chet Morgan	Cleveland, Mississippi
Glenn Moulder	Cleveland, Oklahoma
Jason Grimsley	Cleveland, Texas
Ellis Valentine	Helena, Arkansas
Bill Hohman	Brooklyn, Maryland
Stan Perzanowski	East Chicago, Indiana

World Hometowns

PLAYER	TOWN
Grover Cleveland Alexander	Elba, Nebraska
Tim Wakefield	Melbourne, Florida
Jackie Warner	Monrovia, California
Pius Schwert	Angola, New York
Tom Spencer	Gallipolis, Ohio
Danny Wallin	Neptune, New Jersey
Dick Weik	Waterloo, Iowa
Bill Chappelle	Waterloo, New York
Jim McGuire	Dunkirk, New York
Jim Blackburn	Warsaw, Kentucky
Jot Goar	New Lisbon, Indiana
Jim Thorpe	Prague, Oklahoma
Paul Hinrichs	Marengo, Iowa
J. R. Richard	Vienna, Louisiana
Bill Humphreys	Vienna, Missouri
Don Wert	Strasburg, Pennsylvania
Ken O'Dea	Lima, New York
Brad Komminsk	Lima, Ohio
Beals Becker	El Dorado, Kansas
Fred Beck	Havana, Illinois
Johnny Sain, Jim Walkup	Havana, Arkansas
Sid Schact	Bogota, New Jersey
Rick Henninger	Hastings, Nebraska
Culley Richard	Oxford, Mississippi
Jim Jones	London, Kentucky
Bob Bescher	London, Ohio
Snoops Carey	East Liverpool, Ohio
Mace Brown	North English, Iowa
Jay Johnstone	Manchester, Connecticut
Johnny Tobin	Jamaica Plains, Massachusetts

PLAYER	TOWN
Quincy Trouppe	Dublin, Georgia
Jim Brillheart	Dublin, Virginia
Monte Beville	Dublin, Indiana
Hal Griggs	Shannon, Georgia
Harry Kane	Hamburg, Arkansas
Carl Stimson	Hamburg, Iowa
Sammy Byrd	Bremen, Georgia
Whitey Guese	New Bremen, Ohio
Bill Kerksieck	Ulm, Arkansas
Terry Steinbach	New Ulm, Minnesota
Bob Whitcher	Berlin, New Hampshire
Otis Lambeth	Berlin, Kansas
Mike Naymick	Berlin, Pennsylvania
Ray Kolp	New Berlin, Ohio
Ira Townsend	Weimar, Texas
Bill Dineen	Syracuse, New York
Pete Donahue	Athens, Texas
Bert Bradley	Athens, Georgia
Wayne Redmond	Athens, Alabama
Jack Britton	Athens, Illinois
Jim Baskette	Athens, Tennessee
Whitey Herzog	New Athens, Illinois
Joe "Ubbo Ubbo" Hornung	Carthage, New York
Carl Hubbell	Carthage, Missouri
Buff Williams	Carthage, Illinois
Soup Campbell	Sparta, Virginia
Tom Rogers	Sparta, Tennessee
Rip Coleman	Troy, New York
Doc Adkins	Troy, Wisconsin
Bob Turley	Troy, Illinois
Billy Hitchcock	Inverness, Alabama
Brian and Denny Doyle	Glasgow, Kentucky
Karl Best	Aberdeen, Washington
Tom Umphlett	Scotland Neck, North Carolina
Randy Nieman	Scotia, California
Del Crandall	Ontario, California
Guy Hoffman	Ottawa, Illinois
Gordie Hinkle	Toronto, Ohio
Roger Bowman	Amsterdam, New York
Terry Lyons	New Holland, Ohio

Babe Doty	Genoa, Ohio
Ben Cantwell	Milan, Tennessee
Randy Moore	Naples, Texas
Harley Hisner	Naples, Indiana
Vic Cornell	Florence, South Carolina
Hal Quick	Rome, Georgia
Emmett Rogers	Rome, New York
Ted Savage	Venice, Illinois
Del Paddock	Volga, South Dakota
Gordon McKenzie	St. Petersburg, Florida
Terry Cox	Odessa, Texas
Jim Duffalo	Helvetia, Pennsylvania
Varney Anderson	Geneva, Illinois
Mickey Witek	Luzerne, Pennsylvania
Charlie Biggs	French Lick, Indiana
Ken Richardson	Orleans, Indiana
Heinie Stafford	Orleans, Vermont
Ron Piche	Verdun, Quebec, Canada
Joe Benz	New Alsace, Indiana
Bill Van Dyke	Paris, Illinois
Doc Daugherty	Paris, Pennsylvania
Bob Edmondson	Paris, Kentucky
Chick King	Paris, Tennessee
Eddie Robinson	Paris, Texas
Bob Prichard	Paris, Texas
Si Johnson	Marseilles, Illinois
Harry Wheeler	Versailles, Indiana
Charles Jackson	Versailles, Ohio
Chuck Scrivener	Alexandria, Virginia
Steve Sundra	Luxor, Pennsylvania
Paul Erickson	Zion, Ohio
Mel Hoderlein	Mt. Carmel, Ohio
Danny Hoffman	Canaan, Connecticut
Howie Judson	Hebron, Illinois
Thurman Munson	Canton, Ohio
Bob Hasty	Canton, Georgia
Mel Wright	Manila, Arkansas
Anse Moore	Delhi, Louisiana

Who is the best player from Juneau?

Hall of Famer Addie Joss, born April 12, 1880 in Juneau, Wisconsin.

Who is the first native New Yorker to manage the New York Yankees?

Joe Torre (1996), born in Brooklyn on July 18, 1940.

Masanori Murakami (Giants, 1964–5) was the first native of Japan to play in America's major leagues: Hideo Nomo (Dodgers, 1995–) was the second. Who was the third?

1996 Tigers' pitcher Jeff McCurry, born in Tokyo on January 21, 1970. His father was a captain in the United States Air Force. Jeff came to America when he was just six months old.

On the Mound

Which pitcher had the most wins without ever winning a Cy Young Award?

Cy Young—511.

OK, since the Cy Young award was instituted in 1956—one year after Young's death.

Don Sutton—324.

Who was the only pitcher with over 3,000 strikeouts but fewer than 1,000 walks?

Ferguson Jenkins: 3,192 strikeouts, 997 walks.

Which pitcher recorded the most career strikeouts without ever leading the league in that category?

Don Sutton (3,574). His high was 217 in 1969, when he was with the Dodgers. Ferguson Jenkins of the Cubs led the National League that year with 273.

Nolan Ryan, pitching for the Angels, led the American League in Ks every year from 1972 through 1979 (averaging 302 per year)—except for 1975, when he was sixth with 186. Who beat him for the strikeout title that year?

His teammate Frank Tanana, who struck out 269.

Which pitcher had the most wins in a season without a shutout?

"Bullet" Joe Bush (26, with the 1922 Yankees).

Six pitchers who began their careers in the 1960s went on to win over 300 games. Who were they?

Steve Carlton (329), Don Sutton (324), Nolan Ryan (319), Phil Niekro (318), Gaylord Perry (314), Tom Seaver (309).

Who had the most career wins without ever winning 20 games in a season?

Larry French—197. He pitched for the Pirates, Cubs, and Dodgers from 1929 to 1942, winning a high of 18 games three times.

If this question were reworded to read: "Who had the most career wins with only one 20-game-victory season?", the answer would be Don Sutton—324 wins, but 20+ wins only in 1976, when he was 21-10 for the Dodgers.

Would you select a pitcher for your team if he surrendered more than 7,000 hits?

Yes, you would. He also:

Had the most career wins—511
Started the most games—815
Pitched at least 300 innings for 16 years (the record)
Had the most years with at least 20 wins—16

His name was Cy Young.

Who are the first two brothers to win 20 games each in the same season?

The Perrys—Jim and Gaylord. In 1970, Jim won 24 for the Twins and Gaylord won 23 for the Giants.

GRAND SLAMS BY PITCHERS DEPARTMENT

Only one Hall of Fame pitcher has hit two grand slams in his career. Who is he?

Bob Gibson.

His first grand slam was on September 29, 1965 in San Francisco off another future Hall of Famer, Gaylord Perry, in the eighth inning, to help the Cardinals beat the Giants 8-6.

Gibson's second grand slam was on July 26, 1973 off John Strohmayer as the Cards trounced the Mets 13-1 in the first game of a doubleheader.

Who is the only man in the modern history of the big leagues to pitch a perfect game *and* hit a grand slam?

Hint: He did both in the same year, but not in the same game.

Don Larsen.

His grand slam came at Yankee Stadium in the fourth inning on April 22, 1956, off Frank Sullivan of the Red Sox. On base were Bill Skowron, Jerry Lumpe, and Andy Carey.

Larsen's perfect game was October 8, 1956—Game 5 of the World Series.

Who is the only pitcher to hit grand slams in both leagues?

Lynwood "Schoolboy" Rowe. His first was on July 22, 1939 for the Tigers at home against the Philadelphia A's in the second inning of the second game of a doubleheader. Rowe drove in five runs in that game, but did not get the win, as he was chased in the sixth inning. The Tigers won 11-10.

Rowe smacked his second grand slam as a pinch hitter—take that, DH!—on May 2, 1943, when he was with the Phillies. The game was tied at 4 and the bases were loaded in the sixth inning, when Phillies' Manager Bucky Harris sent Rowe up to pinch hit. The Phillies won 6-5 in 12 innings.

Rowe's career batting average was .263, with 18 home runs. In 1943, he topped all National League pinch hitters with 15 hits and a .306 batting average.

It has been extremely rare for an American League pitcher to come to bat since 1973, when the League adopted the designated hitter as an "experiment." (Pitchers have batted only when the DH has played in the field or has batted as a pinch hitter, or, since 1997, in interleague games.)

Who is the last pitcher to hit a grand slam in the American League?

Steve Dunning of the Indians, on May 11, 1971 against the Tigers. Although Dunning did not win the game, the Indians did, beating Oakland 7-5.

Dunning, who came to the big leagues from Stanford without any time in the minors, was Cleveland's first draft pick in 1970. He fizzled, retiring after the 1977 season with a record of 23-41 and an ERA of 4.56.

Only six other modern pitchers besides Gibson and Rowe have hit two grand slams in their career. Name them.

1. **Tommy Byrne.**
   - His first grand slam came off the Senators' Sid Hudson in the ninth inning of the first game of a doubleheader in Washington on September 18, 1951. Although the season was virtually over, it was the Browns' first grand slam all season. The Browns won 8-0. Pinch-

hitting in the 10th inning of the nightcap, Byrne drove in the run that gave the Browns a 3-2 win. During his career, he batted .238 with 14 home runs.

- Vic Raschi was pitching a two-hit, 3-0 shutout for the Yankees on May 16, 1953, going into the top of the ninth inning. Bud Sheely of the White Sox singled. Fred Marsh ran for him and moved to second on a fielder's choice, with Nellie Fox at the plate. Then Raschi walked Ferris Fain. Next, Minnie Minoso hit into a fielder's choice and was safe at first, erasing Fain at second. Now there were two outs with runners at second and third. The next batter, Tom Wright, singled to center, scoring Marsh and moving Minoso to third. Then Raschi walked "Jungle" Jim Rivera on a 3-2 pitch to load the bases.

  Yankee manager Casey Stengel brought in righty Ewell "The Whip" Blackwell to face righty Vern Stephens. But White Sox manager Paul Richards went to his bench, calling on his best left-handed pinch hitter—pitcher Tommy Byrne. (Over his career, Byrne hit .213, a respectable average for a pitcher, and smacked 20 homers.)

  Byrne took the first four pitches, working the count to 2-2. He parked the next pitch in the right-field stands. Final score: White Sox 5, Yankees 3.

  What a moment—a pinch-hit grand slam by a pitcher to win the game!

2. **Dizzy Trout.**
   - His first grand slam, part of a 13-7 win over the Senators in Washington, came in the ninth inning on July 28, 1949, when Trout was a Tiger. The smash was off Al Gettel, with Pat Mullin, Johnny Lipton, and Aaron Robinson aboard. Trout won the game.
   - If you're going to hit a grand slam, do so in a record-setting game before over 51,000 screaming fans at home! Dizzy Trout's home run off Tommy Byrne in the fourth inning with Johnny Groth, Don Kolloway, and Bob Swift aboard, at home against the Yankees on June 23, 1950, was one of five homers hit by the Tigers in that game—including a record-tying four homers in the fourth inning. Walter "Hoot" Evers had two, while Vic Wertz and Gerry Priddy each contributed one.

     But the Yankees had six homers of their own—two by Hank Bauer and one each by Yogi Berra, Jerry Coleman, Joe DiMaggio, and Tommy Henrich. DiMaggio's homer in the seventh, and Henrich's in the eighth, were both off Trout.

     The Tigers won 10-9 on Evers' second blast, an inside-the-park two-run homer off Joe Page in the bottom of the ninth inning.

The 11 home runs hit in that game are still a record (subsequently tied). Homers accounted for all 19 runs in the game. The win put the Tigers in first place, two games ahead of the Yankees, but the Yankees finished the season in first place, three games ahead of the Tigers.

3. **Camilo Pascual.**
   - August 14, 1960, Senators against the Yankees. Pascual, sporting a .167 batting average, clubbed a bases-loaded homer—the first homer of his career—off the right-field foul pole at Yankee Stadium off Bob Turley to win the first game of a doubleheader for the Senators. On base were Jim Lemon, Bob Allison, and Earl Battey.
   - Pascual hit the second grand slam of his career on April 27, 1965—off Stan Williams in the seven-run first inning—while pitching a two-hitter, leading his Twins to an 11-1 victory over the Indians in Cleveland. Pascual hit .205 over his career, with a grand total of five home runs. Thus, 40% of his home runs were grand slams.

4. **Rick Wise.**
   - His sixth homer of 1971 was his first grand slam, on August 28, 1971. He hit it in the seventh inning off Don McMahon at home for the Phillies and (along with his other homer in that game) helped his team beat the Giants 7-3. Byron Browne, Roger Freed, and Tim McCarver were on base.
   - Wise's second grand slam was on August 21, 1973, when he was a Cardinal. He hit his slammer in a seven-run third inning in Atlanta off Roric Harrison. The Braves rallied with six runs of their own in the sixth and beat the Cardinals 11-7.

5. **Tony Cloninger.**
   - Perhaps his grand slams were the most memorable of all pitchers' grand slams. Why? They happened in the same game, on July 3, 1966, making Cloninger the only National Leaguer—pitcher or not—to hit two grand slams in a single game. An RBI single lifted his total for the day to nine—a record for a pitcher.

     The first blow, a 410-foot smash to center field in Candlestick Park off Bob Priddy, came as part of the seven-run first inning. Three innings later, Cloninger cleared the right-field fence off Ray Sadecki. The two homers gave Cloninger 18 RBIs in four games.

6. **Dave McNally.**
   - During his first six years in the big leagues, through 272 at bats, McNally had failed to connect for any home runs at all, let alone a grand slam. His first grand slam, on August 26, 1968, came as part

of a seven-run Baltimore first inning off Chuck Dobson of the Oakland A's. McNally gave up six hits as he beat the A's 8-2.

- McNally's second homer was a memorable one. On October 13, 1970, he hit one 325 feet into the left-field stands at home at Baltimore's Memorial Stadium, off Wayne Granger (pitching in relief of Tony Cloninger!) of the Reds, with two outs in the sixth inning of Game 3 of the World Series—the only World Series grand slam by a pitcher. On base were Paul Blair, Brooks Robinson, and Davey Johnson. The four runs McNally drove in with that homer helped him get the win, as his Orioles beat the Reds 9-3 and took the Series four games to one.

McNally finished his career with nine home runs and a .133 batting average.

Which pitchers have appeared in at least 1,000 big-league games?

Hint: As of the end of the 1997 season, there were only four.

Hoyt Wilhelm, 1952–1972, 1,070 games. Kent Tekulve, 1974–1989, 1,050 games. Goose Gossage, 1970–1995, 1,002 games. Lee Smith, 1980–1997, 1,023 games. Smith appeared in his 1,000th game on April 6, 1997, with the Expos.

Tekulve and Gossage were teammates for the 1977 Pirates, where they combined for 21 wins and 33 saves.

Which pitchers won at least 100 more games than they lost?

Note that all are Hall of Famers.

	WON	LOST	DIFFERENCE
Cy Young	511	316	195
Christy Mathewson	373	188	185
Grover Alexander	373	208	165
Lefty Grove	300	141	159
Kid Nichols	361	208	153
John Clarkson	328	178	150
Walter Johnson	417	279	138
Whitey Ford	236	106	130
Eddie Plank	305	183	122
Warren Spahn	363	245	118
Jim Palmer	268	152	116
Tom Seaver	311	205	106
Bob Feller	266	162	104
Joe McGinnity	246	142	104
Juan Marichal	243	142	101

Only once in the history of the National League have two left-handed teammates won at least 20 games each. Who were they?

Carl Hubbell (22) and Cliff Melton (20), 1937 Giants.

"Although I won only 31 games in my twenties, I won 121 games in my forties. Who am I?"

Phil Niekro.

Who was the first pitcher to save 45 games in a season in each league?

Brian Harvey. American League: Angels, 1991 (46). National League: Marlins, 1993 (45).

Who was the only Canadian-born pitcher to hurl a no-hitter?

Toronto native Dick Fowler, Philadelphia A's, 1-0 over St. Louis, September 9, 1945.

When did pitching brothers first face each other in the American League?

July 3, 1973. Jim Perry of the Tigers faced Gaylord Perry of the Indians. Gaylord lost 5-4.

In one year, he went 27-9 and led his league in ERA, games started, games completed, innings pitched, and strikeouts. The next year he was out of baseball. Who was he?

Sandy Koufax (a member of the Jewish Sports Hall of Fame in Netanya, Israel). He retired after his stellar 1966 season rather than risk permanent arthritis injury to his left arm.

During his 14-year career, this pitcher won 20 games five times, averaged 19.7 wins per year during his first 10 years, and won 228 games. He completed 82.5 percent of his starts and batted .263 lifetime with 23 triples.
He appeared in three consecutive World Series.
He is not in the Hall of Fame. Who was he?

George Mullin. He spent most of his career (1902–1915) with the Tigers. He was in the Series in 1907 (Tigers lost to Cubs 4-0), 1908 (Tigers lost to Cubs 4-1), and 1909 (Tigers lost to Pirates 4-3), winning three and losing three—all complete games.

Which pitcher has the most wins without ever appearing in a World Series?

Phil Niekro—318.

One of the oldest and most sacred of baseball's many superstitions is that during a no-hitter no teammate may mention the no-hitter to the pitcher—or even talk to him. (Many broadcasters will also not overtly report that the game being described is a no-hitter.)

But Cardinal Bob Forsch wasn't superstitious when he no-hit the Phillies on April 16, 1978. Why not?

Because he was born on January 13, 1950—Friday the 13th.

It's April 22, 1970, and Tom Seaver of the Mets has just been presented with the 1969 Cy Young Award—his first—during ceremonies at Shea Stadium. How does he celebrate?

By striking out 19 Padres, including a record 10 in a row! Seaver won the game 2-1.

In 1914, in one of the strangest good news/bad news combinations ever, he led the National League in losses (23) and saves (6). Who was he?

Red Ames, Cincinnati Reds.

This pitcher hit nine home runs and threw a no-hitter in the same year. Who was he?

Hall of Famer Wes Ferrell of Cleveland. He no-hit the Browns 9-0 on April 29, 1931.

Would you want this pitcher on your team if his World Series marks include the following?
Most walks surrendered—34
Most losses—8
Most hits surrendered—132

Yes. His name is Whitey Ford, and he also started 22 World Series games—a record—and won 10, also a record.

Who was the first relief pitcher to win an ERA title?

Hoyt Wilhelm, Giants, 1952. He pitched to an ERA of 2.43.

Who was the first black player to pitch a no-hitter?

"Sad" Sam "Toothpick" Jones of the Cubs. Jones no-hit the Pirates at Wrigley Field on May 12, 1955 before a "crowd" of 2,918. After walking Ed Freese, Preston Ward, and Tom Saffell in the ninth to load the bases, he struck out Dick Groat, Roberto Clemente, and Frank Thomas to preserve his 4-0 win and his no-hitter.

CLOSE DEPARTMENT

Nolan Ryan holds the major-league record for most strikeouts in a season since 1900–383, set in 1973 when he was with the Angels. This would be quite a feat in any year, but consider that 1973 was the first year of the designated hitter in the American League! Thus every ninth batter was no longer a virtual automatic out.

Who is second on the single-season strikeout list?

Sandy Koufax, the National League record holder. As a Dodger in 1965, he struck out 382.

To surpass Koufax's eight-year-old record—by 1—Ryan had to strike out 16 Twins in 11 innings, setting the record in the last game of the season (September 27, 1973), on the last pitch to the last batter—Rich Reese.

Reese also was the last out in another memorable game. Which one?

Catfish Hunter's perfect game, Oakland versus Minnesota on May 8, 1968. With the count at 3-2, Reese fouled off five pitches in a row before swinging and missing.

What was the most frustrating pitching performance by two opposing pitchers?

On May 1, 1920, Leon Cadore went the distance for the Dodgers, facing Joe Harris of the Boston Braves. Each pitched 26 innings in a 3-hour, 50-minute game that ended—because of darkness—in a 1-1 tie!

"Frustrating? FRUSTRATING? *YOU CALL THAT FRUSTRATING?* I'm Charlie Pick, the Braves' second baseman in that game. I went 0-for-11!"

Would you want this guy in your rotation? In his pitching debut against the Pirates, on July 6, 1955, he walked eight and got no decision.

Yes. His name is Sandy Koufax.

Would you want this pitcher on your team if he:
Lost 274 games in his career?
Led the league in games lost for four consecutive years (1977-tied, 1978, 1979, 1980)?
Set the modern record for most wild pitches in a game—six?
Set a National League record for most wild pitches in an inning—four?

Yes, you would. His name is Phil Niekro, and he won 318 games in his Hall of Fame career.

Who was the first man to lead each league in ERA?

Hoyt Wilhelm. In his rookie season (1952), with the Giants, he led the National League with an ERA of 2.43. Seven years later, as an Oriole, he led the American League with a 2.19 ERA.

Who are the only brothers to throw no-hitters?

No, not the Deans, the Niekros, or the Perrys. Dizzy Dean, Phil Niekro, and Gaylord Perry did indeed throw no-hitters, but Daffy Dean, Joe Niekro, and Jim Perry did not.

The answer is the Forsch brothers. On April 16, 1978, Bob Forsch (Cardinals) no-hit the Phillies 5-0. He pitched another no-hitter on September 26, 1983, against the Expos.

Ken Forsch, with the Astros, pitched a no-hitter against the Braves on April 7, 1979.

Who was the oldest pitcher to win 20 games?

Warren Spahn. He was 42 when he went 23-7 for the 1963 Milwaukee Braves. He finished his career with 363 wins and exactly 363 hits!

Jim Abbott, born without a right hand, pitched a no-hitter for the Yankees on September 4, 1993, against the Indians. Is he the only one-handed pitcher to throw a no-hitter?

While Abbott is the only one to do so in this century, Hugh "One Arm" Daily (born Harry Criss), who lost his left hand in a gun accident, no-hit Philadelphia 1-0 on September 13, 1883, pitching for the National League's Cleveland Spiders.

While pitching in the old Negro Leagues, Satchel Paige frequently guaranteed that he would strike out the first three batters he faced—a boast sure to draw a big crowd. He often did so.

But this nineteenth-century big leaguer—a Hall of Famer—is the only man to strike out the first *nine* batters he faced in a game. Who is he?

Mickey Welch: August 28, 1884, New York Giants versus the Cleveland Spiders.

Who were the first father-and-son pitchers in the big leagues?

Willie Mills (2 games, Giants, 1901) and Art Mills (19 games, Boston Braves, 1927–1928). Neither ever won a game.

Only two pitchers have appeared in at least 400 games in each league. Who were they?

Both were knuckleballers—Hoyt Wilhelm and Charlie Hough.

	AL	NL
Wilhelm	630	440
Hough	402	456

Which pitcher led his league in games, saves, and, as a reliever, wins and losses—all in the same year?

Mike Marshall. In 1974, pitching for the Dodgers, he appeared in 106 games—still the single-season record for a pitcher. As a reliever he won 15, lost 12, and saved 21 games.

Who was the youngest man in this century to pitch a perfect game?

Jim "Catfish" Hunter. He was 22 when he did it for Oakland against the Twins on May 8, 1968.

Who were the only pitchers to strike out at least 200 batters in their first two seasons?

Herb Score, Indians (1955: 245; 1956: 263).
Dwight Gooden, Mets (1984: 276; 1985: 268).

He was the catcher in Babe Ruth's last game as a pitcher (October 1, 1933) and in Ted Williams' only mound appearance (August 24, 1940). Who was he?

Joe Glenn.

Who made the last out in Phil Niekro's no-hitter for the Braves against the Padres on August 5, 1973?

Right fielder and future Blue Jays manager Cito Gaston. He bounced out to third baseman Darrell Evans.

Name the six American League pitchers who have won the Cy Young award and the MVP in the same year.

Denny McLain (Tigers, 1968), Vida Blue (Oakland, 1971), Rollie Fingers (Milwaukee, 1981), Willie Hernandez (Tigers, 1984), Roger Clemens (Red Sox, 1986), Dennis Eckersley (Oakland, 1992).

Name the four pitchers with 35 or more lifetime home runs.

Wes Ferrell—38, Bob Lemon—37, Red Ruffing—36, Warren Spahn—35.

Name the only two players with the same first *and last* names who have pitched no-hitters?

Samuel Jones and Samuel Jones.
Yankee "Sad" Sam Jones no-hit the Philadelphia A's on September 4, 1923.

Sam "Toothpick" Jones (also known as "Sad Sam") pitched a no-hitter for the Cubs, beating the Pirates 4-0 on May 12, 1955.

Who was the first American Leaguer to pitch two no-hitters in the same season?

Allie Reynolds of the Yankees. He did it July 12, 1951, beating Cleveland's Bob Feller—just 11 days after Feller's then-record third no-hitter—and against the Red Sox on September 28.

Which pitcher had the most seasons in which he struck out at least 100 batters?

Don Sutton—21.

This pitcher won 273 games and had 58 pinch hits. Who was he?

Red Ruffing. His lifetime batting average was .269.

Only two pitchers have had over 200 wins and *losing* records. Who were they?

Bobo Newsom and Jack Powell.

During his 20-year career (1929–1953), the "well-traveled" Newsom won 211 games and lost 222. In World Series play, he was 2-2. In 1938, he won 20 games (losing only 16), despite giving up a record 186 earned runs.

Jack Powell won 245 but lost 254 games during his 16-year career (1897–1912) with the Spiders and Cardinals in the National League and the Yankees and Browns in the American.

Which pitchers won at least 30 games three years in a row?

Christy Mathewson (Giants, 1903–05) and Grover Cleveland Alexander (Phillies, 1915–17).

Who was the only pitcher to win All-Star Games for both leagues?

Vida Blue did it for the American League in 1971, and for the National in 1981.

Because the 1981 season was shortened by a 50-day strike, neither league had a 20-game winner that year. But the next season, 1982, was a full one. How many American League pitchers won at least 20 games in 1982?

None—this was one of only three full seasons in which the American League had no 20-game winners (the other two: 1955 and 1960). In 1973 there were a record twelve 20-game winners in the American League, including three for Oakland—Catfish Hunter (21), Vida Blue (20), and Ken Holtzman (21).

The National League had no 20-game winners only in 1931 and 1983. In 1969 there were a league record nine 20-game winners, led by Tom Seaver of the Mets with 25.

Would you want this man to pitch for your team if he:
Gave up 505 home runs, most ever in a career?
Gave up 46 home runs in one season, the league record?
Led the league in home runs allowed for five years—also a league record?
Had a record nine seasons in which he surrendered 30 or more home runs?

Yes, you would. His name is Robin Roberts, and he won 286 games en route to a plaque at Cooperstown.

Which qualifying pitcher had the only sub-2.00 ERA in the 1950s?

Billy Pierce, 1.97 for the 1955 White Sox.

Which two pitchers won over 300 games, yet never struck out as many as 200 batters in a season?

Early Wynn and Warren Spahn. Wynn's high was 184 strikeouts in 1957 with the Indians, and Spahn's high was 191 with the 1950 Braves.

GOOD NEWS, BAD NEWS DEPARTMENT

This pitcher led the American League in both walks and strikeouts for a record six seasons. Who is he?

Nolan Ryan, Angels (1972–4, 1976–8).

Which pitcher had the most career saves without ever leading the league in saves in any single season?

Hoyt Wilhelm. His total of 227 saves put him at #1 on the career save list when he retired, but his high for one season was 27, a number he reached in 1964 with the White Sox. Dick Radatz of the Red Sox led the American League that year with 29.

Who was the first pitcher to win 20 games for a last-place team?

Frank George "Noodles" Hahn, 1901. His record was 22-19, and his Reds went 52-87—a .374 winning percentage.

Which modern rookie pitcher had the most shutouts?

The Yankees' Russ Ford, 1910–8. This mark was subsequently tied by Reb Russell of the White Sox in 1913 and Fernando Valenzuela of the Dodgers in 1981.

Three Hall of Fame pitchers led their leagues with ERAs of above 3.00. Who were they?

Lefty Grove, 1938 Red Sox (3.07); Early Wynn, 1950 Indians (3.20); Warren Spahn, 1961 Braves (3.01).

Who was the first pitcher to win 20 games one year and lose 20 the next year?

George Mullin of the Tigers. He won 21 in 1906 and lost 20 in 1907.

Who was the first man to retire more than 27 batters in a row in one game?

Harvey Haddix, on May 26, 1959, when he pitched 12 perfect innings for the Pirates but lost the game. In fact, after #27 (**Q:** Who was #27? **A:** Opposing pitcher Lew Burdette. Haddix struck him out.) Haddix broke the record with each new batter he retired—nine new records in a row! Ultimately, he retired 36 in a row—a single-game record that will probably stand forever!

Which pitcher had the worst record—perfectly awful—in the American League in 1954?

Don Larsen. He was 3-21 with the Orioles.

Which rookie pitcher won the most games?

Grover Cleveland Alexander—28 for the 1911 Philadelphia Phillies.

This pitcher threw a perfect game in his third major-league start, yet he finished his career with an abysmal 49–80 won-lost mark. Who was he?

Charlie Robertson. His Philadelphia A's beat the Tigers on April 30, 1922.

He lost 20 games, yet still led the league in ERA—the only man to accomplish this unusual feat. Who was he?

Hall of Famer Ed Walsh, White Sox, 1910. He had a 1.27 ERA to go with his 18-20 record.

Not counting Babe Ruth, which pitcher has had the most hits in one season?

George Uhle: 52 for Cleveland in 1923. Uhle appeared in 54 games, and thus had almost one hit per game—a .361 average. He also has the highest lifetime batting average by a pitcher—.288.

Each of these three pairs of pitching brothers won over 100 games. Who were they?

Phil (318) and Joe (221) Niekro, Gaylord (314) and Jim (215) Perry, and Ken (114) and Bob (168) Forsch.

How many times did Hall of Famer Steve Carlton lead the National League in ERA?

Only once—1972 (1.97).

Who was the first pitcher to save three consecutive All-Star Games?

Dennis Eckersley (Oakland), 1989–91.

Who was the first pitcher to lead his league in ERA without pitching a shutout?

Dave Koslo, 1949 New York Giants—2.50.

What was Scott Erickson's ERA before he pitched his no-hitter for the Twins on April 27, 1994?

7.48.

Who was the youngest pitcher to win 20 games in a single season?

Dwight Gooden of the Mets. He won #20 on August 25, 1985, when he was just 21.

Which pitcher with at least 200 wins has the highest career ERA?

Earl Whitehill, 4.36 and 218 wins (Tigers, Senators, Indians, and Cubs, 1923–1939).

For which team did Hall of Famer Eddie Plank play when he won the 300th game of his career-total 305?

The St. Louis Terriers of the Federal League, 1915.

Who are the only brothers to combine for a shutout?

Rick and Paul Reuschel. They pitched it for the Cubs on August 21, 1975 against the Dodgers.

Less than a month later, on September 16, the Reuschels pitched on the *losing* end of a 22-0 drubbing by the Pirates. Tom Dettore, Oscar Zamora, and Buddy Schultz also pitched for the Cubs that memorable day.

In that game, Rennie Stennett of the Pirates went 7-for-7, the first modern player to do so. The game also saw Stennett become the fourth player to have two hits in an inning *twice in the same game!*

He gave up Stan Musial's 3,000th hit on May 13, 1958, making Musial the first man in 16 years (since Paul Waner, on June 19, 1942) to reach 3,000 hits. He was also the losing pitcher when Early Wynn finally won his 300th game on July 13, 1963. Who was he?

Moe Drabowsky, the best pitcher ever to come out of Ozanna, Poland.

Which pitcher had the best single-season strikeout-to-walk ratio since 1900?

Bret Saberhagen, Mets, 1994. He struck out 143 while walking only 13 in 177⅓ innings, an 11-to-1 ratio.

Which Hall of Fame pitcher had over 3,000 strikeouts, yet never led the league in strikeouts in any one year?

Gaylord Perry—3,534. Perry is #6 on the all-time strikeout list.

Who was the first—and so far the only—pitcher to strike out over 300 batters three years in a row?

Nolan Ryan, Angels (1972–4).

Even awful pitchers may have their day. This pitcher, 45-89 lifetime, started his career with a bang. In his pitching debut with the Phillies, on July 24, 1935 (in relief), he struck out three future Hall of Famers in a row—Pirates Lloyd Waner, Paul Waner, and Arky Vaughan. Who was he?

Hugh "Losing Pitcher" Mulcahy.

Who was the only pitcher in the history of the game to have over 400 starts and over 400 relief appearances?

Charlie Hough. During his 24-year career with the Dodgers, White Sox, Rangers, and Marlins, he amassed 440 starts and 418 relief appearances. He retired in mid-1994 with a career 216-216 won-lost record, and 61 saves, in 3,801.1 innings pitched.

Who are the only father-and-son pitchers to win 50 games each?

Joe Coleman Sr. (52) and Jr. (142); Jim Bagby Sr. (127) and Jr. (97); and Mel (164) and Todd Stottlemyre (109 through 1997).

There are many ways to judge a pitcher's effectiveness—wins, losses, winning percentage, batting average against, ERA, "quality starts," etc. One way is to determine his strikeout-to-walk ratio. This comparison deals with statistics solely within the pitcher's control. That is, a pitcher cannot control

whether another player makes an error (which could contribute to a run and then a loss) or whether his team will help him protect a one-run lead.

But only the pitcher gives up walks or records strikeouts. The credit or blame is all his. So Ferguson Jenkins's extraordinary numbers—3,192 strikeouts versus only 997 walks—stand tall. (He struck out 3.2 batters for every one he walked.) So do Nolan Ryan's 5,714 strikeouts.

But this pitcher had more walks than strikeouts. In fact, he never struck out 100 batters in a single season—and still wound up with his likeness on a Hall of Fame plaque. Who was he?

Ted Lyons of the White Sox. He walked 1,121, but struck out only 1,073.

Who was the last pitcher to throw more than three innings in a nine-inning All-Star Game?

Lefty Gomez of the Yankees, who pitched six innings in the 1935 game. (The AL won 4-1.) After this the rule was changed to limit a pitcher to three innings (in a nine-inning game).

In 1953, the New York Yankees won their fifth consecutive World Series—a feat unmatched, and probably unmatchable, in baseball history.

How many 20-game winners did the Yankees have on their pitching staff that year?

None! Whitey Ford won 18 games—the most on the team.

During their reign, from 1949 through 1953, how many different Yankee pitchers won 20 games?

Three—Vic Raschi, Eddie Lopat, and Allie Reynolds.

Were you going to say Whitey Ford? He was a 20-game winner only twice, in 1961 (25) and 1963 (24).

Name six pitchers who played in four decades.

Nick Altrock (1898–1924), Bobo Newsom (1929–1930, 1932, 1934–1948, 1952–1953), Early Wynn (1939–1963), Jim Kaat (1959–1983),* Nolan Ryan (1966–1993), and Jerry Reuss (1969–1990).

Which pitcher won the most games for a team without a single .300 hitter?

Grover Cleveland Alexander, who won 33 for the 1916 Phillies. Their top batter was Gavvy Cravath, who hit .283.

---

*Kaat also had 16 Gold Gloves and 16 lifetime home runs.

It's October 2, the last day of the 1938 season, and Detroit's Hank Greenberg has already hit 58 home runs. He has a chance to tie or break Babe Ruth's record of 60. A crowd of 30,000 fans packs Detroit's Briggs Stadium to see a record set. They do, in fact, see a record set—but not a home-run record. What record is set that day?

Cleveland's Bob Feller struck out a then-modern-record 18 batters and won the American League strikeout crown with a season total of 240 (beating Bobo Newsom's 226). Feller was just 20.

Who was the first rookie pitcher to win an All-Star Game?

Frank "Spec" Shea ("The Naugatuck Nugget") of the 1947 Yankees.

Who was the youngest man to start a game on Opening Day?

Dwight Gooden of the Mets—April 9, 1985. The Mets beat the Cardinals 6-5. Gooden was 20 years, 4 months, and 24 days old.

Since 1900, only four pitchers have had more victories than walks allowed in a season with at least 150 innings pitched. Who are they?

Bret Saberhagen, 1994 Mets (14 wins, 13 walks); Christy Mathewson, 1913 Giants (25 wins, 21 walks) and 1914 Giants (24 wins, 23 walks); and Slim Sallee, 1919 Reds (21 wins, 20 walks).

Who was the only pitcher to record at least 20 saves for 10 consecutive years?

Jeff Reardon, who retired just before the start of the 1995 season. In fact, he did it for 13 consecutive years—1982–94.

How many pitchers did the Philadelphia Athletics use in defeating the Chicago Cubs in the 1910 World Series four games to one?

Two. Jack Coombs pitched 27 innings, and Chief Bender pitched 18.2.

Who recorded the most wins in a career without a no-hitter?

Grover Cleveland Alexander—373 (1911–1930). Only Cy Young and Walter Johnson had more career wins.

On April 28, 1986, when the Red Sox' Roger Clemens struck out 20 Mariners to set the modern major-league record for a nine-inning game, it was his career win number ____.

Twenty. He matched it with another 20-strikeout game on September 18, 1996 in Detroit. In 1993, Clemens became the first graduate of the University of Texas to have his number (21) retired.

This pitcher hurled only 23⅔ innings in the majors, giving up 13 hits and walking 14, yet striking out 11. Although his ERA was a respectable 1.52, he garnered only one win. Yet he's a Hall of Famer. Who was he?

Jimmie Foxx.

Who was the first pitcher to strike out 200 batters in each of nine seasons?

Bob Gibson, Cardinals (1962–66, 1968–69, 1970, 1972). Gibson was the first man inducted into Creighton University's Hall of Fame, primarily on the basis of his achievements on the basketball court.

Which pitcher recorded the most career saves with one team?

Dennis Eckersley, Oakland A's (1987–1995)–320.

Who was the first pitcher to save 30 games in a season for three different teams?

Jeff Reardon–1986 Expos (41), 1987 Twins (31), 1991 Red Sox (40).

Who was the only pitcher with over 150 wins and over 2,000 hits as a batter?

> Hint #1: He played in the nineteenth century.
>
> Hint #2: He's a Hall of Famer.

John Montgomery Ward (1878–1894): 164 wins, 2,104 hits.

Who was the first pitcher to have at least 20 wins in a season while pitching fewer than 200 innings?

Bob Grim, 1954 Yankees–20 wins, 199 innings.

Who was the first pitcher to win 200 games without ever winning 20 in a single season?

Milt Pappas (Orioles, Reds, Braves, Cubs, 1957–1973). He won #200 in 1972. His high was 17 wins, in both 1971 and 1972. Pappas (born Miltiades Stergios Papastegios) won 110 games in the American League (all with Baltimore) and another 99 in the National.

Name the two twentieth-century 300-game winners who never appeared in a World Series.

Gaylord Perry (314) and Phil Niekro (318).

There has not been a player-manager who was a pitcher since 1952. Who was the last one?

Fred Hutchinson, whose 1952 Tigers finished dead last in the American League, 45 games behind the Yankees.

Although not a Hall of Famer, Jim Hegan holds a unique place in baseball annals: he handled eighteen 20-game winners during his 13-year career (1942–1957) with the Cleveland Indians. How many can you name?

PITCHER	YEAR	WINS
Bob Feller	1946	26
Bob Feller	1947	20
Bob Lemon	1948	20
Gene Beardon	1948	20
Bob Lemon	1949	22
Bob Lemon	1950	23
Early Wynn	1951	20
Mike Garcia	1951	20
Bob Feller	1951	22
Bob Lemon	1952	22
Mike Garcia	1952	22
Early Wynn	1952	23
Bob Lemon	1953	21
Early Wynn	1954	23
Bob Lemon	1954	23
Early Wynn	1956	20
Herb Score	1956	20
Bob Lemon	1956	20

Hegan caught seven 20-game seasons for Lemon, four for Wynn, three for Feller, and two for Garcia.

Name the first team to have three pitchers with at least 200 strikeouts in the same season.

The 1967 Minnesota Twins. Wilmer "Dean" Chance struck out 220, Dave Boswell 204, and Jim Kaat 211.

No matter—the team finished third.

Who was the first pitcher to record World Series wins in both leagues?

Jack Coombs. In 1916, with the National League's Brooklyn Robins, he beat the Red Sox 4-3 in Game 3.

Previously, he had won three World Series games pitching for the American League's Philadelphia A's in 1910.

Who were the first National League teammates to save at least 20 games in the same season?

Greg Minton and Gary Lavelle of the 1983 Giants. Minton saved 22, while Lavelle saved 20. But they weren't enough, as the Giants finished in fifth place, 12 games behind the Dodgers.

Who was the only pitcher from Rhode Island to start an All-Star game?

Dave Stenhouse (Senators), a native of Westerly, did it on July 30 at Wrigley Field, in the second 1962 game.

WHEN I GIVE UP A HIT, IT'S A DOOZIE DEPARTMENT

These two pitchers—one a Hall of Famer—are the only starters to surrender more home runs than walks in a single season. Who were they?

Hall of Famer Robin Roberts, Phillies, 1956: 46 homers, 40 walks. Gary Nolan, Reds, 1976: 28 homers, 27 walks.

"Gee Dad, I'm sorry you had the most losses in the league this season. If *I* ever become a major league pitcher, I hope *I* don't lead the league in losses." He did anyway. Who were they?

Herm Pillette, 1923 Tigers (14-19) and Duane Pillette, 1951 Browns (6-14).

In the history of the game, only three pitchers have struck out 300 batters in a single season, won 300 games, and struck out 3,000 during their careers. Who were they?

Walter Johnson, Nolan Ryan, and Steve Carlton.

Of those pitchers who won at least 300 games, who had the most saves?

Recognizing that the criteria for a save have changed over the years, the answer is Lefty Grove, who had 55 saves during his career to go with his 300 wins. The 300-game winners with the fewest saves are Pud Galvin and Tom Seaver, with one save each.

Who was the youngest man to notch his 300th win?

The appropriately named "Kid" Nichols. He was 31 on July 7, 1900, when he won #300 (on his way to 361); an 11-4 victory for his Boston Braves over the Chicago Cubs.

Which reliever with over 300 saves had the fewest relief appearances?

Dennis Eckersley. Although he was a starting pitcher from 1975 to 1987, starting 361 games for the Indians, Red Sox, Cubs, and A's, he became a reliever with the A's in 1987 (moving to the Cardinals with manager Tony LaRussa in 1996). Through 1997, Eckersley appeared in 660 games in relief, earning 389 saves.

Lee Smith, by contrast, saved more games (478), but also had 1,017 relief appearances. (He also started six games early in his career.) Thus, Eckersley saved 59% of the games in which he pitched in relief, compared to Smith's 47%; Rollie Fingers had 907 relief appearances, 341 saves, 38%; Jeff Reardon had 880 appearances, 366 saves, 42%.

Only two pitchers lost more than 300 games. Who were they?

Hall of Famers Cy Young—313 (to go with his 511 wins) and Pud Galvin—308 (360 wins, 1879–1892).

In 1984, what relief specialist had more saves than strikeouts?

Dan Quisenberry. The Royals' stalwart saved 44 games but struck out just 41.

Who was the last pitcher to compile more wins in a single season than another *team* in the league?

Hall of Famer Jack Chesbro. In 1904, he won 41 games for the New York Highlanders (later Yankees). The lowly Washington Senators won only 38 games that season.

"I won a World Series game in a year in which I didn't win a single big-league game. I was *not* a relief pitcher. Who am I?"

Virgil "Fire" Trucks, Detroit Tigers, 1945. Trucks was in the U.S. Navy during most of 1945, and was not discharged until after World War II was over. He pitched only five innings during the regular season—in the pennant clincher, on the very last day of the season.

But when the Series started, Trucks was ready, and won Game 2, beating the Cubs 4-1. The Tigers took the Series 4-3.

You're Bob Gibson. It's September 3, 1975, the final game of your Hall of Fame career. What do you do with your last pitch?

You give up a grand slam to Pete LaCock of the Cubs—the only grand slam of LaCock's career.

Who started the most games?

Cy Young—818. Too easy?

Name five other pitchers who started at least 700 games.

Nolan Ryan (773), Don Sutton (756), Phil Niekro (716), Steve Carlton (709), and Tommy John (700).

It happens to most pitchers sooner or later, during a season or during a career. But it didn't happen to the Mets' Dwight Gooden until April 9, 1990—Gooden's seventh year in the majors—in an Opening Day game against the Pirates. What was it?

He had a losing record, for even part of a season. The amazing Dr. K's season-by-season stats always showed more Ws than Ls until he lost the first game of the 1990 season and was officially 0-1. From 1984–1989, while winning 100 games, Gooden lost only 39 and never lost more than two games in a row.

Who was the first knuckleballer to win 20 games in a season?

Emil "Dutch" Leonard, Washington Senators, 1939 (20-8).

Who was the first pitcher to strike out at least 200 batters in eight consecutive years?

Hint: This Hall of Famer's first name is George.

Tom Seaver. He set this record on September 1, 1975, as a Met, when he struck out his 200th batter of that season—Manny Sanguillen of the Pirates. The next year, Tom Terrific extended his record to a ninth 200+ strikeout season.

On September 19, 1986, Joe Cowley of the White Sox pitched a no-hitter. When did he record his next win?

He didn't. That was the last win of his big-league career—making him the only man so far to pitch a no-hitter for his final win. (It was not Cowley's final game, or even his final decision, though. In 1987, he went 0-4 for the Phillies.) His final record was 33-25.

No pitcher did it during the 1930s, 1950s, or 1970s. Did what?

Record career win #300.

Who was the only major-league pitcher married to a Pitcher?

Jim Brosnan. His wife's birth name was Anne Pitcher.

The Brooklyn Dodgers won only one World Championship—in 1955. Their team featured such greats as future Hall of Famers Pee Wee Reese, Roy Campanella, Duke Snider, and Jackie Robinson.

Which Dodger had the highest batting average in that memorable season?

Don Newcombe. In 117 at bats, the pitcher had 42 hits, for a .359 average.

After his pitching career was over, this man became the commissioner. Who was he?

> *Hint #1: At 24, he was the youngest coach in the history of the National Basketball Association.*
>
> *Hint #2: He's a Hall of Famer—a basketball Hall of Famer.*

Dave DeBusschere. He pitched for the White Sox in 1962–3. Switching to basketball, the 6'6" DeBusschere played for the Detroit Pistons and the New York Knicks from 1962–1974, and was the Pistons's player-coach 1964–7. He entered the Basketball Hall of Fame in 1982. DeBusschere was the second commissioner of the American Basketball Association.

When was the first time pitchers with palindromic last names faced each other?

August 3, 1994, when Robb Nen of the Marlins faced Dave Otto of the Cubs. The Marlins won 9-8 in Chicago.

During his illustrious career, which includes appearing in 1,023 games, Lee Smith saved more games than any other pitcher—478. For how many different pitchers did he record saves?

101.

On August 24, 1940, he pitched the only two innings he would ever toss in the major leagues. He gave up three hits, no walks, and no runs, and struck out one batter—Rudy York. His ERA was 4.50. He never pitched again. Yet his number was retired, and he is in the Hall of Fame. Why?

Because his name is Ted Williams.

WHAT'S THE CONNECTION?

───────

Ken Griffey Sr., Stan Musial, Ken Griffey Jr.

All born in tiny Donora, Pennsylvania.

Babe Ruth, Al Jolson.

Both were residents of St. Mary's Industrial School in Baltimore, Maryland.

Ted Williams, Jackie Robinson, Moe Berg.

The only players awarded the Presidential Medal of Freedom.

Williams presented his medal to the San Diego Hall of Champions Sports Museum while he was in San Diego, his hometown, for the 1992 All-Star Game.

Jackie Robinson's medal was awarded posthumously in 1984 by President (and former Cubs broadcaster) Ronald "Dutch" Reagan.

The brilliant, mysterious, and eccentric Moe Berg—lawyer, linguist, spy, and sometime catcher—declined the 1946 honor, but the medal is in the permanent collection of the National Baseball Hall of Fame and Museum in Cooperstown.

Lou Gehrig, Harmon Killebrew.

Both hit 49 home runs twice, but never 50.

Gehrig reached 49 in 1934 and 1936, and Killebrew did it in 1964 and 1969.

Rabbit Maranville, Pud Galvin, Mordecai "Three Finger" Brown, Cy Young, Roger Connor, Honus Wagner, Luke Appling, Sunny Jim Bottomley, Tommy McCarthy, Bill Dickey.

They're all Hall of Fame players who managed in the big leagues—but only for one year!

Billy Martin, Cliff Young, Chico Ruiz, Joe DeSa, Alvin Montgomery, Frankie Frisch, Tony Boeckel, Mike Miley, Bob Moose, Bill Suero, Billy Bruton, Danny Monzon, Bob Klinger, Mel Ott, Turk Farrell, Mike Sharperson, Danny O'Connell.

All died as a result of car crashes.

Mike Pazik, Minnie Rojas, Bob Meusel, Don Larsen, Roy Campanella, Ed Kirkpatrick, Mike Jones, Carlos Quintana, Amos Rusie, Zack Wheat, Andre Robertson, Roberto Clemente, Lenny Dykstra, Glenn Burke, Andre Thornton, the 1954 Yankees, the 1993 Angels, Charlie Bennett, Ron Gant.

All survived car crashes.

Joe Hovlik, Bobby Fenwick, Bobby Thomson, Bert Blyleven, Kurt "Dutch" Kreuger, Elmer Valo, Mark Hutton, Harry Wright, Al Campanis (seven games at second base, 1943 Dodgers), Jake Gettman, Tony Solaita, Brian Lesher, Al Pardo, John Michaelson, Art Jorgens, Jack Doyle, Otto Hess, Masanori Murakami, Henry Chadwick, Olaf Henriksen, Danny Graves.

They were all born outside the Western Hemisphere.

Okay, name the only Peruvian who played in the big leagues.

Tom Lynch (Chicago Cubs, 1884), from Peru, Illinois.

Stan Musial, Ken Griffey Jr., but not Ken Griffey Sr.

They share a birthday: November 21. Musial was born in 1920 and Griffey in 1969.

Catfish Hunter, Al Kaline, Mel Ott, Bob Feller, Sandy Koufax, Ted Lyons, Herb Pennock, Frank Chance, Ernie Banks, George Sisler.

These Hall of Famers came to the big leagues without playing in the minors. So did future Hall of Famers Dave Winfield and Robin Yount.

Whitey Ford, Sandy Koufax, Phil Rizzuto, Hank Greenberg, Jim Palmer, Lou Gehrig, Frankie Frisch, Wee Willie Keeler, Mickey Welch, George Wright.

These Hall of Famers were all born in New York City.

Bucky Dent, Jim Palmer.

Both were adopted. Palmer is the only adoptee in the Hall of Fame.

Larry Lintz, Joe DiMaggio, Tug McGraw.

All were born in Martinez, California.

Hall of Famer Roger Bresnahan, Dan McGann.

Both were severely injured by the same pitcher on successive plate appearances. On June 18, 1907, Reds pitcher Andy Coakley hit Bresnahan in the head with a pitch, rendering him unconscious. He was given the last rites of the Catholic Church. McGann was the next batter: Coakley broke his wrist. Both Bresnahan and McGann resumed their careers.

Nolan Ryan, Rickey Henderson.

On May 1, 1991, Ryan (Texas) pitched his seventh no-hitter, beating Toronto 3-0. The same day, in the fourth inning, Oakland's Henderson stole third—his 939th stolen base, breaking Lou Brock's career record and leading the A's to a 7-0 win over the Yankees. Henderson was caught stealing in the first and fifth innings by Yankee catcher Matt Nokes.

Another connection: Henderson was Ryan's 5,000th strikeout victim.

Connie Mack, Earle Mack.

Both father and son hit a single and a triple in their first big-league games—October 7, 1886 and October 15, 1910, respectively.

Sunny Jim Bottomley, Paul Waner.

Both hit into unassisted triple plays—the only Hall of Famers to do so.

On May 7, 1925, in Pittsburgh, Bottomley, of the Cardinals, lined to Pirate shortstop Glenn Wright, who doubled Jim Cooney off second and tagged yet another Hall of Famer, Rogers Hornsby, coming from first.

On May 30, 1927—also in Pittsburgh—in the fourth inning, Paul Waner lined to Jim Cooney, who stepped on second base (to get yet another Hall of Famer, Lloyd Waner), then tagged Clyde Barnhart off first base. Coincidentally, Glenn Wright watched this unassisted triple play from the Pirate bench.

Thus Cooney is the only man to play on both ends of an unassisted triple play.

Rod Carew, Cesar Tovar.

As Minnesota Twins, on May 18, 1969, they stole home in the same inning! The Tigers' Mickey Lolich was on the mound.

Ty Cobb, Ted Lyons, and Bucky Dent.

They all played in the first big-league games they saw.

On August 3, 1905, Ty Cobb played in his first big-league game for the Tigers.

Lyons made his first mound appearance, with the White Sox, in relief in a 7-2 losing effort against the Browns on July 2, 1923.

Bucky Dent (born Russell Earl O'Dey) played in his first game on June 1, 1973—also for the White Sox.

Hall of Fame umpire Al Barlick umpired in the first major-league game he ever saw.

Rodney Childress, Glenn Nelson, Rocco Colavito, Robert Rhawn, John Stone, Rocco Krsnich, Everett Bridges. Umpire: John Rowe.

Name the all-"Rocky" team. And don't forget John Coppinger, whose middle name really is "Rocky".

Grover Cleveland Alexander, Christy Mathewson.

Both won exactly 373 games—the most ever in the National League.

Bump Wills, Toby Harrah.

On August 27, 1977, these Texas Rangers hit inside-the-park home runs (off Yankee Ken Clay) *on consecutive seventh-inning pitches* to lead their team to an 8-2 win at Yankee Stadium.

Al Kaline, Babe Ruth, Mel Ott, Sandy Koufax, Rogers Hornsby, Harmon Killebrew, Jimmie Foxx, Mel Ott, Ty Cobb, Bob Feller.

All started their Hall of Fame big-league careers as teenagers.

Johnny Mize, Ralph Kiner.

They are the only men to tie each other for the league home run lead twice. In 1947 they each belted 51; the very next year they tied again with 40.

Kiner won the home run crown outright in 1946 (23), 1949 (54), 1950 (47), and 1951 (42). In 1952 he tied with Hank Sauer with 37.

Mize was the home run champ in 1939 (28) and 1940 (43).

Fred Merkle, Zack Taylor, Burleigh Grimes, Jack Doyle, Sal Maglie, Lefty O'Doul, Wee Willie Keeler, Tony Lazzeri.

Each played for the New York Yankees, the New York Giants, and the Brooklyn Dodgers.

No-hitters by White Sox pitchers Jim Scott (no-hitter through nine innings vs. Washington, May 14, 1914); Joe Benz (vs. Indians, May 31, 1914); and Eddie Cicotte (vs. St. Louis, April 14, 1917); Charlie Robertson's perfect game (vs. the Tigers, April 30, 1922).

Hall of Famer Ray Schalk was the catcher in all four—a record for catchers.

Ozzie Smith, Eddie Murray.

These future Hall of Famers both attended Los Angeles's Locke High School.

Dazzy Vance, Lefty Grove.

They are the only pitchers to lead the National and American Leagues, respectively, in strikeouts during their first seven years in their leagues.

Bob Feller, Mike Witt.

Feller (Indians) no-hit the White Sox 1-0 in Chicago on April 16, 1940, Opening Day.

Witt (Angels) pitched a no-hitter—and a perfect game to boot!—on September 30, 1984, the *last* day of the season, beating the Rangers 1-0.

Bill Dickey, Rabbit Maranville, Ray Schalk, Harry Hooper.

Though all four are Hall of Famers, none ever led his league in any offensive category.

Ryne Sandberg, Roy Smalley Jr., Willie Mays Aikens, Mickey Mantle, Ken Griffey Jr., Larry Johnson, Rogers McKee.

All were named after major leaguers. Ryne Sandberg was named for Ryne Duren; Mickey Mantle for Mickey Cochrane. Larry Johnson's full name is Larry Doby Johnson, while McKee was named Rogers Hornsby McKee. Honorable mention: Chuck Klein Stobbs, Jack Dempsey Cassini. And don't forget Curt Schilling's son, Gehrig.

Moe Berg, John Montgomery Ward, Tony LaRussa, Miller Huggins, Branch Rickey, Eddie Grant, Donn Clendenon, Hughie Jennings, Yankee broadcaster and later announcer of *This Week in Baseball* Mel Allen.

All were or are lawyers. In December 1995, LaRussa got a W in New York Supreme Court when a judge ruled that he was not legally required to have any contact with, or even to acknowledge the existence of his daughters Andrea and Averie. LaRussa was divorced from their mother in 1973, and voluntarily surrendered his visitation rights. He has since remarried and had two daughters with his new wife—the only children he recognizes. The judge fined the lawyer for the older daughters for bringing a frivolous lawsuit.

Hoyt Wilhelm, umpire Nestor Chylak.

Both were wounded in the Battle of the Bulge (December 1944–January 1945), the last great land battle of World War II. Earl Johnson (pitcher for the Red Sox and Tigers, 1940–1941, 1946–1951) also saw action in the battle, as did Dick Whitman, a backup outfielder for the Dodgers and Phillies (1946–1951). Wilhelm's wound forced him to hold his head at a slight angle.

Eddie Mathews, Hank Aaron, Joe Adcock, Frank Thomas.

These Milwaukee Braves hit back-to-back-to-back-to-back homers in the seventh inning on June 8, 1961 against the Reds in Cincinnati. Jim Maloney gave up the first two taters. Adcock and Thomas hit their blasts against Marshall Bridges. But the Braves lost 10-8.

Danny Graves, Richie Hebner, Edd Roush, Andy Seminick, Joe Quinn.

In the off-season, Hebner (Pirates third baseman, 1969–1975) kept in shape as a gravedigger. Seminick (catcher for the Phillies and Reds, 1943–1957), worked in the off-season as an undertaker. Hall of Famer Roush was a gravedigger, and later a cemetery manager in Indiana. Joe Quinn—a native Australian—was a mortician.

Talk about down under!

Phil Rizzuto, Johnny Evers, John Clarkson, Lloyd Waner, Jimmy Collins, Wee Willie Keeler, Jesse Burkett.

None of these Hall of Famers weighed more than 160 pounds.

Phil Rizzuto: 160 pounds; Johnny Evers: 125; John Clarkson: 155; Lloyd Waner: 150; Jimmy Collins: 160; Wee Willie Keeler: 120; Jesse Burkett: 155.

Hank Aaron, José Canseco, George Bell, Zack Wheat, Christy Mathewson, Lindy McDaniel, Heinie Manush, Wilbert Robinson, Clyde Milan, Bing Miller, Richie Allen, Eddie Murray, Heinie Groh, Johnny Evers, Buck Ewing, Fred Clarke, Bill Dickey, Jim O'Rourke, Honus Wagner, Marty Marion, George Kell, George Kelly, Carney Lansford, Graig Nettles, Robin Yount, Tom Paciorek.

Each had a brother who played briefly in the big leagues. Allen and Paciorek had two.

Jim Hunter, umpire Bill Klem, Jim Crawford, George Metkovich.

All shared the same nickname—"Catfish." Players faced virtual automatic ejection for using that sobriquet to Klem's face.

Jim Palmer, Sandy Koufax, Bo Belinsky, John Candelaria—two connections.

Each was born in New York City, and each threw a no-hitter.

Gene Autry, Bowie Kuhn.

Each is a descendant of a defender of the Alamo.

Autry, first owner of the California Angels, is a descendant of Mikah Autry. Former Baseball Commissioner (1969–1984) Kuhn is a direct descendant of Jim Bowie.

Steve Garvey, Ron Cey, Reggie Smith, Dusty Baker.

As 1977 Dodgers, they became the first four teammates to hit at least 30 home runs in the same season. Garvey: 33; Smith: 32; Cey: 30; Baker: 30.

Jim Thorpe, Clarence McKay, "Ace" Parker, Red Badgro, Ernie Nevers, Greasy Neale, George Halas, Paddy Driscoll, umpire Cal Hubbard.

These former big-league baseball players and umpire are in the Pro Football Hall of Fame in Canton, Ohio.

Sandy Koufax's perfect game (Dodgers), September 9, 1965; no-hitters by Bill Singer (Dodgers), July 20, 1970, and Nolan Ryan (Angels), May 15, 1973.

The catcher in all three games was Jeff Torborg.

Stan Musial, Willie Mays, Hank Aaron.

They are the only three men to play in a record 24 All-Star Games.

Harmon Killebrew, Bob Allison.

On July 18, 1962, in Bloomington, Minnesota, these Twins became the first teammates to hit grand slams in the same inning. Killebrew's came off Jim Perry, while Allison's was off Barry Latman in the Twins' 11-run first inning. Allison drove in Killebrew, who had walked after scoring. Killebrew homered again in the third. The Twins beat the Indians 14-3.

A's, Royals, Cowboys.

The three Kansas City major-league teams.

The A's were in Kansas City from 1955 to 1967, and the Royals began play in 1969. The Kansas City Cowboys were in the National League in 1886.

Babe Ruth, Jackie Robinson, Lou Gehrig, Roberto Clemente.

They are the only major leaguers to appear on United States postage stamps. ("Mighty Casey" was also featured on a 1996 issue.)

But they are not the only American players to appear on stamps. On March 15, 1996, Nicaragua issued a set of stamps (four cordobas each) featuring Honus Wagner, Roberto Clemente, Ty Cobb, Babe Ruth, Mike Schmidt, Johnny Bench, Tom Seaver, Rogers Hornsby, and Lou Gehrig. A separate souvenir sheet honors Reggie Jackson (10 cordobas).

In 1988, Grenada issued stamps featuring 81 past and present big leaguers including Alvin Davis, Mark McGwire, George Bell, Roberto Clemente, Cal Ripken Jr., Bob Feller, Dan Quisenberry, Kirby Puckett, Robin Yount, Don Drysdale, Charlie Hough, Andre Dawson, Ty Cobb, Gary Carter, Hank Aaron, Gaylord Perry (in a Mariners uniform), Babe Ruth, and Pete Rose.

Alvin Davis?????

St. Vincent's stamps honored Willie Mays, Al Kaline, Red Schoendienst, and Carl Yastrzemski [misspelled Yastrezmski] with $2 stamps.

Charles Guth, Frederick Veil, Stanley Harris, Darrell Brandon, Fred Waters, Newton Jacobs, Russell Dent.

Name the all-"Bucky" team.

Grover Cleveland Alexander, Tony Lazzeri, Louis Sockalexis, Hal Lanier.

All were epileptics.

Tony Oliva, Bob Allison, Jimmie Hall, Harmon Killebrew.

These visiting Twins hit back-to-back-to-back-to-back homers in the 11th inning against the Kansas City Athletics on May 2, 1964. Oliva, Allison, and Hall hit theirs off Danny Pfister, while Killebrew's was off Vern Handrahan. Final score: Minnesota 7, Kansas City 3.

Jackie Robinson, Ferguson Jenkins.

They are the only two players in both the American and Canadian Baseball Halls of Fame.

Yogi Berra, Phil Rizzuto, Ron Santo, Joe Torre, Babe Pinelli, Rico Petrocelli, Gus Mancuso, Ernie Lombardi, Tony Lazzeri, Dom, Joe, and Vince DiMaggio, Frank Crosetti, Tony Cuccinello, Tony Conigliaro, Rocky Colavito,

Dolph Camilli, Zeke Bonura, Ping Bodie, Roy Campanella, Joe Garagiola, Carl Furillo, Billy Martin, Mary Lou Retton.

All have been enshrined in the National Italian American Sports Hall of Fame, in Arlington Heights, Illinois, which requires that the athlete be (1) retired, and (2) at least 25% Italian.

Woody Held, Pedro Ramos, Tito Francona, Larry Brown.

These Indians hit back-to-back-to-back-to-back homers in the sixth inning of the second game in a twin bill against the Angels on July 31, 1963 in Cleveland. Paul Foytack gave up all four homers. The Indians won 9-5.

Arky Vaughan, Roberto Clemente.

Both were Pittsburgh Pirate Hall of Famers; both wore #21; both died young (Vaughan was 40 and Clemente 38); and both died in the water. Vaughan drowned in a boating accident on August 30, 1952, Clemente when his plane crashed into the ocean on December 31, 1972.

Jocko Conlan, Johnny Cooney, Freddie Fitzsimmons.

They are the only three players since 1912 to umpire in big-league games *during their playing careers.*

In 1935, Conlan—a White Sox bench warmer—filled in when an umpire took ill. He liked the job, and went on to a Hall of Fame umpiring career.

Cooney (Braves) filled in behind the plate during a Dodgers-Braves game in Boston on June 28, 1941, when the umpires were late. Fitzsimmons, of the Dodgers, worked the bases in that game—assisting umpires Al Barlick and Babe Pinelli.

Larry Doby, Joe DiMaggio, Smoky Joe Wood, Hank Aaron, Yogi Berra, Phil Rizzuto, Hall of Fame broadcaster Ernie Harwell, umpire Larry Barnett, Buck O'Neil, Al Lopez, Jackie Robinson, Marge Schott, Cito Gaston, Willie Mays, Mo Vaughn, Ralph Branca.

All have been awarded honorary degrees.

Larry Doby, the first black in the American League, was awarded an honorary degree by Connecticut's Fairfield University on May 18, 1997.

In May 1994, New York University gave Joe DiMaggio an honorary degree in recognition of his "philanthropist and humanitarian support." It was his fourth honorary degree.

In recognition of Smoky Joe Wood's achievements as a big-league pitcher (Red Sox and Indians, 1908–1920, 116-57), and then as its baseball coach (1922–1942), Yale University awarded him an honorary Doctor of Humane Letters degree shortly before his death in 1985, when he was 96.

[No, he was not George Bush's coach (1947–48). That was former big leaguer Ethan Allen, a member of the American Baseball Coaches Association Hall of Fame in Omaha, Nebraska.]

Hank Aaron received an honorary Doctor of Public Service degree from Spring Hill College—in his hometown of Mobile, Alabama—on May 10, 1992.

Aaron was awarded another honorary degree in June, 1992—this time a Doctor of Humane Letters from Columbia College in Chicago, in recognition of his being a "perfect exemplar of individual excellence and commitment to secure genuine equality of opportunity in professional sports and in American life."

Atlanta's Emory University bestowed an honorary degree on Aaron on May 8, 1995, with the following proclamation:

> Home-Run King, Diligent Citizen:
> A young man not yet able to vote,
> you left family and home to follow your life's great calling.
> North and South you pursued, as well,
> your nation's destiny of colorblind opportunity.
> Along the way you entered the large and
> consequential realm of American myth.
> Through perseverance and fortitude, you showed
> good fences make good targets.
> In our springtime of anxiety
> about America's pastime and future,
> your career—in baseball and since—reminds us that,
> however simple the games of our youth,
> our collective history has no simple eras.
> For your heart—its strength and striving toward good—and for your
>   hands—their power and building of good—we confer on you
> the degree of Doctor of Laws, *honoris causa.*

On May 16, 1996, Yogi Berra was awarded an honorary degree by New Jersey's Montclair State College.

On April 28, 1995, Hofstra University in Hempstead, New York, awarded an honorary Doctor of Humane Letters degree to Hall of Famer Phil Rizzuto. The very next month, Iona College in New Rochelle, New York, awarded Rizzuto an honorary Doctor of Laws degree.

Ernie Harwell, who has broadcast baseball on radio and television since 1940 for the Dodgers, Giants, Orioles, Angels, and Tigers, was awarded an honorary Doctorate of Letters by Adrian College in Adrian, Michigan, in 1985.

Veteran American League umpire Larry Barnett was awarded an honorary Doctor of Public Service degree by Ohio's Bowling Green State University on

May 6, 1995, in recognition of his many charitable endeavors, including work for disabled veterans. He has also been given the Presidential Volunteer Action Award. In 1988, Barnett was considered for the Presidential Medal of Freedom, which was ultimately given to Mother Teresa.

Barnett was behind the plate when, in Game 3 of the 1975 Red Sox–Reds World Series in Cincinnati, he was involved in one of the most controversial calls in World Series history. He called "no interference" on Reds batter Ed Armbrister.

On March 15, 1995, Sarasota Florida High School awarded an honorary diploma and a varsity baseball letter to Buck O'Neil, a star of the Negro Leagues. Segregation laws prevented O'Neil from attending the school in the '20s.

Al Lopez was awarded an honorary Doctor of Humane Letters degree by the University of South Florida in Tampa—his hometown—on April 29, 1989. At the time, the Hall of Fame catcher and manager was retired and was living in Tampa.

Howard University awarded honorary degrees on June 7, 1957, to two men whose pioneering work helped change the face of America—Rev. Dr. Martin Luther King, Jr., and Jackie Robinson, who had retired the year before.

Robinson was also given honorary doctorates by Franklin Pierce College, Sacred Heart University, Pace University, and the University of Maryland.

Reds owner Marge Schott was awarded an honorary degree by Maryville College in St. Louis in 1991.

Edwin "Cito" Gaston, then manager of the Blue Jays, was given an honorary Doctor of Laws degree by the University of Toronto on June 10, 1994, after guiding the Blue Jays to consecutive World Championships in 1992 and 1993.

In 1991, Bowling Green gave an honorary degree to Willie Mays.

Red Sox first baseman Mo Vaughn was awarded an honorary Doctor of Humane Letters by the University of Massachusetts at Boston on May 31, 1977.

New York's Long Island University awarded an honorary degree to Ralph Branca on June 1, 1997.

Lou Gehrig, actor Stacy Keach.

Keach was born on June 2, 1941, the day Gehrig died.

Max Flack, Cliff Heathcote.

They were traded for each other between games of a Cardinals-Cubs doubleheader on May 30, 1922. They played against each other in the first game, then switched teams (Flack going from the Cubs to St. Louis, and Heathcote the other way) for the second game. This is the only time this has happened.

Joe DiMaggio, O. J. Simpson.

They both attended Galileo High School in San Francisco (DiMaggio for only one year). Joe's brothers also went there, as did future big leaguers Gino Cimoli, Dario Lodigiani, Mario Mieretti, Dino Restelli, and Dr. Bobby Brown.

Roger Bresnahan, Stan Musial, Babe Ruth, Lefty O'Doul, George Sisler.

They all started their careers as pitchers.

Denis Menke and Jimmy Wynn.

As Astro teammates, they hit grand slams in the same inning—the ninth—against the Mets on July 30, 1969.

Stan Musial, Ted Williams, Matty Alou, Danny Heep, Dane Iorg, Tris Speaker, José Canseco, Dave Kingman, Rick Cerone, Rocky Colavito, Wade Boggs, Dave Winfield.

They each pitched in one game in the big leagues. Hall of Famers Harry Hooper, Cap Anson, Honus Wagner, George Kelly, King Kelly, Jake Beckley, Jimmie Foxx, Bobby Wallace, Walter Alston, Ed Barrow, Fred Clarke, and George Sisler pitched briefly, too.

Tom Seaver, Rod Carew.

On August 4, 1985, Seaver, then with the White Sox, recorded his 300th career win (on Phil Rizzuto Day at Yankee Stadium). A few hours later, and 3,000 miles away, Carew, then with the Angels, got his 3,000th hit off Frank Viola of the Twins. The Twins won 6-5 as Carew singled in the third.

Manny Trillo, Jack Hamilton, Al Jackson, Ned Garver, Nellie Fox, Jo-Jo Moore, Ben Chapman, Gene Lamont, Rickey Henderson.

All were born on Christmas Day.

Actor Danny DeVito, Tom Seaver.

Born on the same day—November 17, 1944.

Eddie Collins, Sam Crawford, Joe Jackson.

Each came in second in the league in batting three times, but none ever won the batting crown. Willie Mays came in second four times (1955, 1957, 1958, 1960), but he won in 1954, when he hit .354. Ty Cobb won the title a record 12 times and came in second 3 times. Rod Carew won the American League batting title seven times and came in second only once, in 1983, when he hit .339 to Wade Boggs' .361.

Charles "Piano Legs" Hickman, Norm Cash.

Both finished #2 in his league for the home run title three times without ever winning. Hickman—1902–3, 1906; Cash—1962, 1965, 1971.

Mel Ott came in second a record seven times—but he won the title six times, on the way to hitting 511 homers.

George Brett, Mike Schmidt.

Both had 1,595 career RBIs.

Harry Heilmann, Yogi Berra, Billy Williams.

Each came in second three times in the race for the league RBI title without ever winning it.

Bobby Thomson, Sonny Corleone, Dave Winfield.

Sonny (played by James Caan in *The Godfather*) was shot to death on October 3, 1951, the day of Thomson's home run, which beat the Dodgers in the third game of the National League playoff, thus winning the pennant for the Giants. The broadcast of the game can be heard from a radio at the tollbooth during the shooting scene. Dave Winfield was busy being born that day.

Gary Carter, Arky Vaughan, Al Rosen, Ted Williams, and Willie McCovey.

They are the only men to homer twice in one All-Star Game.

Vaughan—1941, Williams—1946, Rosen—1954, McCovey—1969, Carter—1981.

Eddie Mathews and Willie Mays.

They are the only two men with over 500 home runs who never led the league in RBIs in a single season.

Mickey Lolich, Hoyt Wilhelm, Joe Niekro, Allie Reynolds.

Although these pitchers enjoyed long careers, each hit only one home run in his entire major-league career.

Lolich's came in Game 2 of the 1968 World Series on October 3, 1968, off Nelson Briles in the third inning. His Tigers beat the Cardinals, 4-3.

Wilhelm, who broke in with the Giants, homered in his first major-league at bat, on April 23, 1952, off the Braves' Dick Hoover in the fourth (the Giants won 9-5). Wilhelm won the game.

Niekro's sole homer came off his brother, Phil, on May 29, 1976. Joe was with the Astros and Phil was with the Braves.

Allie Reynolds came to bat 857 times in his 13-year career (1942–1954). His one homer came as part of a Yankee seven-run first inning on Opening Day in Washington, DC on April 19, 1948. (The Yanks beat the Senators 12-4. President Truman threw out the first ball.)

Ken Holtzman pitched for the pennant-winning Oakland A's in 1974, and, due to the designated hitter rule in the American League, never came to bat. But on October 16, 1974, in Game 4 of the World Series, he hit his only homer. (He went 2-for-4 in the Series, with his homer, a double, an RBI, a walk, and 2 runs scored.) Oakland beat the Dodgers 4-1.

IT WAS THE BEST OF TIMES, IT WAS THE WORST OF TIMES DEPARTMENT

Wilbur Wood, Phil Niekro.

Each led his league in wins in a season in which he had 20 losses.

In 1973, with the White Sox, Wood led the American League with 24 wins. But he also had 20 losses.

In 1979, Braves pitcher Phil Niekro led the National League in both wins (21) *and* losses (20).

Andy Kosco, Mickey Owen.

Kosco (Yankees, Twins, Dodgers, Milwaukee, Red Sox, Reds) was born on October 5, 1941, the day Mickey Owen dropped the third strike in the World Series—one of the most memorable errors in World Series history. His error led to a Yankee victory.

Bucky Dent, Alan Trammell.

They are the only shortstops to be World Series MVPs. Dent—Yankees, 1978; Trammell—Tigers, 1984.

Dallas Green, Yogi Berra, Casey Stengel, Joe Torre.

All four men managed both the Yankees and the Mets.

Dave Winfield, Frank Robinson, Eddie Murray, Rusty Staub.

They each homered in 32 different ballparks.

Babe Ruth, Claudell Washington, Johnny Mize, Dave Kingman, Larry Parrish, Darryl Strawberry.

These are the only men to hit three home runs in a single regular-season game in both leagues.

Ruth hit three homers on May 21, 1930 with the Yankees, and on May 25, 1935 with the Braves—his last home runs.

Mize hit three home runs in one game a record six times, including five in the National League (on July 13 and 20, 1938 and May 13 and September 8, 1940 for the Cardinals and on April 24, 1947 for the Giants) and one in the American (on September 15, 1950 for the Yankees).

Washington did it on July 14, 1979 for the White Sox in a 12-4 rout of the Tigers at home, and on June 22, 1980 for the Mets.

Dave Kingman hit three homers in a single game as a Chicago Cub on July 28, 1979 at Shea Stadium against the Mets. On April 16, 1984, Kingman drove in eight runs while hitting three home runs (including a grand slam) for the Oakland A's at Seattle.

On May 29, 1977, Larry Parrish of the Montreal Expos smacked three homers against the Cardinals in St. Louis. He also hit three home runs—in consecutive at bats—for the Expos on July 30, 1978 in a 19-0 drubbing of the Braves in Atlanta. The Expos collected a record 58 total bases in that game.

Parrish hit three homers again for the Expos against the Braves in Atlanta on April 25, 1980, and hit three for the Texas Rangers against the Yankees on April 29, 1985, in the fourth, sixth, and eighth innings at home at Arlington Stadium.

Darryl Strawberry's first three-home-run game came on August 5, 1985, when he was a Met, against the Cubs in Chicago. He homered in the first inning off rookie Derek Notelho with two men on, and again in the third inning—a solo shot, also off Notelho. Strawberry was walked intentionally in the fifth. He had another solo shot in the seventh inning off Ron Meredith. Powered by Strawberry's three blasts, the Mets beat the Cubs 7-2 to move into first place in the National League East.

As a Yankee, Strawberry hit three homers in one game a mere 11 years and one day later, on August 6, 1996—all three shots off Kevin Tapani of the White Sox in New York.

Pete Rose, Willie Davis.

Each smacked hit #2,000 on the same day—June 19, 1973. But there the similarity ends: Davis finished with 2,561, while Rose had more than 2,000 *more* hits, finishing his career with a record 4,256.

Sid Fernandez, Charlie Hough, Ron Darling.

These three pitchers are all natives of Honolulu.

Bobby Thomson, Hank Aaron.

Aaron became the Braves' regular outfielder when Thomson broke his ankle on March 13, 1954, during spring training.

Catfish Hunter, Jerry Ujdur, Ron Santo, Bill Gullickson.

All were diabetic.

Willis Rementer, Charles Schmidt, Arthur Weis, Elmer Nieman, Charles Sutclife, Charles Wensloff, Harold Wynegar, Clell Hobson, Alfred Benton, Francis Albert, Clarence Metzger, Claude Edge, Floyd Henry, Wallace Davis.

Name the all "Butch" team.

What do John Kennedy, 35th President of the United States, and John Kennedy, a utility infielder with the Senators, Dodgers, Yankees, Pilots, Brewers, and Red Sox from 1962 to 1974 (32 home runs in 12 years), have in common besides their name?

They share the same birthday: May 29. The President was born in 1917, and the ballplayer—not to be confused with still another John Kennedy, who played for the Phillies in 1957—was born in 1941.

Christy Mathewson, umpire Red Ormsby, Hall of Fame executive Larry MacPhail.

All three were gassed in World War I.

Rosy Ryan, Frank Demaree, Mickey Lolich.

Their first major-league home runs were in the World Series.

Ryan, a pitcher for the Giants, hit his on October 6, 1924, in Game 3 of the Series. The Giants won the game 6-4, but lost the Series to the Senators 4-3. The only other homer of Ryan's 248-game career came in 1925.

Demaree hit his on October 2, 1932, in Game 4 of the Series. Chicago lost the game 13-6 and the Series 4-0 to the mighty Yankees. Demaree went on to hit 72 regular season homers.

Lolich's first homer, after 381 at bats, came on October 3, 1968 in Game 2 of the Series for the Tigers, who won the game 8-1 and the Series 4-3 over the Cardinals.

Elmer Smith, Yogi Berra, Mickey Mantle, Chuck Hiller, Dave McNally.

They are the only men to hit grand slams in the World Series.

Lou Gehrig, Hank Greenberg.

Both averaged .92 RBIs per game—the highest in history.

Babe Ruth, Jimmie Foxx, Frankie Frisch, Kiki Cuyler, Sunny Jim Bottomley, Heinie Manush, Earl Averill Sr., Mickey Cochrane.

These Hall of Famers all wore #3.

Hank Aaron, Hoyt Wilhelm.

They were honored together on Aaron-Wilhelm Night in Atlanta on May 26, 1970, recognizing Aaron's 3,000th hit (on May 17, 1970) and Wilhelm's

1,000th game on the mound—at the time, a unique achievement for a pitcher. A separate Hank Aaron Day was held on May 23, 1968.

Albert Belle, Reggie Jackson, Tony Gwynn, Ken Griffey Jr., Chipper Jones, Wade Boggs.

They all had candy bars named after them. (Griffey was accorded this unusual honor in 1989, his rookie season!) Actually, Boggs' was called a "352 Bar," after the then-Red Sox–star's career batting average at the time.

Perhaps they were friends with Jack Clark, Frank Hershey, Rudy York, Ed Mars, Mike Heath, and Roger Maris and Mickey Mantle—"the M&M Boys."

The Altoona Rail Kings, an independent team in the Heartland League, have their own candy bar—the R.K. Bar. A portion of the profits from its sales benefits local youth sports programs.

Don Money, Cecil Cooper.

These Brewer teammates hit grand slams *in the same inning* off Boston's Mike Torrez and Chuck Rainey at County Stadium on April 12, 1980.

Ted Lyons, Luke Appling.

They are the only modern Hall of Famers who played for over 20 years for the same team without appearing in a World Series. Lyons was a White Sox pitcher (1923–1942, 1946—21 seasons) and Appling was the Sox' star shortstop (1930–1950—20 years). They were teammates from 1930 to 1942.

Joe Charboneau, Willie McCovey, Dave Righetti, Bob Hamelin.

These Rookies of the Year all spent part of their sophomore years in the minors.

McCovey, Giants, Rookie of the Year in 1959
Charboneau, Cleveland, 1980
Righetti, Yankees, 1981
Hamelin, Kansas City, 1994

Dan Bankhead, Cuno Barragan, Jim Bullinger, Andre David, Dave Eiland, Bill Lefebvre, Mitch Lyden, Dave Machemer, Eddie Morgan, Bill Roman, Don Rose, José Sosa, Hoyt Wilhelm.

Each of these ballplayers—all forgettable except for Wilhelm—hit his only home run in his first big-league at bat.

Lew Krausse Sr., Lew Krausse Jr.

On June 11, 1931, when he was a 19-year-old pitcher for the Philadelphia Athletics, Lew Sr. was the youngest man in the major leagues.

On June 16, 1961, Lew Jr., pitching for the Kansas City A's, was the youngest major leaguer at 18. He was also one of the few pitchers who made his big-league debut as a starter.

In his last high school game, Lew Jr. struck out 24 batters. When he signed his contract with the A's on June 9, 1961, he received a bonus of $125,000 (to be spread out over five years)—a record at the time. His base salary was $7,000 per year.

Lew Sr. retired with a 5-1 career record (an .833 winning percentage). Lew Jr.'s record (after 12 years with the A's, Orioles, Cardinals, and Braves) was 68-91, for a .428 winning percentage.

Bombo Rivera, Manny Trillo, Pepe Frias, Chucho Ramos, Charlie Cuellar.

They all shared the same real first name: Jesus.

Paul Molitor, Joe Carter.

On April 9, 1994, these two Blue Jays reached career milestones on the same ball. In the bottom of the ninth, in a game against the Mariners in Seattle, Molitor got his 2,500th hit (off Bobby Thigpen). The ball was put back in play, and the next batter, Carter, hit it for a two-run homer, giving him his 1,000th career RBI. Carter kept the ball.

October 1, 1932; September 28, 1938; October 3, 1951; July 24, 1983.

The dates of four "named" home runs.

- The "Called Shot"—Babe Ruth's blast off the Cubs' Charlie Root on October 1, in Game 3 of the 1932 World Series.
- The "Homer in the Gloamin'," Gabby Hartnett's shot to left in the dusk off the Pirates' Mace Brown, with two out and the score tied in the bottom of the ninth inning on September 28, 1938, on an 0-2 pitch at Wrigley Field. The homer helped the Cubs to the pennant.
- The "Shot Heard 'Round the World"—October 3, 1951. Bobby Thomson's series-winning homer off Ralph Branca ended the 1951 Giants-Dodgers National League play-off.
- The "Pine Tar Shot" of July 24, 1983, hit by George Brett off the Yankees' Goose Gossage.

Stan Musial, Harmon Killebrew, Jimmie Foxx, Zack Wheat.

None of these Hall of Famers was ever thrown out of a game.

Sandy Koufax, Harvey Kuenn.

Kuenn had the ignominious distinction of making the last out in a Sandy Koufax no-hitter *twice*.

First, he bounced back to the mound on May 11, 1963 to wrap up Koufax's 8-0 no-hitter over the Giants. Then, on September 9, 1965, Kuenn struck out (on three straight fastballs) to end Koufax's perfect game over the Cubs.

Fred Parent, Ron Hassey, Patsy Dougherty, Ossee Schreckengost, Jim Gilliam, Joe Christopher, Wes Covington, Reggie Jackson.

Each played in two perfect games.

Ted Williams, Jim Bunning, Allie Reynolds.

Williams made the last out in no-hitters by both Reynolds (September 28, 1951) and Bunning (July 20, 1958).

Joe DiMaggio, Earle Combs, Lloyd Waner, Billy Herman.

As rookies, these future Hall of Famers each had at least 200 hits.

Hank Aaron, Don Wilson, Ken Holtzman.

Aaron made the last out in no-hitters by both Houston's Wilson on June 18, 1967, and Holtzman of the Cubs on August 19, 1969.

Rollie Fingers, Catfish Hunter, Ferguson Jenkins.

These three Hall of Fame pitchers batted in the American League after the introduction of the designated hitter in 1973. Fingers and Hunter pinch-hit for Oakland in 1973. Fingers did so again in 1975 (0-1). Hunter batted again in 1976 (once, without a hit). Jenkins came to bat twice for Texas in 1974 and got one hit.

Sandy Alomar, Mel Stottlemyre, George Sisler, Sam Hairston, Dixie Walker.

Each had two sons play in the big leagues. Sandy's sons are Roberto and Sandy Jr., Mel's are Todd and Mel Jr., George's are Dick and Dave, Sam's are John and Jerry, and Dixie's are Harry "The Hat" and Dixie Jr.

Bill Skowron, Lou Piniella, José Cruz, Dwight Evans.

They were never booed—or so they might have thought. Perhaps the crowd was just shouting "MOOOOOOOOSE," "LOUUUUUUUUUUU," "CRUUUUUUUUUUZ," or "DOOOOEEE" for Evans, whose nickname was Dewey. But "Boo" Ferris may actually have been booed.

Chuck Klein, Roberto Clemente, Early Wynn, Lefty Grove, John Kruk.

Klein: exactly 300 home runs. Clemente: exactly 3,000 hits. Wynn and Grove: exactly 300 wins. Kruk finished his career with a batting average of precisely .300 (with exactly 100 home runs).

Roy Campanella, Ray Dandridge, Martin Dihigo, Josh Gibson, Monte Irvin.

The only men in both the American and Mexican baseball Halls of Fame. The Mexican one is in Monterrey.

Allen Sothoron, Phil Douglas, Urban Shocker, Dana Fillingim, Allan Russell, Marvin Goodwin, Burleigh Grimes, Clarence Mitchell, Dick Rudolph, Dutch Leonard, Jack Quinn, Red Faber, Stan Coveleski, Ray Caldwell, Bill Doak, Doc Ayers.

These pitchers were allowed to finish their careers as spitballers when the wet one was banned after the 1920 World Series.

Babe Ruth, Frankie Frisch.

Both Hall of Famers? Yes. So are lots of others. Both stars in New York? Yes, but again, so were lots of others. There must be some other connection. How about this: both had the same roommate—Jimmie Reese. Reese's playing career was brief: just 232 games with the Yankees in 1930 and 1931, when he roomed with Ruth (or, as he put it years later, with Ruth's luggage), and with the Cardinals in 1932, when he roomed with Frisch. He coached for the Angels from 1973 to 1992.

1.   The Dodgers turn a triple play against the Boston Braves at home on April 26, 1949. With Johnny Sain at second and Eddie Stanky at first after singles, Alvin Dark hits a pop fly to short left center field. The runners try to advance, but have to go back after Gene Hermanski snares the ball. Hermanski throws to Jackie Robinson at second base to double Sain off the bag. Robinson then throws on to Gil Hodges at first to get Stanky.

2.   The Dodgers turn a triple play on June 15, 1996 against the Atlanta Braves. In the first inning, with Hideo Nomo on the mound, Marquis Grissom singles and Mark Lemke walks. Chipper Jones is up next, and the runners are going. Jones pops out to shortstop Juan Castro in short left field. Castro throws to Delino DeShields at second to retire Grissom, then on to Eric Karros at first to get Lemke.

What they have in common is that Hall of Fame broadcaster Ernie Harwell called both games! In 1949, he was the radio voice of the Dodgers. For the 1996 game, Harwell, who has broadcast for the Tigers since 1960, was doing the game for the CBS radio network.

Luke Appling, Joe Cronin, Lou Gehrig, Ralph Kiner, Mel Ott, Duke Snider, Earl Weaver.

These Hall of Famers all had the same number—4—retired in their honor.

Appling, White Sox; Cronin, Red Sox; Gehrig, Yankees; Kiner, Pirates; Ott, Giants; Snider, Dodgers; Weaver, Orioles.

Warren Spahn, Denny Lemaster.

These are the only pitchers ever to surrender home runs to Dodger Hall of Famer Sandy Koufax, one of the great pitchers, yet one of the truly abysmal batters, in history.

The first, off Warren Spahn of the Milwaukee Braves, was on June 13, 1962. Koufax connected for his second and final career home run on July 20, 1963, off Denny Lemaster of the Braves.

Miller Huggins, Wee Willie Keeler, Phil Rizzuto, Sandy Koufax, Lou Gehrig, Waite Hoyt, Frankie Frisch, Fred Lindstrom, Duke Snider, Hal Newhouser, Whitey Ford, Mickey Welch, Charles Comiskey, Bill Veeck.

These Hall of Famers played or managed in their hometowns—or, in Veeck's case, owned his hometown team.

- Bill Veeck, a native of Chicago, and perhaps the only Hall of Famer who actually lived in a big-league ballpark (he lived at Wrigley Field when his father was president of the Cubs) owned the White Sox from 1959 to 1961. He reacquired the club in 1976 and resold it in 1980. During the course of his unique career, he owned the Cleveland Indians (1946–1949) and the St. Louis Browns (1951–1953).
- Miller Huggins, of Cincinnati, played for the Reds (1904–1909), then the Cardinals (1910–1916). Although he managed the Cardinals from 1913 to 1917, and the Yankees from 1918 to 1929, becoming one of the immortal managers in the history of the game, he never managed in Cincinnati and did not play in a World Series.
- Phil Rizzuto of New York City played his entire major-league career as the shortstop for the New York Yankees from 1941 to 1942 and 1946 to 1956. He played in the World Series in 1941, 1942, 1947, 1949, 1950, 1951, 1952, 1953, and 1955 and was in a total of 26 World Series games at home at Yankee Stadium, plus another 17 at Ebbets Field in Brooklyn and 3 at the Polo Grounds against the Giants. Total: 46 World Series games in his hometown.

  Rizzuto hit home runs in Game 5 of the 1942 Series at home against the Cardinals, and again in Game 5 of the 1951 Series at home against the Giants.
- Lou Gehrig—perhaps the greatest player to spend his entire career in his hometown (New York City)—was the Yankee first baseman from 1923 to 1939. During that time he hit 251 home runs at home. He won the batting crown in 1934 (.363), the RBI crown in 1927 (175), 1928 (142), 1930 (174), 1931 (184), and 1934 (165), and the home run title in 1931 (46), 1934 (49), and 1936 (49).

  He is the only man to win the Triple Crown in his hometown, a feat he accomplished in 1934. (Batting average .363, 49 homers, 165 RBIs.)

Gehrig appeared in the World Series in 1926, 1927, 1928, 1932, 1936, 1937, and 1938, and played 17 World Series games at home. He hit 10 homers in World Series play, including 4 at home, and he was on World Champion teams in 1927, 1928, 1932, 1936, 1937, and 1938.

In 1936, and again in 1937, the Yankees' World Series opponents were also from New York City—the Giants. Gehrig played six games at the Polo Grounds in those series (in three games each year); so even though those games were not at his home park, they were in his hometown.

- During his 21-year career, Brooklyn-born Waite Hoyt pitched for the Giants in 1918 and then for the Yankees from 1921 to 1930. In 1932, he pitched for both the Dodgers and the Giants.

He appeared in the World Series in 1921, 1922, 1923, 1926, 1927, and 1928, pitching in five games at Yankee Stadium (including two wins) plus one at the Polo Grounds.

- Frankie Frisch was born in the Bronx. He played for the New York Giants from 1919 to 1926, then for the St. Louis Cardinals from 1927 to 1937.

As a Giant, he played in all eight games in the 1921 World Series against the Yankees. He played in all five games of the Giants-Yankees all–New York City best-of-nine Series in 1922 (which the Giants won 4-0, with one game ending in a tie), and all six games of the Giants-Yankees 1923 Series—again, a subway series. All of these games were in his hometown.

In 1924, Frisch played for the Giants against the Senators, appearing in all seven games—three at home.

As a Cardinal, he played against the Yankees in the 1928 World Series (playing two games at Yankee Stadium).

- Duke Snider, a native of Los Angeles, spent 16 of his 18 big-league years with the Dodgers, 11 in Brooklyn and 5 in Los Angeles. In 1959, his Los Angeles Dodgers beat the Chicago White Sox 4-2. Snider played in four games in the 4-2 Dodger victory, but his homer in that series was in Game 6 in Chicago.

- Mickey Welch, a 307-game winner from Brooklyn, never played in the modern World Series, for his career spanned 1880–1892, well before the first modern Series in 1903. Welch's career started for Troy (1880–1882), and he was with the Giants from 1883 to 1892.

- Hal Newhouser, a Hall of Famer from Detroit, played for his hometown Tigers for 15 of his 17 years. He was a Tiger from 1939 to 1953, and was considered the best pitcher of the World War II era. But he was no fluke. Yes, he led the American League with 29 wins in 1944 and 25 in 1945, when many major leaguers were in military service. But in 1946, with the big leaguers back, Newhouser led the league in wins again with 26. In

1946 he also led the league with an ERA of 1.94, and in 1947 he led the American League with 24 complete games.

His Tigers beat the Cubs 4-3 in the 1945 World Series. Newhouser was 2-1, losing Game 1 at home—his only World Series appearance at home. Games 1, 2, and 3 were played in Detroit, with the remaining four in Chicago, as wartime restrictions cut down on travel. Newhouser's two wins, in Games 5 and 7, were on the road.

- Whitey Ford, a native of Manhattan, probably can retire the cup for hometown World Series pitching records. He appeared in 11 different World Series, starting a record total of 22 World Series games. He pitched in 11 at Yankee Stadium and won 7 there. He also appeared in two games at Ebbets Field against the Brooklyn Dodgers.
- Fred Lindstrom played in the big leagues for 13 years, primarily with the Giants and the Pirates. He was with the Dodgers in 1936, but in 1935 he played 90 games for his hometown Chicago Cubs.

Cal Ripken Jr., Marv Throneberry.

Both wore #8 for the Baltimore Orioles.

PRIZE GUYS

Only one man won the big three awards during his career—Rookie of the Year, MVP, and Cy Young. Who was he?

Don Newcombe, Dodgers. Newcombe was the major-league Rookie of the Year in 1949, although he started the year with Montreal in the International League. He won Cy Young and MVP honors in 1956.

Who was the first Rookie of the Year elected to the Hall of Fame?

Jackie Robinson, the very first Rookie of the Year (1947), was elected to Cooperstown in 1962.

Who is the only man to be named World Series MVP twice—with two different teams?

Reggie Jackson. 1973—Oakland A's (He was also American League MVP that year); 1977—Yankees.

Has anyone else ever been named World Series MVP twice?

Yes. Sandy Koufax—Dodgers, 1963, 1965; Bob Gibson—Cardinals, 1964, 1967.

He threw seven no-hitters, struck out 5,714, and led the league in strikeouts seven times. How many Cy Young Awards did Nolan Ryan win?

None.

Who was the first reliever to win the Cy Young Award?

Mike Marshall, Dodgers, 1974.

Lou Gehrig won the Triple Crown in 1934. Was he the American League's MVP?

No. Gehrig came in fifth in the MVP voting, behind Mickey Cochrane (who won), Charlie Gehringer, Lefty Gomez, and Schoolboy Rowe.

Who was the youngest player to be named MVP in two consecutive seasons?

Hal Newhouser, Tigers—1944 and 1945. Newhouser was 24 in 1945.

Who was the only National Leaguer to win the Most Valuable Player award in his first year in the league?

Kirk Gibson, Dodgers, 1988.

Who was the only Yankee to be Rookie of the Year and later MVP?

Thurman Munson: Rookie of the Year—1970, American League MVP—1976.

Who is the youngest man to win the Cy Young Award?

The Mets' Dwight Gooden. He was 20 in 1985.

Who are the only father-in-law and son-in-law to win MVP awards?

Lou Boudreau, Indians (1948) and his son-in-law Denny McLain, Tigers (1968).

Who are the only Heisman Trophy winners to play in the major leagues?

Vic Janowicz and Bo Jackson.

Janowicz played for Ohio State and won the Heisman Trophy in 1950—the third junior to do so. (In a game against Iowa, he scored 46 points himself, leading his team to an 83-21 win.) In 1954–1955, he played for the Washington Redskins.

He played for the Pirates in 1953 and 1954, appearing in 83 games, mostly as a catcher, hitting .214 with two home runs.

Jackson was a world-class runner and a star running back at Auburn, and won the Heisman award in 1985. He had a successful but injury-shortened baseball career with the Royals, White Sox, and Angels, and was voted Most Valuable Player of the 1989 All-Star Game. (There's a combination unlikely to be repeated soon: Heisman Trophy winner and All-Star MVP.) Jackson severely injured his hip while playing football for the NFL's Los Angeles Raiders against the Cincinnati Bengals on January 13, 1991 in a playoff game (Raiders

20, Bengals 10). In 1993, he underwent hip replacement surgery. He retired from baseball just before the 1995 season and returned to Auburn to earn his degree in December of that year.

Name three MVPs with the same last name.

Jackie (1949), Brooks (1964), and Frank Robinson (1961, 1966).

Who won MVP awards separated by the most years?

Willie Mays of the Giants: 1954 and 1965—11 years apart.

What was the first year in which the MVPs in both leagues were first basemen?

1994. American League: Frank Thomas, White Sox. National League: Jeff Bagwell, Houston.

> **Do Bagwell and Thomas have anything else in common?**
>
> Yes. They were born on the very same day—May 27, 1968.
>
> Thomas was born at 4:35 a.m. Bagwell's birth certificate, a copy of which we obtained, does not show a time of birth.

> ### Thanks to Barb Kozuh, of Big Hurt Enterprises, who obtained the time of his birth for us from Thomas's mother, Charlie Mae Thomas.
>
> ---

Similarly, Barry Lyons and Steve Lyons—unrelated—were both born on June 3, 1960.

Who was the only man to win an MVP award but never play in an All-Star Game?

Kirk Gibson. A career .268 hitter with 255 career home runs, Gibson was an All-American football star at Michigan State. He had a 17-year career with the Tigers, Dodgers, Royals and Pirates (1979–1995) that was more dramatic than productive; he played over 150 games in only one season (1985—154).

He was the National League's Most Valuable Player in 1988, when he was with the Dodgers.

During his years with the Yankees (1982–1995), Don Mattingly had seven teammates who had been Rookies of the Year—not all with the Yankees. Name them.

> Lou Piniella: Rookie of the Year in 1969 with the Kansas City Royals, and a Yankee from 1974 to 1984.

John Montefusco: Rookie of the Year in 1975 with the Giants. A Yankee from 1983 to 1986.

Steve Howe: Rookie of the Year in 1980 with the Dodgers. A Yankee from 1991 to 1996.

Dave Righetti: Rookie of the Year as a Yankee in 1981, he was with New York in 1979 and from 1981 to 1990.

Steve Sax: 1982 Rookie of the Year as a Dodger, he teamed with Mattingly from 1989 to 1991.

Darryl Strawberry: Rookie of the Year as a 1983 Met. He was a Mattingly teammate in 1995 for 32 games.

Derek Jeter: Rookie of the Year in 1996. He was a Mattingly teammate in 1995, when he played in 15 Yankee games.

The James E. Sullivan Award has been presented annually since 1930 by the United States Amateur Athletic Union to the outstanding amateur athlete of the year. Winners have included Dick Button (figure skating), Sammy Lee (Diving), Mike Powell (long jump), and Janet Evans (swimming).

But only once has the honor gone to a baseball player. He was given the award in recognition of his abilities as a college player. He later became a big leaguer. Who was he?

Jim Abbott, who received the award in 1987. He was a standout pitcher for the University of Michigan before being named to the 1988 United States Olympic Team. Thereafter, he pitched for the Angels, the White Sox, the Yankees, and then the Angels again.

Hank Aaron had more lifetime home runs, runs, games, and RBIs than any other player. He hit over 30 home runs in 15 different years. How many Most Valuable Player Awards did he win?

Just one, in 1957. That year, with the Milwaukee Braves, he led the National League with 44 homers and 132 RBIs, as well as 118 runs scored, while hitting .322. He was #2 in hits (198) and #1 in total bases (369).

In one year, he was MVP of the National League, MVP in the League Championship Series, and MVP in the World Series, which his team won. Who was he?

Willie Stargell, Pirates, 1979. (He tied for National League MVP with Keith Hernandez.)

Which former big leaguer is the only baseball player to be MVP in the National Football League?

Clarence "Ace" Parker—NFL MVP in 1940, elected to the Football Hall of Fame in 1972. His baseball career consisted of 94 games with the Philadelphia

A's (1937–1938). Parker was the first American League rookie to homer in his first pinch-hit at bat, April 30, 1937.

Name at least one player at each position who has been MVP in two consecutive years.

P	Hal Newhouser, 1944–45
C	Yogi Berra, 1954–55
1B	Jimmie Foxx, 1932–33
	Frank Thomas, 1993–94
2B	Joe Morgan, 1975–76
3B	Mike Schmidt, 1980–81
SS	Ernie Banks, 1958–59
LF	Barry Bonds, 1992–93
CF	Mickey Mantle, 1956–57
RF	Roger Maris, 1961–62
	Dale Murphy, 1982–83

Who is the first active player to have a major award named after him?

Lou Brock. In 1978, the National League announced that the Lou Brock Stolen Base Award would be given annually to the league's most prolific base stealer.

What is the official name of the MVP trophy?

The Kenesaw Mountain Landis Award.

Who was the first catcher to be named Rookie of the Year?

Johnny Bench, Reds, 1968.

Who is the only pitcher to win the Triple Crown of Pitching—most wins, most strikeouts, and lowest ERA in a single season—for a last-place team?

Steve Carlton, 1972 Phillies—27 wins (of his team's 59), 310 strikeouts, and 1.97 ERA.

Dodger catcher Mike Piazza was voted National League Rookie of the Year in 1993. In which round was he drafted?

The 62nd: 1,388 players were selected before him.

In his rookie season he hit 35 home runs, drove in 100 runs, and was rewarded with Rookie of the Year and All-Star honors. But he also led his league in strikeouts. Who was he?

Ron Kittle, White Sox, 1983—150 Ks, .254 batting average, 132 hits.

Who were the only pitching teammates to finish 1-2 in MVP voting?

Hal Newhouser and Dizzy Trout, 1944 Tigers.

He was not the MVP the year he won the National League Triple Crown. Who was he?

Chuck Klein, 1933 Phillies. He was National League MVP in 1932, but when he won the Triple Crown (28 homers, .368 batting average, and 120 RBIs) in 1933, Giants' pitcher Carl Hubbell was named Most Valuable Player. Hubbell's stats were 23-12, 1.66 ERA, and 308.2 innings (all league leaders) with 10 shutouts.

Klein was traded to the Cubs in the 1934 off-season for Ted Kleinhans, Mark Koenig, Harvey Hendrick, and $65,000.

Who was the first unanimous choice for Most Valuable Player?

Al "Flip" Rosen, Cleveland, 1953—.336 batting average, 43 homers, and 145 RBIs. Rosen was also the first Jewish MVP.

In 1951, the MVPs in both leagues played the same position in the same city—the only time this has ever happened. Who were they?

American League: Yogi Berra, catcher, New York Yankees. National League: Roy Campanella, catcher, Brooklyn Dodgers.

No other catchers in either league got even one MVP vote that year!

Who was the first MVP to bat eighth in his team's batting order?

Marty Marion, 1944 Cardinals' shortstop.

Who was the first American Leaguer to be a unanimous choice for Rookie of the Year?

Carlton Fisk, Red Sox, 1972.

Who was the first pitcher to win the Cy Young award twice—with two different teams?

Gaylord Perry: Indians, 1972; Padres, 1978.

Since 1949, each league has given a separate Rookie of the Year award. A number of winners—such as Johnny Bench and Willie McCovey—have gone on to Cooperstown. But in some years, the National and American League Rookies of the Year *both* wound up in Cooperstown.

In how many years have the National and American League Rookies of the Year both gone on to the Hall of Fame? Who were the players?

It's only happened twice: in 1956, the National League Rookie of the year was Cincinnati's Frank Robinson, while the White Sox' Luis Aparicio won in the American League.

In 1967, Tom Seaver (Mets) and Rod Carew (Twins) were selected, at the start of their Hall of Fame careers.

Future additions to this list might include the 1977 pair: Andre Dawson (Expos) and Eddie Murray (Orioles).

Only three times since each league gave its own Cy Young Award have both recipients been elected to the Hall of Fame. Name the years and the pitchers.

1972: Gaylord Perry (Cleveland) and Steve Carlton (Philadelphia). 1973 and 1975: Jim Palmer (Orioles) and Tom Seaver (Mets).

Eddie Murray was American League Rookie of the Year in 1977. Which other former Rookies of the Year also amassed 3,000 hits?

Willie Mays (Giants, 1951), Pete Rose (Reds, 1963), and Rod Carew (Twins, 1967).

Who is the first pitcher to win a Cy Young award without winning at least 20 games?

Tom Seaver, 1973 Mets (19–10). But his won-lost record does not tell the whole story. He led the National League in complete games (18), strikeouts (251), and ERA (2.08).

Who was the only man to have been both MVP and Manager of the Year?

Joe Torre: MVP–National League, 1971, Cardinals; Manager of the Year–Braves, 1982.

Who is the first man to be traded the year after he won the Cy Young Award?

Frank Viola. On July 31, 1989, after going 24-7 with the 1988 Twins (including an All-Star appearance), "Sweet Music" was traded to the Mets.

Two men once used the same locker in the same stadium. One was the Most Valuable Player in the American League, and the other was named Player of the Year in the National Football League in the same year. Both played on championship teams that year, too. And both became Hall of Famers in their respective sports. Who were they?

Mickey Mantle, Yankees, and Frank Gifford, New York Football Giants, in 1956. They shared a locker at Yankee Stadium.

Only two eligible players who have won two Most Valuable Player awards are not in the Hall of Fame. Who are they?

Roger Maris, Yankees (1960, 1961).
Dale Murphy, Braves (1982, 1983).

THE WORLD SERIES

Who were the first brothers to face each other in a World Series?

Jimmy and Doc Johnston. In the 1920 Series, Jimmy Johnston played third base for the Dodgers, while Wheeler Page "Doc" Johnston played first base for the Indians. The Indians won 5-2.

These brothers played in the same city and opposed each other in three World Series in a row. Who were they?

"Long" Bob and Emil Frederick "Irish" Meusel. Bob played 10 years for the Yankees, plus one for the Reds, and finished with a lifetime batting average of .309. His older brother played for the Senators, Phillies, Giants, and Dodgers during his 11-year career, compiling a lifetime batting average of .310—one point higher than Bob's.

Bob was in the World Series with the Yankees in 1921, 1922, and 1923. Opposing him those years was Irish, a member of the Giants. The Giants won in 1921 and 1922, and the Yankees in 1923.

Who are the only first basemen named World Series MVPs?

Donn Clendenon, Mets, 1969, and Willie Stargell, Pirates, 1979.

These brothers won two games each in the same World Series—the only time this has ever happened. Who were they?

Dizzy and Daffy Dean, 1934 Cardinals. They beat the Tigers 4-3.

Who is the youngest manager to win a World Series?

Bucky Harris was just 27 when, as player-manager in 1924, he helped his Senators beat the Giants 4-3. (He hit .333 with two homers and seven RBIs.)

When was the only time that brothers homered for each team in one World Series game?

On October 15, 1964, in the seventh game of the Series, Ken Boyer homered for the Cardinals and his brother Clete homered for the Yankees. (Both brothers played third base.) The Cards won the game and the Series 4-3.

Who was the first rookie manager to win a World Series?

Tris Speaker, Cleveland, 1920. While still an active player, the future Hall of Famer managed the Indians for 60 games the previous year, but 1920 was his first full season. His Indians beat the Dodgers 5-2.

Who is the only man to play in a World Series in a year in which he did not play in the regular season?

Clyde McCullough, 1945 Cubs.

A part-timer during virtually all of his career (1940–1956), McCullough was a catcher and occasional pinch hitter who appeared in more than 100 games in only 3 of his 15 seasons.

He was in the Navy during the entire 1944 and 1945 seasons, and was discharged only in time to appear in the Series. In his one at bat, in the ninth inning of the seventh game, Hal Newhouser struck him out. The Tigers went on to win the Series 4-3.

Who is the only former prisoner of war to play in a World Series?

Mickey Grasso, who had been held by the Germans in North Africa during World War II. He caught 322 games for the Giants, Senators, and Indians (1946–1955).

In 1954, he played in the World Series for the Indians, appearing in one game with no at bats.

Augie Donatelli, who umpired in the National League for 24 years, including four All-Star Games and five World Series, began his umpiring career as a prisoner of war. He enlisted in the United States Army Air Corps and flew 18 missions as a B-17 tail gunner before being shot down over Berlin in 1944. He was a prisoner of war for 15 months in Stalag VI in East Prussia, where he umpired softball games.

Bert Shepard's P-38 was shot down over Germany during World War II. His leg was destroyed, and he was a prisoner of war. Later, with an artificial leg, he became the batting-practice pitcher for the Washington Senators. His dream of pitching in the big leagues finally came true—at least for 5⅓ innings on August 4, 1945, in the second game of a twin bill in Washington against the Red Sox. He walked one, struck out two, and allowed three hits and an earned run. Tom McBride drove in 6 runs for the Red Sox in the 12-run fourth inning with a bases-loaded double followed by a bases-loaded triple.

Phil "Babe" Marchildon, a native of Penetanguishene, Ontario, who pitched for the Philadelphia Athletics and Red Sox (1940–1942, 1945–1950), was a tail gunner in the Royal Canadian Air Force during World War II. In 1944, his plane was shot down over the Baltic on his 26th mission. He lost 40 pounds during the nine months he spent as a German prisoner of war. Marchildon's career record was 68-75 with a 3.93 ERA.

The World Series was a best-of-nine affair in 1903, 1919, 1920, and 1921. How many of those Series went the full nine games?

None.

The American League Boston Pilgrims won the 1903 Series—the first—5-3 over the National League's Pittsburgh Pirates.

In 1919, the Cincinnati Reds beat the Chicago White Sox 5-3.

The Cleveland Indians beat the Brooklyn Dodgers 5-2 in 1920.

The 1921 Series, the last of the best-of-nine style, saw the New York Giants beat their Polo Grounds tenants, the Yankees, 5-3.

Why did Thomas Wilson throw out the first pitch of Game 2 of the 1915 World Series on October 9 (Red Sox against the Phillies at Philadelphia)?

Because he was the President of the United States. Thomas *Woodrow* Wilson was the first President to throw out a first pitch in a World Series. But that was not Game 1 of the Series.

Who was the first President to throw out the first pitch in the first game of a World Series?

Calvin Coolidge—October 4, 1924, as the Giants beat the Senators 4-3 in Washington. The Senators went on to take the Series 4-3.

Who had the most lifetime hits without being in a World Series?

Adrian "Cap" Anson—3,081. His career ended in 1897, before the first Series.

Who is the only man to hit four home runs in one World Series—twice?

Duke Snider, Dodgers, 1952 and 1955.

When was the last World Series in which both teams were piloted by player-managers?

It has not happened since 1934, when Frankie Frisch's Cardinals beat Mickey Cochrane's Tigers 4-3.

Who was the youngest player in a World Series?

Hall of Famer Fred Lindstrom. He was 18 when he played third base for the Giants in 1924. He went 10 for 30 (.333), hit two doubles, scored a run, and drove in four runs, but the Senators beat the Giants 4-3.

Only two men have played in the All-Star Game and the World Series in both leagues. Who were they?

Frank Robinson and Reggie Smith. Robinson appeared in the All-Star Games of 1956, 1957, 1959, 1961, 1962, and 1965 (all with the Reds), 1966, 1969, and 1971 (Orioles), and 1974 (Angels). He played in the 1961 World Series with the Reds, and in the 1966, 1969, and 1971 Series with the Orioles.

Smith, a powerful switch-hitter, was an All-Star in 1969 and 1972 (Red Sox), 1974 and 1975 (Cardinals), and 1977 and 1978 (Dodgers). He was in the 1967 World Series for the Red Sox, and the 1977 and 1978 Series with the Dodgers.

Only one man played in all 44 World Series games between the Yankees and the Brooklyn Dodgers: 1941 (five games), 1947 (seven), 1949 (five), 1952 (seven), 1953 (six), 1955 (seven), and 1956 (seven). Who was he?

Harold Henry "Pee Wee" Reese.

Whose first and last World Series were separated by the most years?

Willie Mays—22 years apart. Giants, 1951; Mets, 1973.

In between, he appeared in the fall classic in 1954 and 1962 with the Giants.

Who is the only rookie pitcher to win three games in a World Series?

Babe Adams, 1909 Pirates. The Pirates beat the Tigers 4-3.

Who was the first man to pitch five complete games in one World Series?

Charles "Deacon" Philippe. He did it in the very first World Series in 1903 for the Pittsburgh Pirates against the Boston Pilgrims (also known as the Puritans and later Red Sox). He won three and lost two. Boston won the Series 5-3.

Who was the last man to pitch five complete games in one World Series?

Charles "Deacon" Philippe, 1903.

Who hit the first grand slam in a World Series?

Elmer Smith of Cleveland, in Game 5 of the 1920 Series, on October 10, off Burleigh Grimes of the Dodgers.

In that game, Jim Bagby of the Indians became the first pitcher to hit a home run in a World Series.

Were those the only memorable events of that game?

No. Bill Wambsganss turned the only unassisted triple play in the World Series—and only the second in big-league history—in the fifth inning.

Who is the only World Series MVP who did not play on a winning team?

Even though Bill Mazeroski's home run in the bottom of the ninth inning of Game 7 on October 13 won the 1960 Series for the Pirates—the first time a World Series was decided on a homer in the bottom of the ninth inning of the seventh game—Bobby Richardson was the Series MVP. He hit .367 for the Yankees, collecting 12 RBIs—including a record 6 in Game 3.

Who was the only man to steal seven bases in a seven-game World Series twice?

Lou Brock, Cardinals, 1967 and 1968.

What did Walter Johnson do in his first World Series game?

He lost. Johnson pitched in the big leagues for 18 years (721 games, 376 wins, 250 losses) before appearing in his first World Series. On October 4, 1924, pitching for the Senators in Game 1 against the Giants, he struck out 12 in 12 innings but lost 4-3 to Art Nehf.

Who was the last Cub manager in a World Series?

Charlie "Jolly Cholly" Grimm, in 1945. The Cubs lost to Detroit 4-3.

Who was the last Cub manager to *win* a World Series?

Frank Chance, in 1908. The Cubs beat the Tigers 4-1.

Who was the oldest pitcher to start a World Series game?

Freddie Fitzsimmons. He was 40 on October 4, 1941, when he started Game 3 of the Series for Brooklyn against the Yankees, but did not figure in the decision as the Dodgers lost the game 2-1 and the Series 4-1.

When was the first Sunday night World Series game?

October 17, 1976: Game 2, Reds versus Yankees at Cincinnati. The Reds won the game 4-3 and the Series 4-0.

He was caught stealing twice in one World Series game—rare enough. Then, in a later game in the same Series, he was caught stealing again— twice. Who was he?

Frank Schulte, Cubs: Game 1, October 17, and Game 5, October 23, 1910.

"I hit over 300 home runs in my career. In my first World Series at bat, I smacked a grand slam. Who am I?"

José Canseco, Oakland A's, October 15, 1988, in the first game of the series in Los Angeles.

Who is the only man to be picked off twice in one World Series game?

On September 9, 1918, in Game 4, in Boston, Red Sox catcher Sam Agnew and pitcher Babe Ruth picked off Max Flack of the Chicago Cubs in the first and fourth innings, respectively.

In the 1918 Series, the Cubs played their home games at the White Sox home, Comiskey Park, as it had a larger seating capacity than Wrigley Field.

Who is the only West Pointer to play in a World Series?

Walter French. He attended West Point from July 1920 to September 1922, but did not graduate. He was selected as a football All-American halfback. His major-league career (A's, 1923, 1925–1929, .303) started the next year. In 1925, French also played pro football for the Pottsville Maroons. He came to bat once as a pinch hitter in the 1929 World Series, but struck out. The A's won anyway, 4-1.

When his baseball career was over, French went back to the military, retiring in 1959 as an Air Force lieutenant colonel.

Thanks to West Point Historian Dr. Steven Grove for this information on French.

Who was the last player-manager to win a World Series?

Lou Boudreau of the Indians, 1948. The Indians beat the Braves 4-2.

Who is the only pitcher to win two World Series games *and* serve as a McGovern delegate at the 1972 Democratic Convention?

Jim Bouton, Yankees, 1964. The author of *Ball Four* won Games 3 and 6, but the Yankees lost to the Cardinals 4-3. Bouton: 2-0. McGovern: 0-1.

He was the only man to play for championship teams in the major leagues and the NBA—both teams in the same city! Who was he?

6'8" pitcher Gene Conley: World Champion 1957 Boston Braves, and NBA Champion Celtics, 1959, 1960, and 1961.

When was the first World Series game under the lights?

October 9, 1949, Game 5. Although it started as a day game, by the top of the ninth inning of this final game of the Dodgers-Yankees Series at Ebbets

Field, darkness was falling. Paul Minner was on the mound when Commissioner Happy Chandler ordered the lights turned on.

Who were the only undefeated World Series managers?

George Stallings, Hank Bauer, and Lou Piniella never lost a World Series game.

Stallings steered the Boston Braves to four straight wins over the Philadelphia A's in 1914.

Bauer managed the Baltimore Orioles to a 4-0 sweep of the Dodgers in 1966. That was his only World Series as a manager.

Piniella's Cincinnati Reds swept the A's 4-0 in 1990.

Casey Stengel of the Giants hit the first Yankee Stadium World Series home run—an inside-the-parker—on October 10, 1923 in the first game of the Series against the Yankees. Who hit the second one?

Casey Stengel, two days later in Game 3. But the Giants lost to the Yankees 4-2.

Who is the only man to pitch opening games in consecutive World Series for two different teams?

Don Gullett—Reds, 1976; Yankees, 1977. He won Game 1 5-1 in 1976, as his Reds swept the Yankees 4-0.

In Game 1 of the 1977 Series, he started for the Yankees, but reliever Sparky Lyle came on in the 9th inning to win the game and beat the Dodgers 4-3 in 12 innings. The Yankees took the Series 4-2.

Who is the first player to have two multiple–home run games in one World Series?

Willie Mays Aikens, Royals, Games 1 and 4 of the 1980 Series. In Game 1 he homered twice off Bob Walk. In Game 4 his homers were off Larry Christenson and Dickie Noles. The Phillies beat the Royals four games to two.

Who is the only man to manage a team to a World Series victory, then became a major-league umpire?

Clarence "Pants" Rowland. He managed the White Sox from 1915 to 1918 and won the 1917 World Series 4-2 over the Giants. He was an American League umpire from 1923 to 1927.

How many World Series winners did Honus Wagner play on?

One—the 1909 Pirates, who beat the Tigers 4-3.

Who is the only man to play on four World Championship teams in his first four years in the big leagues?

Joe DiMaggio, Yankees—1936, 1937, 1938, 1939.

Ralph Kiner hit 369 homers during his 10-year career. How many did he hit in World Series play?

None. He never appeared in a World Series.

Who is the only pitcher to strike out four batters in one inning in a World Series?

Orval Overall, Cubs. In the first inning of Game 5, on October 14, 1908, he struck out Charlie O'Leary of the Tigers—#1—then walked Matty McIntyre. Next, he struck out Ty Cobb—#2. Then Sam Crawford singled. Claude Rossman was the next batter, and with two strikes he swung at but missed a wild pitch and wound up on first base. Strikeout #3, WP—two outs, bases loaded. The next batter was Germany Schaefer, and Overall struck him out, too—#4. He had 10 strikeouts in the game. Before a crowd of 6,210 fans, Overall won the game 2-0, as the Cubs won the Series 4-1.

How many home runs did Willie Mays hit in his four World Series?

In his 20 World Series games (71 at bats), the man who blasted 660 career regular season homers—#3 on the all time list—had no home runs.

How many World Series games did Bob Feller win?

Although considered the dominant pitcher of his time, Feller never won a World Series game. His Cleveland Indians appeared in the 1948 Series, in which Feller lost two games—his only Series appearances. Nevertheless, his Indians beat the Boston Braves 4-2.

But Feller's career was spectacular in every other respect: "Rapid Robert" led the American League six times in wins, five times in innings pitched, seven times in strikeouts, and four times in shutouts. He finished his career in 1956 with 266 wins versus only 162 losses. Fans will forever speculate on what his final statistics would have been had he not lost four of his potentially most productive years, 1942–1945, to combat service in the United States Navy during World War II.

This pitcher appeared in 15 World Series games, #3 on the all-time list behind Whitey Ford (22) and Rollie Fingers (16). He pitched 77⅓ innings (#8 on the all time list) and won seven games (tied for #2). He saved four games (also tied for #2) and pitched two World Series shutouts (Christy Mathewson had four, while Three Finger Brown and Whitey Ford each had

three). His total combined saves and wins—11—is unmatched in World Series annals.

Only two men had more World Series strikeouts than his 62—Ford (94) and Bob Gibson (92). Only Ford (34) walked more than his 32. Who is this non-Hall of Famer?

Allie Reynolds. Reynolds is not in the Baseball Hall of Fame, but he was the President of the National Hall of Fame for Famous American Indians in Anadarko, Oklahoma—hometown of Cal McLish and Butch Huskey.

How many pitches did Don Larsen throw on October 8, 1956 in his perfect Game 5 in the World Series?

97.

Who is the youngest man to pitch a World Series shutout?

Jim Palmer, Orioles. He was 20 on October 6, 1966, when he blanked the Dodgers 6-0 in Game 2 of the Series. Baltimore swept L.A. 4-0.

This man pitched for 16 years and won 217 games. He came to bat 821 times, but his only home run was in his first World Series game. Who is he?

Mickey Lolich. His homer came off the Cardinals' Nellie Briles on October 3, 1968, in the third inning of Game 2 of the World Series, when he was with the Tigers. Detroit won the game 8-1 and the Series 4-3.

Only two pitchers in World Series history have hit two home runs. Who are they?

Hint: One is a Hall of Famer.

Dave McNally—Orioles, 1969, Game 5; 1970, Game 3 (one with one man on and one a grand slam) and Hall of Famer Bob Gibson—Cardinals, 1967, Game 7; 1968, Game 4 (two solo shots).

He retired the side on three pitches in a World Series game twice—in the same Series. Who was he?

Christy Mathewson, Giants, Games 2 and 8, October 9 and October 16, 1912.

Who was the only pitcher to appear in all seven games of a World Series?

Darold Knowles, Oakland A's, in the 1973 Series against the Mets: two saves, 0.00 ERA.

Who was the first left-hander to win three games in one World Series?

Harry Brecheen, Cardinals versus Boston, 1946: Games 2 (October 7), 6 (October 13), and 7 (October 15).

Who was the only man to play for the 1923 World Champion Yankees (their first championship) *and* the 1927 New York football Giants—their first championship too?

Henry "Hinkey" Haines. He played 28 regular season games for the Yankees and was 0-for-1 with a run scored in World Series play.

This Hall of Fame player went on to manage. But he lost every World Series game he ever managed. Who was he?

Gabby Hartnett. He guided the Cubs to the National League pennant in 1938, but they were swept 4-0 by the Yankees. That was Hartnett's only World Series managerial experience.

He appeared at 25 World Series and 18 All-Star Games. Who was he?

Al Schacht—"The Clown Prince of Baseball."

Only three men in history have hit World Series home runs in three different decades. Who are they?

Joe DiMaggio—Yankees: 1937, 1938, 1939; 1947, 1949; 1950, 1951.

Yogi Berra—Yankees: 1947; 1950, 1952, 1953, 1955, 1956, 1957; 1960, 1961.

Eddie Murray—Orioles: 1979; 1983; Indians: 1995.

"I played in a World Series. My college roommate played in the Super Bowl. Who am I? Who is he?"

Mike Aldrete, who played with the Yankees in the 1996 Series. His roommate at Stanford was John Elway (class of '83), who led the Denver Broncos into the Super Bowl in 1986, 1987, and 1989.

Who is the only nonpitcher to hit a home run in his only World Series at bat?

Jim Mason, Yankees' shortstop, in the seventh inning of Game 3, October 19, 1976. The Reds swept the Yankees 4-0.

One of baseball's most memorable moments occurred on October 10, 1926, in Game 7 of the World Series, when the Cardinals' Grover Cleveland Alexander came into the game in the seventh inning with two outs and the bases loaded to strike out Yankee Tony Lazzeri. Which pitcher did Alexander relieve?

Hall of Famer Jesse Haines, probably the only knuckleball pitcher who actually held the ball with his knuckles. Haines could not continue because of a blister on his pitching hand.

For a fascinating insight into how baseball games were broadcast before television, instant replays, and endless chitchat about statistics and extraneous off-the-field events, see *The New York Times* of October 27, 1926, which contains a full transcript of the Graham MacNamee/Phillips Carlin WJZ radio broadcast of this climactic game.

In the first 92 years of World Series history, he was the only man to homer in his first *two* at bats. Who was he?

Gene Tenace, A's, October 14, 1972, Oakland versus Cincinnati, Game 1.

Who tied that mark?

Andruw Jones of the Atlanta Braves, in Game 1 of the 1996 World Series in New York on October 20, 1996. Jones, the first native of Curaçao to play in the big leagues, had a two-run homer and a three-run homer, followed by a single, in his very first World Series game. He was 19—the youngest man ever to homer in a World Series. The Braves won the game 12-1, but lost the Series to the Yankees 4-2.

Who was the youngest World Series MVP?

Bret Saberhagen, 1985 Royals—he was 21. The Royals beat the Cardinals 4-3.

These three were teammates on the World Champion 1948 Cleveland Indians. Perhaps they said to their sons, "Maybe someday *you'll* play in the World Series." The sons did.

Who are these three sets of fathers and sons who have each appeared in a World Series?

Bob Kennedy played three World Series games in the outfield for the 1948 Cleveland Indians. His son Terry was a catcher with the Padres in the 1984 Series and with the Giants in 1989.

Ray Boone had one at bat—as a pinch hitter—for the same 1948 Cleveland Indians. (He struck out.) His son Bob, also a catcher, was with the Phillies in 1980.

Jim Hegan was the Indians' catcher in 1948 and 1954. His son Mike appeared in the 1964 Series with the Yankees, and in the 1972 Series with Oakland.

Finish this sentence: "Had Willie Mays not made his famous catch of Vic Wertz's 440-foot drive into deep center field in the Polo Grounds on September 29, 1954, in Game 1 of the Giants-Indians World Series, it would have been . . ."

Wertz's fifth hit in the game—and he'd have been the first man to have five hits in one World Series game.

Who *was* the first player to have five hits in one World Series game?

Paul Molitor, Brewers versus Cardinals, Game 1, October 12, 1982.

Who is the only man in history to make the last out in two consecutive World Series?

Charles "Boss" Schmidt: 1907 and 1908.

In the top of the ninth inning of Game 5, October 12, 1907, with two outs and the bases loaded, against the Cubs at Detroit with the Tigers down 2-0, Schmidt (a catcher) pinch hit for Jimmy Archer and flied out to Joe Tinker in left field. (Schmidt went 2-for-12 in the Series.) The Cubs won the game and the Series 4-0. (Game 1 ended in a tie.)

The very next year, on October 14, 1908, the two teams met again in the Series and another decisive Game 5. Again the game was in Detroit; Schmidt came to bat in the bottom of the ninth inning with none on and two outs and Chicago ahead 2-0. Schmidt (1-for-14) grounded out.

Schmidt is the reluctant holder of the record for most stolen bases allowed by a catcher in a World Series game: seven, in Game 3, October 10, 1907, in 10 innings.

Who umpired in the most World Series?

Hall of Famer Bill Klem—18, between 1905 and 1940. He also umpired the first game at the Polo Grounds (in 1907), the first official All-Star Game (in 1933), and five no-hitters.

Who played in the big leagues the longest before making his first appearance in the World Series?

Joe Niekro. After 21 seasons, he made his World Series debut with the Twins on October 21, 1987 in Game 4 of the Series against the Cardinals. He pitched two innings without a decision, notching a walk and a strikeout and allowing one hit.

Which was the last World Series without any home runs?

Red Sox versus Cubs, 1918—the Sox won 4-2. In this, Babe Ruth's third World Series, he had no home runs in five at bats.

How many World Series winners did Ty Cobb play on?

None.

The record–holders for most consecutive errorless World Series games at each position are all Yankees—all but one.

Which non-Yankee holds the record for most consecutive errorless World Series games at his position?

Ron Cey, third base. See below.

P	Whitey Ford, Yankees	18
C	Yogi Berra, Yankees	30
1B	Bill Skowron, Yankees	31
2B	Billy Martin, Yankees	23
3B	Ron Cey, Dodgers	22
SS	Phil Rizzuto, Yankees	21
OF	Joe DiMaggio, Yankees	45

Who played on the most World Series losers?

Pee Wee Reese and Elston Howard—six.

Reese was on the Dodgers when they lost in 1941, 1947, 1949, 1952, 1953, and 1956. He was on one winner, in 1955—the Brooklyn Dodgers' only World Championship.

Howard—who homered in his first World Series at bat as a Yankee, against the Dodgers in the second inning of Game 1 on September 28, 1955—was on the losing end of the World Series with the Yankees in 1955, 1957, 1960, 1963, and 1964. He was also on the losing Red Sox team in 1967. But he was with Yankee winners in 1958, 1961, and 1962.

Which National Leaguer played in the most World Series games?

Frankie Frisch—50. He was with the Giants in 1921, 1922, 1923, and 1924, and the Cardinals in 1928, 1930, 1931, and 1934 (eight World Series in 13 years!). In his 197 at bats (fourth on the all-time list) he had no home runs!

How many World Series winners did Willie Mays play on?

One—in 1954. His Giants beat the Indians 4-0.

Which unlikely batter holds the record for receiving the most bases-loaded walks in one World Series game?

Jim Palmer! On October 11, in Game 2 of the 1971 Orioles-Pirates series, Palmer walked twice with the bases loaded. In fact, he did it in successive innings (fourth and fifth)! Need more excitement? Brooks Robinson reached base five times in a row in that game—three hits and two walks. The Orioles won the game 11-3, but the Pirates won the Series 4-3.

In Game 6 of the 1977 World Series, New York's Reggie Jackson hit three home runs on three consecutive first pitches by three different pitchers. (Babe Ruth also hit three home runs in one World Series game—he did it twice, in both 1926 and 1928.)

What did Jackson do in the at bats that preceded these three historic homers?

He hit a home run in his last at bat in Game 5. Then, in the second inning of Game 6, in the plate appearance preceding his three homers, he walked on four straight pitches. Thus four home runs in four swings on consecutive at bats—in a World Series!

Who is the oldest pitcher to start a World Series game?

Jack Quinn. On October 12, 1929 he started Game 4 for the Philadelphia A's, who went on to beat the Cubs four games to one. Quinn was 46.

Who are the only pitchers ever to win both Game 6 and Game 7 of one World Series?

Ray Kremer (Pirates, 1925) started and finished Game 6 against the Senators in Pittsburgh, then pitched in relief in Game 7, with the Pirates trailing. When they went ahead, he got that win, too.

Harry Brecheen (Cardinals, 1946) started and finished Game 6 against Boston, then picked up a victory in Game 7 with two innings of relief.

In the 1976 World Series, this player hit .529—the highest batting average ever for a player on a losing team. Who was he?

Thurman Munson. His Yankees lost 4-0 to the Reds. Johnny Bench hit .533 (8-for-15) to top Munson's 9-for-17.

In the history of baseball, only two men have ever pitched *and* played the outfield in the World Series. One was Babe Ruth. Who was the other?

Smoky Joe Wood.

Ruth appeared as a pinch hitter for the Red Sox in the 1915 Series and pitched for them in the Series of 1916 and 1918, going 3-0.

As a Yankee, he appeared in the World Series as an outfielder in 1921, 1922, 1923, 1926, 1927, 1928, and 1932, but did not pitch in the Series for the Yankees.

Smoky Joe Wood compiled an excellent 116-57 record with an ERA of just 2.03 between 1908 and 1920 as a pitcher with the Red Sox and Indians.

When his pitching arm gave out, he stayed in the game and played another five years, primarily as an outfielder with the Cleveland Indians. His lifetime batting average was .283.

He appeared in the fall classic as a pitcher in 1912 with the Red Sox (3-1) and as an outfielder in 1920 with the Cleveland Indians.

It happened on October 5, 1922, in Game 2 of the World Series, and has not happened since. It will never happen again. What was it?

The game ended in a 3-3 tie between the Giants and the Yankees because of darkness—the last such tie, but not the only one.

Game 1 of the 1907 Cubs-Tigers Series (Ty Cobb, in this, his first World Series game, went 0-5) and Game 2 of the 1912 Red Sox–Giants Series also ended in darkness—and ties.

Who was the first man to appear in more than 50 World Series games?

Joe DiMaggio.

Joe played in all six games of the 1936 Series (Yankees 4-2 over the Giants), all five games of the 1937 Series (Yankees 4-1 over the Giants), all four games of the Yankees' 1938 sweep of the Cubs, all four games of the Yankees' 1939 sweep of the Reds, all five games of the 1941 Series (Yankees 4-1 over the Dodgers), and all five games of the Yankees' 4-1 loss to the Cardinals in 1942.

Although the Yankees were in the Series in 1943, Joe was in the Army and missed the season and the Series.

The Yankees were back in the Series in 1947, and Joe played all seven games in the Yankees' 4-3 victory over the Dodgers, all five games of the Yankees' 4-1 victory over the Dodgers again in 1949, and all four in the Yankees' 4-0 sweep of the Phillies in 1950.

In 1951, DiMaggio played in his last Series, appearing in all six games in the 4-2 triumph over the Giants.

Joe's last game was on October 10, 1951, the final game of that six-game Series, which the Yankees won by a score of 4-2 over the Giants.

Who is the only man to hit over .400 in two consecutive World Series?

Lou Brock, Cardinals: .414 in 1967, .464 in 1968.

Retired Numbers

Who is the only player to have his number retired by a team for which he did not play?

Hint: He is also the only man to have one team retire two different numbers in his honor.

Jackie Robinson. In April 1997, the Montreal Expos retired #20 in honor of Robinson, who played for the Montreal Royals during his brief minor-league career. #20 was permanently imprinted right on the field at Olympic Stadium, to the right of home plate. That same month, like all other big-league teams, the Expos retired #42 in Robinson's honor.

The Yankees retired #8 for Bill Dickey and Yogi Berra. Only one other team has retired the same number for two different players. Which team, which number, and which players?

The Montreal Expos—#10: Rusty "Le Grande Orange" Staub, and André Dawson.

Who is the only player to have his number retired by three different teams?

Nolan Ryan: #30—Angels (1972–1979); #34—Astros (1980–1988); #34—Rangers (1989–1993).

Only four other men have had their numbers retired by *two* teams. Who are they?

> Casey Stengel: #37—Yankees, Mets.
> Hank Aaron: #44—Braves, Brewers.
> Rod Carew: #29—Twins, Angels.
> Rollie Fingers: #34—A's, Brewers.

What is the highest retired number?

85. August A. Busch Jr., owner of the Cardinals, retired in 1984, when he was 85 years old.

Which players had their numbers retired while they were still active—and were then traded?

Harold Baines, whose #3 was retired by the White Sox in 1989. Baines was traded to the Rangers on July 29, 1989. He was reacquired by the White Sox in 1996, and his number was "unretired."

The Angels retired Nolan Ryan's #30 in 1990, while he was still with the Texas Rangers.

Eddie Murray's #33 was retired by Baltimore. He subsequently played for the Dodgers, the Mets, and the Indians. In mid-1996, he went back to the Orioles, who unretired his number.

Which team has unretired three numbers?

The Orioles. In addition to Murray's #33, the Orioles unretired Earl Weaver's #4 and Frank Robinson's #20 when Weaver and Robinson came back to manage the team.

Which is the highest retired number for a player?

Don Drysdale's #53. Between 1956 and 1969, the Dodger Hall of Famer won 209 and lost 166.

Who is the only man in the history of the major leagues to have his number retired on opening day of his team's inaugural season?

> *Hint—he never played for that team, or for any other.*

Carl F. Barger, #5, Marlins. The president and chief operating officer of the Marlins from their inception, he died of a heart attack at the baseball winter meetings on December 9, 1992. American League President Bobby Brown, former Yankee infielder and a retired cardiac surgeon, was unable to revive Barger. Four months later, on the Marlins' first Opening Day, April 5, 1993, the team dedicated its first season to Barger and retired #5 in his honor.

Why #5? Barger was a great admirer of Joe DiMaggio, the immortal Yankee Clipper, who wore #5.

Which other teams retired numbers for men who never played or managed a single game?

The California Angels and the St. Louis Cardinals. In honor of their owner, Gene Autry, the Angels retired #26 in 1982, in recognition of his devotion to the team and desire to win—the 26th man on the team.

As previously noted, in 1984, the Cardinals retired #85 in honor of their owner, August A. Busch Jr.

Of retired numbers 1 through 10, nine have multiple retirees. That is, more than one team has retired #1, #2, and so on, for different players. But only one of those 10 numbers has only one retiree in the big leagues. Who is he—the only man to have that number retired?

Mickey Mantle, New York Yankees—#7.

When did the Tigers retire Ty Cobb's number?

They didn't—numbers were not worn in Cobb's day. Recognizing this, the Tigers did not officially retire *any* numbers until 1980, when Al Kaline was elected to the Hall of Fame. No Tiger has worn Kaline's #6 since. In 1983, similar honors were bestowed on Charlie Gehringer's #2 and Hank Greenberg's #5.

Two other players have had their numbers retired, even though they wore no numbers. Who were they?

Christy Mathewson and John McGraw of the Giants. Numbers were not worn in their era. Likewise, when National League Hall of Fame umpires Bill Klem, Jocko Conlan, and Al Barlick were honored at ceremonies at Wrigley Field on September 10, 1995, their numbers were retired, even though those umpires did not wear numbers. They were assigned the honorary numbers 1, 2, and 3, respectively.

Spurgeon "Spud" Chandler may be the most famous potato in baseball history. What about the most infamous?

No, not Spud Davis. The answer is the baseball-sized peeled potato pocketed by catcher Dave Bresnahan before the August 31, 1987 Eastern League game between his AA Williamsport Bills and the Reading Phillies. Bresnahan threw the potato during a pickoff throw to (and beyond) third base and kept the ball to tag out the runner. He was fined $50 and thrown out of the game. The Cleveland Indians released him from their Class AA team the next day. But on May 30, 1988, Williamsport retired Bresnahan's number 59.

What's the connection? Steve Garvey, Tony Oliva, Ken Boyer, Thurman Munson, Roger Maris, Minnie Minoso, Rusty Staub, Bill Mazeroski, Jimmie Reese, Gary Carter, Harold Baines, Don Wilson, Danny Murtaugh, Mike Scott, Elston Howard, José Cruz, Jim Gilliam, Mel Harder.

None has been elected to the Hall of Fame, yet each has had his number retired.

THE HALL OF FAME

Who is the only Hall of Famer to play in two perfect games?

Reggie Jackson. He was with Oakland when Catfish Hunter threw his perfect game against the Twins on May 8, 1968, and with the Angels when Mike Witt was perfect against the Rangers on September 30, 1984.

Name the only two Hall of Fame pitchers with losing major-league records.

Satchel Paige (28-31) and Rollie Fingers (114-118).

This Hall of Famer's plaque names five other Hall of Famers. Who is he?

Carl Hubbell. His Cooperstown plaque notes that in the 1934 All-Star Game, he struck out Babe Ruth, Lou Gehrig, Jimmie Foxx, Al Simmons, and Joe Cronin in succession.

This beloved Hall of Famer appeared in the World Series during his first four full years in the big leagues. Although he played 17 more years, he would never play in the fall classic again. Who was he?

Stan Musial, Cardinals (1941–1963). In 1941, Musial appeared in just 12 games. In 1942, the Cardinals beat the Yankees 4-1 in the Series; in 1943, the Yankees beat the Cardinals 4-1; in 1944, the Cardinals beat the Browns 4-2; in 1945, Musial was away on military service; in 1946, the Cardinals beat the Red Sox 4-3. The Cardinals did not return to the World Series again until 1964, the year after Musial retired, when they beat the Yankees 4-3.

You're Duke Snider. When you were inducted into the Baseball Hall of Fame in Cooperstown, New York in 1980, your old Compton, California High School basketball teammate Pete and his uncle Joe were in the audience. Pete had probably never been to the Baseball Hall of Fame before. But he's a Hall of Famer too. Who was he?

The late Pete Rozelle, former National Football League Commissioner and Football Hall of Famer, whose plaque is at Canton, Ohio, not Cooperstown. Joe Rozelle was Snider's first baseball coach. As a writer for the Long Beach (California) *Press-Telegram,* Pete touted Snider's baseball abilities, and he became known as "Duke Snider's press agent."

Thanks to Stanley Newman for this anecdote.

Who is the only Hall of Famer to appear in the World Series for three different teams?

Burleigh Grimes: Brooklyn Dodgers, 1920 (L); St. Louis Cardinals, 1930 (L), 1931 (W); Chicago Cubs, 1932 (L).

Others such as Don Baylor (Boston, 1986; Minnesota, 1987; Oakland, 1988) and Mariano Duncan (Cincinnati, 1990; Philadelphia, 1993; Yankees, 1996) have also played in the Series for three different teams, but Grimes is the only Hall of Famer.

Who is the only Hall of Famer who actually played baseball in Cooperstown, New York?

"Happy" Jack Chesbro. He lived in Otsego County, New York in 1896-7 and pitched for a semipro team there. But he never knew that he was to be immortalized at the Baseball Hall of Fame. Chesbro died on November 6, 1931, before Cooperstown was selected as the site for the Hall of Fame, into which he was inducted in 1946.

The 1950 Philadelphia A's were managed by Hall of Famer Connie Mack. Their general manager was also a Hall of Famer. Who was he?

Mickey Cochrane. The team finished at 52-102, in the American League cellar.

This Hall of Fame catcher came to the big leagues as a pitcher, and threw a shutout in his first game. Who was he?

Roger Bresnahan.

Which Hall of Famer was once chief of the Honolulu Fire Department?

Alexander Cartwright.

Name the five left fielders from the 1920s who are in the Hall of Fame.

Zack Wheat, Al Simmons, Harry Heilmann, Goose Goslin, and Heinie Manush.

When Detroit Tiger second baseman Frank O'Rourke contracted measles during the 1926 season, who succeeded him and went on to a Hall of Fame career?

Charlie Gehringer, "The Mechanical Man." He was the Tigers' second baseman from 1926 to 1941.

"You'll never be as good as—hey, I think this kid's a player!"

Why is Sanford Braun a Hall of Famer?

When his parents divorced and his mother remarried, he took the last name of his stepfather, a lawyer named Irving Koufax.

What is the most common last name among Hall of Famers?

Robinson: Brooks, Frank, Jackie, and Wilbert.

Too easy? What is the last name shared by three Hall of Famers?

Johnson: Walter, Ban, and Judy.

Three of the first black players to join their respective teams are in the Hall of Fame. Who were they?

Jackie Robinson (Dodgers, 1947), Monte Irvin (Giants, 1949), and Ernie Banks (Cubs, 1953).

Name the three Yankee catchers in the Hall of Fame.

Bill Dickey (1,789 games, 1928–1946), Yogi Berra (2,116 games, 1946–1963), and Branch Rickey (52 games, 11 as a catcher, 1907, when the team was still known as the Highlanders). Rickey, who virtually invented the farm system for the Cardinals, then, as the Dodgers' general manager, broke the big leagues' color line by signing Jackie Robinson, was elected to the Hall of Fame for his executive abilities, not his on-the-field talent.

He played for four years (1905, 1906, 1907, and 1914), with a .239 batting average and three home runs.

Who is the only Hall of Famer inducted during a year in which he played?

No, not Roberto Clemente (see the following). It's Lou Gehrig. Recognizing the incurable illness that had forced him to retire on May 2, 1939, the Baseball Writers Association of America (BBWAA) waived the five-year waiting period and elected Gehrig to the Hall of Fame by acclamation on December 8, 1939.

Clemente died as his plane, overloaded with relief supplies for earthquake-ravaged Managua, Nicaragua, crashed and sank on December 31, 1972. On April 29, 1973, the normal five-year waiting period before eligibility was waived, and Clemente was elected by 393 of the 424 voters by the BBWAA. He was inducted posthumously on August 6, 1973. No one has ever identified the 31 writers who did not vote for him.

Twenty-three voters did not approve of Willie Mays' enshrinement. Likewise, Cy Young was not good enough for 48 writers, and Walter Johnson didn't measure up in the eyes of 37.

Name the only switch-hitting pitchers in the Hall of Fame.

Urban "Red" Faber, .134; Rube Marquard, .179; Three Finger Brown, .195; Early Wynn, .214; Kid Nichols, .226; Ted Lyons, .233.

Who is the only writer in the actual Hall of Fame—*not* the so-called writers' wing (actually a plaque) created in 1962 for winners of the J. G. Taylor Spink Award for great baseball writers?

Henry Chadwick, inducted in 1938. His Hall of Fame plaque reads: BASEBALL'S PREEMINENT PIONEER WRITER FOR HALF A CENTURY. INVENTOR OF THE BOX SCORE. AUTHOR OF THE FIRST RULE-BOOK IN 1858. CHAIRMAN OF RULES COMMITTEE IN FIRST NATION-WIDE BASEBALL ORGANIZATION.

Who is the only Hall of Famer from the Orient?

Dazzy Vance, born in Orient, Iowa.

And who is the only former major-leaguer—not a Hall of Famer—who lives in Orient?

Bill Hands (Giants, Cubs, Rangers, Twins, 1965–75). A 20-game winner for the 1969 Cubs, and winner of 111 games overall, he lives in Orient, New York.

Who is the only Hall of Famer from Morocco?

Sam Rice, born in Morocco, Indiana.

Who is the only Hall of Famer who had two sons play in the big leagues?

George Sisler. His sons are Dick and Dave.

Dick played for the Cardinals, Phillies, and Reds (1946–1953), batting .276 (a mere 64 points below his father's lifetime .340 average). He also coached and managed.

Dave Sisler pitched for the Red Sox, Tigers, Senators, and Reds from 1956 to 1962, compiling a 38-44 (.463) record. This was better than his father's pitching record of 5-6 (.455). But George could also hit. He finished his career with 2,812 hits, and batted .407 in 1920 and .420 in 1922—both for the St. Louis Browns. His 246 hits in 1922 is still the single-season record.

At the time of his death in 1958, this Hall of Famer held the National League career records for, among other things, the most home runs, runs batted in, total bases, and walks. Who was he?

"Master Melvin" Ott: Giants, 1926–1947. 511 home runs; 1,660 RBIs; 5,041 total bases; 1,708 walks.

Which team had seven future Hall of Famers and was managed by an eighth, yet did not win the pennant?

The 1928 Philadelphia A's, who finished second to the Yankees by 2½ games. The team, managed by Connie Mack, featured Ty Cobb, Tris Speaker, Eddie Collins, Mickey Cochrane, Lefty Grove, Jimmie Foxx, and Al Simmons.

Who is the only Seattle Pilot with a namesake in the Hall of Fame?

Billy Williams—that is, William Williams, of Newberry, South Carolina. He played in four games, with 10 at bats, for the hapless Pilots. He is *not* to be confused with Hall of Famer Billy Leo Williams of Whistler, Alabama—2,488 games, 426 home runs.

"I played in the big leagues. My two brothers are in the Hall of Fame. Who am I?"

Sam Wright, shortstop for the Boston Red Caps (National League) and Cincinnati Reds, 1876, 1880–1881—12 games, .109 batting average. His brothers George and Harry are both in Cooperstown.

Name the only Hall of Fame catcher whose brother was also a big-league catcher.

Bill Dickey. His brother George caught 170 games and pinch-hit during his six-year career with the Red Sox and White Sox between 1935 and 1947.

His 13-year career landed him in the Hall of Fame. His son appeared in one major league game. Who was he?

Fred Lindstrom. From 1924 to 1936, with the Giants, Pirates, Reds, and Dodgers, he hit .311.

His son Charlie played in one game for the White Sox on September 28, 1958. He walked once, hit a triple, scored a run, and had an RBI.

He played for 18 years, during which time he never hit above .282 in a full season. He never stole more than 30 bases in a season, and hit only 12 homers in his entire career. He never led his league in any offensive category. His lifetime batting average was a meager .253. Yet he is a Hall of Famer. Who was he?

Catcher Ray "Cracker" Schalk. His career batting average is the lowest for all non-pitchers in Cooperstown. But he was considered one of the finest catchers of his day (1912–1929), and caught a record four no-hitters, including a perfect game.

Who was the first American League shortstop elected to the Hall of Fame?

Bobby Wallace, elected in 1953. He played for the Spiders, Browns, and Cardinals from 1894 to 1918 (also pitching 57 games), and managed for three more years.

This Hall of Famer, born in England, was on the field at the first American League game (April 24, 1901) between Chicago and Cleveland—the other games that day were rained out—and the first World Series (1903). He was also present at the first games played at Shibe Park (April 12, 1909), the original Comiskey Park (July 1, 1910), Fenway Park (April 20, 1912), and Yankee Stadium (April 18, 1923). Who was he?

Umpire Tom Connally. He umpired eight no-hitters, including Addie Joss's perfect game on October 2, 1908.

Who are the only Hall of Famers to homer in their first major league at bats?

Earl Averill and Hoyt Wilhelm. Averill, of the Indians, did it on April 16, 1929–Opening Day!–against the Tigers' Earl Whitehill.

Wilhelm hit his shot on April 23, 1952 for the Giants. It was the only homer of his 21-year career. He tripled in that first game too–also for the only time in his career.

Only three Hall of Famers batted right and threw left. Can you name them?

Eppa Rixey, Sandy Koufax, and Rube Waddell–all pitchers.

Rickey Henderson will join this group.

Which Houston Astros are in the Hall of Fame?

Robin Roberts, Eddie Mathews, Joe Morgan, and Nellie Fox.

Although he spent most of his 19-year career with the Phillies, in 1965 and 1966 Roberts pitched 23 games for the Astros.

After 15 years with the Braves (Boston, Milwaukee, and Atlanta), Mathews played 101 games for Houston in 1967 before finishing his career with Detroit.

Morgan spent 10 years with the Astros, then had eight stellar seasons with the Reds, another with the Astros in 1980, and a few with the Giants, Phillies, and A's during his great 22-year career.

After an outstanding career with the Philadelphia A's and the White Sox in the American League, Fox finished his career playing first, second, and third base for the Astros in 1964 and 1965.

Nolan Ryan, who was with the Astros from 1980 to 1988, will be the fifth former Astro with a plaque at Cooperstown.

For completeness, we should also mention Yogi Berra, who was an Astros coach from 1986 to 89.

Who is the only man in the American, Mexican, and Cuban Baseball Halls of Fame?

Martin Dihigo.

Who is the only Nobel Peace Prize Winner in a baseball hall of fame?

Lester B. Pearson, an amateur player who went on to become Prime Minister of Canada (1963–1968) and recipient of the 1957 Nobel Peace Prize. He was enshrined in the Canadian Baseball Hall of Fame in 1983.

Who is the first Hall of Famer who made it to the big leagues through the amateur draft?

Johnny Bench. He was selected by the Reds in round 2 of the 1965 draft, and elected to Cooperstown in 1989.

The brother of this Hall of Famer won a silver medal in the Olympics. Who were they?

Matthew "Mack" Robinson, Jackie's brother, won the medal in the 200 meters, second behind Jesse Owens at the 1936 Berlin games. Owens's time was 20.7 seconds to Robinson's 21.1.

Which members of the 1919 Chicago "Black Sox" are in the Hall of Fame?

Second baseman Eddie Collins, elected in 1939, and catcher Ray Schalk, elected in 1955. Red Faber, elected in 1964, was also on the team that year, but did not play in the Series.

The *1918* White Sox were called the Black Sox for reasons having nothing to do with throwing games. Penny-pinching owner Charles Comiskey decided to save money by charging his players for laundering their uniforms. The players declined to pay, and wore their uniforms unwashed until Comiskey relented.

Which Hall of Famer played the most years in the majors without being in a World Series?

Shortstop Bobby Wallace: 25 years (1894–1918).

Which star had over 2,000 career at bats as a designated hitter—the first in the Hall of Fame?

Reggie Jackson: 2,198 at bats as a DH.

What was unusual about Hall of Famer Billy Herman's big-league debut?

On August 29, 1931, in the first game of his distinguished 15-year career at second base (Cubs, Dodgers, Braves, Pirates), Herman singled in the first inning, in his first at bat. But the next time up, he fouled a ball off his own head and knocked himself unconscious.

How many Hall of Famers played over 1,000 games at two positions?

Four—Babe Ruth, Ernie Banks, Rod Carew, and Stan Musial.

Ruth played 1,054 games in left field and 1,133 in right field. He also pitched 163 games.

During his 10 years with the Cubs, Banks played 1,125 games at shortstop and 1,259 at first base, with a few games at third and in the outfield.

Carew started his 19-year career in 1967 at second, where he played 1,130 games. In 1976, he started spending most of his fielding time at first base, and wound up playing 1,184 games there. He also appeared occasionally at shortstop and third base, and he played one game in the outfield.

Musial played 1,896 games in the outfield and 1,016 at first base.

These last men to play for three relocated teams—the New York Giants, the Kansas City Athletics, and the Boston Braves (either original franchises or their descendants)—are all Hall of Famers. Who are they?

Willie Mays, last of the New York Giants. His career ended in 1973.

Reggie Jackson, the last man in the big leagues who played for the Kansas City A's. Reggie retired after the 1987 season.

Eddie Mathews, the last Boston Brave in the big leagues. He played through the 1968 season.

Hall of Famer Phil Niekro, the last Milwaukee Brave to play in the majors. He played through 1987.

Who are the only Hall of Famers to be elected Governor?

Happy Chandler and Morgan Bulkeley.

Before he succeeded Judge Kenesaw Mountain Landis as Baseball Commissioner in 1945, Chandler had been Governor of Kentucky (1935–1939) and a United States Senator (1939–1945). After he left the Commissioner's office in 1951, he was again elected Governor of Kentucky (1955–1959). In 1957, Chandler was named to the Kentucky Sports Hall of Fame, and he was the commissioner of the short-lived Continental Professional Football League (1965).

In recognition of his service as Mayor of Hartford (1879–1887), Governor of Connecticut (1889–1893), and Senator from Connecticut (1905–1911), Morgan G. Bulkeley was selected as the first president of the National League, a position he held for just one year—1876.

Willie Mays hit his first home run off another future Hall of Famer. Who?

Warren Spahn, Boston Braves, May 28, 1951.

Four men who served in succession as Giants manager became Hall of Famers. Who were they?

John McGraw (1902–1932), Bill Terry (1932–1941), Mel Ott (1942–1948), and Leo Durocher (1948–1955).

Which Hall of Famer who actually played in the modern big leagues had the fewest hits?

Walter Alston, St. Louis Cardinals, 1936: one at bat, no hits. Lon Warneke of the Cubs struck out the future great Dodger manager on September 27, the last day of the season, as Alston batted for Johnny Mize, who had been ejected in the seventh inning. (Alston also made an error.)

Which Hall of Fame pitcher had the fewest big-league hits?

Satchel Paige—12.

Which Hall of Fame pitcher—excluding Babe Ruth—played the most games at other positions?

Bob Lemon played 14 games in the outfield and 2 at third base. Walter Johnson played 15 in the outfield between 1913 and 1920. But John Clarkson tops the list, having played 27 games in the outfield, 4 at third base, and 2 at first.

Which Hall of Fame pitcher—again, other than Babe Ruth—had the most hits in his career?

Walter Johnson: 547.

In 1952, this player pitched in only one game, did not retire anybody, and never pitched again. Yet his number was retired, and his plaque is on the wall in Cooperstown. Who was he?

Stan Musial. Both his Cardinals and the opposing Cubs were out of the 1952 pennant race, so on September 28, the last day of the season, he started on the mound—perhaps the only time the league's leading batter was a starting pitcher. Musial's batting average was a league-leading .336.

The first Cub batter was Frank Baumholtz, whose .328 average was second in the league. A career lefty who finished his 10-year (Reds, Cubs, Phillies) career with a .290 batting average, Baumholtz batted righty against Musial for the first time in his life, and reached second base on an error.

Musial won the batting title with a .336 average, and Baumholtz—later inducted into the Ohio University Athletic Hall of Fame and the Ohio Baseball Hall of Fame—finished at .325.

These two Hall of Famers are the only pitchers who gave up home runs to Babe Ruth in 1927, when he hit 60, and hits to Joe DiMaggio 14 years later, when he hit in 56 consecutive games in 1941. Who were they?

Ted Lyons and Lefty Grove.

Lyons, of the White Sox, surrendered Ruth's home run number 54 on September 18 in the second game of a twin bill at Yankee Stadium. Fourteen years later, on July 13, 1941, he surrendered two singles to DiMaggio.

Grove, of the Philadelphia A's, gave up Ruth's 57th home run in New York on September 27, 1927. And on May 25, 1941, DiMaggio singled off Grove, then with the Red Sox.

From 1965 to 1984, Jim Palmer pitched 558 games (3,947⅓ innings). He gave up 3,349 hits, including 303 home runs, in his 268-152 career. How many of those homers were grand slams?

None.

Jim "Catfish" Hunter's 15-year big league career landed him in the Hall of Fame. How many grand slams did he surrender?

When Hunter retired, he had given up more home runs (374) than any other American League pitcher, but he gave up only one grand slam—to Tony Conigliaro of the Red Sox.

"I played on 15 All-Star Game–losing teams, and I am a Hall of Famer. Who am I?"

Brooks Robinson. He also played on three winners.

Which modern Hall of Fame pitcher recorded the fewest wins in the big leagues?

Satchel Paige (28). He had spent most of his career in the Negro Leagues.

Which modern Hall of Fame pitcher recorded the fewest losses?

Satchel Paige (31).

Which onetime Yankee is in the Pro Football Hall of Fame in Canton, Ohio?

George Halas ("Papa Bear"). He was with the Yankees for 12 games in 1919 as an outfielder and pinch hitter.

Lou "The Mad Russian" Novikoff (Cubs, 1941–1944, Phillies, 1946), is not in the Baseball Hall of Fame in Cooperstown, New York. But he is in a Hall of Fame. Which one?

In 1965, Novikoff was inducted into the International Softball Congress Hall of Fame in Long Beach, California (not to be confused with the United States Slo-Pitch (not "Slow-Pitch") Softball Association National Headquarters and Hall of Fame in Petersburg, Virginia).

Who was the only Hall of Famer married to a Hall of Famer?

The late Dodger pitcher, Don Drysdale, enshrined in 1984, was married to Nancy Meyers. She was inducted into the Basketball Hall of Fame in Springfield, Massachusetts.

Can you name another big leaguer—this one not a Hall of Famer—married to a Hall of Famer?

Ray Knight, who played for the Reds, Astros, Mets, Orioles, and Tigers from 1974 to 1988 and managed the Reds in 1996–7, is married to Golf Hall of Famer Nancy Lopez. She was inducted into the Golf Hall of Fame in Pinehurst, North Carolina on July 20, 1987.

Who is the only pitcher whose sister is a Hall of Famer?

Randy Moffitt (43-52, Giants, Astros, Blue Jays, 1972–1983). His sister, Billie Jean Moffitt King, entered the Tennis Hall of Fame in Newport, Rhode Island in 1987.

Who was the lightest hitter in the Hall of Fame?

Hall of Fame pitcher Candy Cummings did *not* tip the scales, at a mere 120 pounds.

This Hall of Famer was managed by Casey Stengel of the Boston Braves in 1942 and again 23 years later when Stengel ran the Mets in 1965. Who was he?

Warren Spahn.

Which future Hall of Famer was the New York Highlanders' catcher when the Washington Senators stole a then-record 13 bases in one game on June 26, 1907?

Branch Rickey.

Is Jim Thorpe in the Hall of Fame?

Yes, the 1912 Olympic decathlon and pentathlon gold medalist is in the Pro Football and American Indian Halls of Fame. He played in the major leagues for six years (1913–1915, 1917–1919), with only a .252 batting average. In 1917, the only season in which he played over 100 games, he hit .237. Baseball was probably his worst sport. He is not in the Baseball Hall of Fame.

These men each won the Triple Crown *twice*. Yet this amazing feat is not mentioned on their Hall of Fame plaques. Who were they?

Rogers Hornsby and Ted Williams.

On August 17, 1917, these two future Hall of Famers were arrested for playing ball on Sunday. Who were they?

Christy Mathewson and John McGraw—managers, respectively, of the Reds and Giants. At the time, New York law prohibited Sunday games—even games played for the benefit of World War I soldiers' families, as the Reds-Giants contest had been the previous day. The case was dismissed.

Which Hall of Famer had the shortest life?

Ross (born Royce) Youngs. He died on October 22, 1927 at age 30.

Although he played only nine full seasons in the big leagues (1917–1926, one season short of the usual requirement for eligibility), Youngs was elected to the Hall of Fame in 1972 by the Veterans' Committee 45 years after his death.

Sandy Koufax was also inducted in 1972, when he was 36—the youngest living person to be enshrined.

Only eight Hall of Famers were born outside the United States. Who were they?

Umpire Tom Connolly (England); Rod Carew (Panama); Ferguson Jenkins (Canada); Luis Aparicio (Venezuela); Juan Marichal (Dominican Republic); Henry Chadwick (England); Harry Wright (England); and Martin Dihigo (Cuba). Dihigo played all nine positions in one Negro League game.

Who succeeded Hall of Famer Jimmy Collins as Philadelphia A's third baseman in 1909?

Frank "Home Run" Baker—also a Hall of Famer.

Who are the three Yankee center fielders in the Hall of Fame?

Joe DiMaggio, Mickey Mantle, and Earle Combs.

This Hall of Famer's playing career lasted just two years—1934 and 1935, when he played 128 games for the White Sox. He never managed in the majors. Yet he has been enshrined in Cooperstown. Why?

Because after his playing days were over, John "Jocko" Conlan became an umpire. In fact, his umpiring career started while he was still a player. In a 1935 game, umpire Emmett "Red" Ormsby became ill during a game between the Browns and the White Sox. Conlan, a benchwarmer, was asked to fill in for Ormsby. He did—in fact he called teammate and future Hall of Famer Luke Appling out at third base—and liked it.

Conlan's 1941–1965 major-league umpiring career included five no-hitters. Inducted in 1974, along with Mickey Mantle, Whitey Ford, and Cool Papa Bell, he's the only umpire in the Hall of Fame who was also a major-league player. (Some Hall of Fame players also umpired, however.)

Name three Hall of Fame players who also had careers as major-league umpires.

Bobby Wallace, James "Pud" Galvin, and "Orator" Jim O'Rourke.

These Hall of Fame pitchers posted the following career World Series strikeout numbers: Waite Hoyt, 49; Christy Mathewson, 48; Jim Palmer, 44; Don Drysdale, 36; Lefty Grove, 36.

But one Hall of Fame *batter* struck out 54 times in the World Series. Who was he?

Mickey Mantle.

"My name is on a Hall of Fame plaque, but I am not a Hall of Famer. Who am I?"

There are three correct answers.

Wes Ferrell. His brother Rick's plaque reads in part: OFTEN FORMED BATTERY WITH BROTHER WES.

Frank Selee. Tommy McCarthy's plaque reads in part: ONE OF BOSTON'S 'HEAVENLY TWINS,' UNDER MANAGER FRANK SELEE. (Hugh Duffy, also a Hall of Famer, was the other "Twin.")

Larry Doby's name appears on Bill Veeck's plaque. The innovative owner signed Doby to play for the Cleveland Indians in 1947—making Doby the first black player in the American League. (Doby went on to an excellent career—.283, 253 home runs, 970 RBIs.)

This is a two-parter: First, name the umpires who have been enshrined in Cooperstown. (Easy, right?) Second, who is the only one to umpire in both the National and American Leagues? (Not so easy.)

Seven umpires have been inducted into the Hall of Fame: Tommy Connolly, Jocko Conlan, Billy Evans, Bill McGowan, Al Barlick, Bill Klem (born Klimm), and Cal Hubbard.

Connolly umpired in the National League from 1898 to 1899, and in the American League from 1901 to 1931.

Which Hall of Fame pitcher has the highest lifetime ERA?

Red Ruffing—3.80. But his record was 273-225.

In 1906, rookie Ty Cobb, all of 19, played the outfield for the Detroit Tigers. The Tigers also had a 46-year-old outfielder who played eight games that year and who, like Cobb, would become a Hall of Famer. Who was he?

"Big" Sam Thompson.

Who was the first Hall of Famer to die?

Michael Joseph "King" Kelly, on November 8, 1894. He was inducted into Cooperstown in 1945—51 years later.

"I'm a Hall of Famer. During my career, my teammates have included these other Hall of Famers: Juan Marichal, Warren Spahn, Willie Mays, Rollie Fingers, Ferguson Jenkins, Frank Robinson, Reggie Jackson, Duke Snider, Phil Niekro, and Willie McCovey.

"I have also been the teammate of future Hall of Famers George Brett, Dave Winfield, Dennis Eckersley, Ozzie Smith, and Goose Gossage.

"Who am I?"

Gaylord Perry.

Which Hall of Fame pitcher had the lowest batting average?

Sandy Koufax (776 at bats, 75 hits, .09664, rounded to .097)? A good guess, but incorrect. Go lower.

Satchel Paige (with 12 hits to show for his 124 at bats, he was just a bit more productive at the plate, with an .09677 average, also rounded to .097)? No, he's not the answer either.

The correct answer is Hoyt Wilhelm, with 38 hits in 432 at bats for a lifetime batting average of .088 (.08796).

We don't count Los Angeles Dodgers' manager Tommy Lasorda, who had but one hit (a single) in his 14 at bats, for an average of .071.

This man received a Hall of Fame vote while he was still an active player! Later, he was indeed elected to the Hall of Fame. Who was he?

Joe DiMaggio. Jack Lang, Executive Secretary of the Baseball Writers Association of America—the man who calls to let you know you have been elected to Cooperstown—reports that Joe DiMaggio got one vote in 1945, when he was in the army but still considered an active big leaguer. After the war, Joe resumed his spectacular career, retiring after the 1951 season. He was elected to the Hall of Fame in 1955.

Which Hall of Famer had the most pinch-hit home runs?

Willie McCovey—16.

Only one Hall of Famer hit above .300 with at least 30 homers and 100 RBIs in his rookie season. Who was he?

Ted Williams, Red Sox, 1939 (.327, 31, 145).

Who was the first Hall of Famer to wear glasses?

Charles James "Chick" Hafey (Cardinals and Reds, 1924–1937). He was enshrined in 1971.

This Hall of Famer had two seasons in which he drove in over 100 runs while hitting no more than 11 home runs. Who was he?

Enos Slaughter. 1950 Cardinals: 10 homers, 101 RBIs. 1952 Cardinals: 11 homers, 101 RBIs.

Who was the only Hall of Fame pitcher to strike out four consecutive batters *in one inning?*

Don Drysdale of the Dodgers, April 17, 1965. In the second inning, facing the Phillies, he struck out Wes Covington, who reached first base when catcher Johnny Roseboro allowed a passed ball on strike three. "Big D" then struck out Tony Gonzalez, Dick Stuart, and Clay Dalrymple, but he lost the game 3-0 to Chris Short.

Walter Johnson and Bob Gibson also struck out four batters in one inning, but not consecutively.

Twelve players have hit at least 30 home runs in six consecutive seasons. All are Hall of Famers except this man. Who are they, and who is he?

The 11 Hall of Famers who have accomplished this impressive offensive feat are Babe Ruth, Mickey Mantle, Jimmie Foxx, Harmon Killebrew, Willie

Mays, Willie McCovey, Hank Aaron, Ralph Kiner, Mike Schmidt, Eddie Mathews, and Lou Gehrig.

The one not in the Hall of Fame is Fred McGriff, who hit at least 30 homers each year from 1988 to 1994.

These two Hall of Famers managed in the big leagues. So did their sons. Who are they?

Connie and Earle Mack, and George and Dick Sisler.

What did Hall of Famer George Sisler do in his first game?

The future Triple Crown winner (1922) pitched for the Browns and beat his idol, the Senators' Walter Johnson, on August 29, 1915. Sisler pitched a total of 24 games over his career, going 5-6 with 12 starts.

Dizzy Dean certainly had Hall of Fame credentials—150-83, plus leading the National League at one time or another in wins, winning percentage, games, complete games, shutouts, games started, and innings pitched.

But one of the criteria for Cooperstown eligibility is that a man play in the big leagues for 10 seasons. This has been waived a few times, for example in the cases of Ross Youngs and Addie Joss.

In how many of his 12 seasons did Dizzy Dean appear in just one game?

Three. In 1930, his first season, Dean appeared in only one game—which he won. He also pitched just one game in both 1941 and 1947, pitching one inning and four innings, respectively.

When Grover Cleveland Alexander won his 300th game on September 20, 1924, playing against the Giants, eight other future Hall of Famers were also on the field. Name them.

Alexander's Cub teammate Gabby Hartnett, plus these opposing Giants: manager John McGraw, Fred Lindstrom, Frankie Frisch, Ross Youngs, Hack Wilson, Bill Terry, and George Kelly.

Which two Hall of Famers pitched Opening Day no-hitters?

It's easy to name Bob Feller, who no-hit the White Sox for the Indians on April 16, 1940, Opening Day.

But 1995 inductee Leon Day also pitched a no-hitter on May 5, Opening Day of the 1946 season, for the Newark Eagles of the Negro Leagues, over the Philadelphia Stars.

Whose Hall of Fame plaque has the fewest words?

Hint: had it not been for him, there might not be any plaques!

Former National League President and Commissioner of Baseball Ford Frick—just 19 words (after his name): SPORTSWRITER-SPORTSCASTER. FOUNDER OF BASEBALL HALL OF FAME. PRESIDENT OF NATIONAL LEAGUE 1934–1951. COMMISSIONER OF BASEBALL 1951–1965.

Who is the only Hall of Famer buried outside the United States?

Martin Dihigo, buried in Cienfuegos, Cuba.

Alexander Cartwright, whose grave is in Oahu, Hawaii, is the only other Hall of Famer buried outside the continental United States.

Name a left-handed third baseman in the Hall of Fame.

Wee Willie Keeler. At the start of his career, he played 26 games at third base; over the next 16 years he switched from his usual position in the outfield to play another 18 games at the hot corner.

The Waners and the Wrights are the only sets of brothers in the Hall of Fame. Can you name two Cooperstown brothers-in-law?

Tim Keefe and John Montgomery Ward. They married sisters, both daughters of Charles Dana Gibson (the artist who created the Gibson girl): Keefe married Clara, and Ward married Helen.

In the late 1800s, Ward's wife, Helen Dauvray, created the Dauvray Cup, to be awarded to any team that won the American Association–National League championship series three times. The cup was never awarded. See "The Helen Dauvray Cup," in *The National Pastime*, No. 17, 1997, p. 73.

Who are the only half brothers in the Hall of Fame?

Rube and Bill Foster.

Name the only Hall of Famer who played over 2,500 games at just one position for his entire career.

Luis Aparicio—2,581 games at shortstop.

Many Hall of Famers won Gold Gloves and silver bats. But only one cut a gold record. Which one?

Phil Rizzuto. Meatloaf's (real name Marvin Lee Aday) album *Bat Out of Hell* contains the song "Paradise by the Dashboard Light" (written by Jim Steinman), which includes Scooter's voice calling the bottom of the ninth inning in a game.

On May 22, 1978, the album was officially certified gold (500,000 copies sold) by the Recording Industry Association of America, and on August 25, 1978, it went platinum (1,000,000 sold).

Rizzuto has another show-business connection: he was the very first mystery guest on *What's My Line?*, the long-running TV quiz show, on February 2, 1950.

Name the four members of the Baseball Hall of Fame who once played for the Harlem Globetrotters.

Bob Gibson (1957–58), Ferguson Jenkins (1968–69), Lou Brock (1968–69), and Satchel Paige (1965–66). Bill Foster once managed the Globetrotters.

Seven Giant infielders from the 1920s have been enshrined at Cooperstown. Name them.

1B—George Kelly, Bill Terry; 2B—Frankie Frisch, Rogers Hornsby; 3B—Fred Lindstrom; SS (plus 1B, 2B, 3B)—Dave Bancroft, Travis Jackson.

Name two Hall of Famers whose names differ by only one letter.

George Kell and George Kelly.

Who is the only Hall of Famer to hit into four triple plays?

Brooks Robinson.

1. On June 2, 1958, in Baltimore against the Senators, Lenny Green singled and Jim Marshall walked. Robinson then lined out to shortstop Rocky Bridges (out 1), who stepped on second base to get Marshall (out 2). Bridges then threw to first baseman Julio Becquer to retire Robinson (out 3). The Senators won 2-1.

2. On September 10, 1964, against the Senators in Washington with the bases loaded in the fifth inning, Robinson grounded to John Kennedy at short; Kennedy threw to Don Blasingame at second to record the first out. Blasingame then threw to Joe Cunningham at first base to get the second out on Robinson. Meanwhile, the runner from third base scored. Luis Aparicio, who had been on second base, also tried to score, but Cunningham threw a bullet to catcher Mike Brumley at the plate to nail Aparicio for the third out: 6-4-3-2—a run-scoring triple play! Baltimore won 12-5, with 17 hits.

3. On August 18, 1965, in Baltimore, against the Red Sox, Robinson hit into a first-inning double play with Paul Blair and Boog Powell aboard. Robinson grounded to Frank Malzone at third base; Malzone threw to Felix Mantilla at second to force Powell. Mantilla then threw on to Tony Horton at first base to get Robinson. Meanwhile, Blair tripped rounding third and

was trapped between third and home. Horton threw to Malzone to get Blair for the third out: 5-4-3-5. Baltimore won 3-2.

4. On August 6, 1967, in the fifth inning of the second game of a double-header at home against the White Sox, with two men on, Robinson grounded to third baseman Ken Boyer, who stepped on third. Boyer then threw to Don Buford at second base, and Buford threw to Tommy McCraw at first to retire Robinson.

This Hall of Famer played in over 1,300 games—but only one in his last season. Who was he?

Buck Ewing. He came to bat just once in his last game, in 1897, for the Reds. Dizzy Dean played in only one game in 1947, his final season.

Who were the only two Hall of Famers to play on World Championship teams in both leagues?

Enos Slaughter, St. Louis Cardinals (National League), 1942, 1944, 1946; New York Yankees (American League), 1956, 1958.

Eddie Mathews, Milwaukee Braves (National League), 1957; Detroit Tigers (American League), 1968.

Who are the only Hall of Famers who never retired?

Big Ed Delahanty, Addie Joss, and Roberto Clemente. All died while still active players.

A number of Hall of Famers have collected over 200 hits in a single season. (That's why they're Hall of Famers.) But only one has ever done so while batting under .300 for a full season. Who is he?

Lou Brock, 1967 Cardinals: 206 hits, .299 batting average in 689 at bats.

Although he had 3,023 hits, and seven seasons in which he scored over 100 runs, Brock never drove in 100 in a single season.

Earl Weaver was once beaned so badly during his minor-league playing career that he bled from his nose for 13 days. But he went on to manage the Baltimore Orioles during their glory years (1968–1982, 1985–1986). In 1996, he was inducted into the Hall of Fame.

How many Hall of Famers and future Hall of Famers can you name who were managed by Weaver?

Frank Robinson, Brooks Robinson, Jim Palmer, and Reggie Jackson. Future Hall of Famers include Cal Ripken Jr. and Eddie Murray.

Joe DiMaggio, Eddie Mathews, and Johnny Mize all ended their careers the same way. How?

The very last games these Hall of Famers played were in the World Series.

DiMaggio's last game was Game 6 of the 1951 World Series, October 10 at Yankee Stadium. The Yankees won the game 4-3 and beat the Giants in the Series 4-2.

Mize's last game was Game 6, of the 1953 Series, October 5 at Yankee Stadium. He grounded out as a pinch hitter in the eighth inning as his Yankees beat the Dodgers 4-3 and took the Series 4-2.

Mathews' last game was Game 4, October 6, 1968. His Tigers lost that game to the Cardinals 10-1, but won the Series 4-3.

Willie Mays's last major-league at bat was also in a World Series. Who was the future Hall of Famer he faced?

Mays singled off A's pitcher Rollie Fingers on October 14, 1973 in Game 2 of the A's-Mets World Series. The game lasted a record four hours and 13 minutes, and used 11 pitchers—also a World Series record.

"During my playing days, my roommates on the road were Babe Ruth, Tony Lazzeri, Joe DiMaggio, and Phil Rizzuto. Now they're all Hall of Famers. Who am I?

"Hint: I'm a Hall of Famer, too."

Lefty Gomez. He also roomed with Tommy Henrich.

Which Hall of Famers played for the New York Yankees, the New York Giants, and the Brooklyn Dodgers?

Burleigh Grimes, Waite Hoyt, Willie Keeler, and Tony Lazzeri.

Name all the Mets in the Hall of Fame.

Casey Stengel (manager, 1962–1965), Rogers Hornsby (coach, 1962), Bob Gibson (coach, 1981), Richie Ashburn (1962), Warren Spahn (1965), Yogi Berra (1965), Willie Mays (1972–1973), Duke Snider (1963), Tom Seaver (1967–1977, 1983), and soon Nolan Ryan (1966, 1968–1971). Ralph Kiner, Bob Murphy, and Lindsey Nelson have all been honored with the Ford C. Frick Award—Hall of Fame recognition for the three original Met broadcasters.

When Jackie Robinson played his historic first game with the Brooklyn Dodgers on April 15, 1947, against the Boston Braves, two other future Hall of Famers were on the field. One was Pee Wee Reese. Who was the other?

Umpire Al Barlick.

Who is the only 300-game winner to have won more than twice as many games as he lost?

Lefty Grove (300-141, 3.06 ERA). Whitey Ford is the only other pitcher with at least 200 wins who won more than twice as many as he lost (236-106).

Who spoke when Lou Gehrig inducted into the Hall of Fame?

Good question! Gehrig was elected on December 8, 1939, in a special vote during the winter meetings, but never formally inducted. Although people were elected between 1940 and 1945, there were no induction ceremonies from 1940 through 1945. Gehrig's plaque was probably mounted at the Hall of Fame some time in 1940.

UNBREAKABLE RECORDS?

CAL RIPKEN JR.'S HISTORIC SHATTERING of Lou Gehrig's incredible consecutive-games-played mark in 1995 proved that any baseball record is theoretically breakable. Indeed, Lou Gehrig's monument in Yankee Stadium says in raised letters that Gehrig's "amazing record of 2,130 consecutive games should stand for all time..."

This chapter includes unusual marks, records, and incredible statistics which we believe will never be broken.

00.

Uniform number worn by Omar Olivares, 1995 Phillies, to match his initials. No one will ever wear a lower number.

Al Oliver (Rangers, Phillies, Expos, Dodgers, Giants, Blue Jays, and Pirates) wore number 0. He said it was an *O* for Oliver, not a zero.

0.

Number of strikeouts recorded by Emil Levsen of Cleveland, who pitched two complete games (6-1, 5-1) in a doubleheader sweep of the Red Sox, August 28, 1926.

It is almost unimaginable for a modern pitcher to start both games of a doubleheader even if one were scheduled, so this record for fewest strikeouts for a pitcher who completes both ends of a doubleheader seems safe.

0.

Number of home runs hit by batting champions Ginger Beaumont (.357, 1902 Pirates), Zack Wheat (.335, 1918 Dodgers), and Rod Carew (.318, 1972 Twins). This "record" can be equaled, but never topped.

⅛.

The only fractional uniform number worn in a big-league game—by Eddie Gaedel, Browns, August 19, 1951. No one will ever again wear a fractional number.

.367.

Ty Cobb's lifetime batting average. While this record is reachable, it has remained unchallenged since Cobb retired in 1928.

3'7".

Eddie Gaedel's height. It is inconceivable that there will ever be a shorter batter, as midgets are now banned from the big leagues. When Gaedel came to bat, on August 19, 1951, home plate umpire Ed Hurley questioned his legitimacy as a player with a big-league contract. But Browns' owner Bill Veeck had anticipated such a question, so he had a copy of Gaedel's contract in hand to show Hurley.

At the time, the only restriction in existence was that a player was not eligible to appear in a big-league game unless his contract *had been sent* to the league president. After Gaedel's at bat, that rule was revised to prevent further such stunts, which were considered detrimental to the serious business of baseball. From that day on, no player has been permitted to appear in a big-league game without the league president's *prior approval.*

.424.

The highest single-season batting average since 1900—Rogers Hornsby, Cardinals, 1924.

1.

Number of perfect games thrown in a World Series in a career. Only achieved by Don Larsen, October 8, 1956.

1.

Number of perfect World Series games caught, held by Yogi Berra.

1.

Number of baseballs used in a big-league game (the Reds' 9-6 victory over the Cubs in Cincinnati on June 29, 1913). There were no homers and no foul balls hit into the stands.

1.

Number of home runs hit at home by the 1945 Washington Senators.

2.

Number of no-hitters pitched on the same day. On June 30, 1990, Dave Stewart of Oakland no-hit the Blue Jays 5-0 in Toronto. Later, the Dodgers' Fernando Valenzuela no-hit the Cardinals 6-0—the first time two no-hitters (one in each league) were pitched on the same day.

2.

Number of consecutive no-hitters pitched by the Reds' Johnny Vander Meer (June 11, 1938, 3-0 over the Braves, and June 15, 1938, 6-0 over the Dodgers). Those were the only no-hitters in the National League in 1938. It would take three in a row to beat this mark.

With a 119-121 career won-lost tally, Vander Meer was one of the most illustrious pitchers to retire with a losing record.

2.

Number of triple plays started in the same game by one player—Gary Gaetti of the Twins (July 17, 1990, vs. Boston).

2.

Number of cities in which Joel Youngblood got hits on the same day—August 14, 1982—for two different teams. After getting a hit for the Mets in Chicago, Youngblood was traded to the Expos. Later that day, he had a hit for the Expos in Philadelphia.

2.

Most games won by a pitcher in a World Series that seven teammates were trying to lose—by Dickie Kerr, 1919 White Sox.

2.

Number of big-league games between different teams attended by one President of the United States on one day. On May 4, 1910, William Howard Taft was in St. Louis. First he watched the first two innings of the National League Cardinals' 12-3 drubbing of the Reds at Sportsman's Park. He left and then watched part of the game at Robinson Field, where the American League Browns and Cleveland Indians tied 3-3 in a contest called because of darkness.

2.

Number of Triple Crowns won by Rogers Hornsby (1922, 1925) and Ted Williams (1942, 1947).

2.

Number of complete-game shutout victories won on the same day by Ed Reulbach—September 26, 1954, Cubs over the Dodgers.

2.

Number of All-Star Games started in the same year by the same man—Dodger Don Drysdale, 1959.

Two All-Star Games were played each year from 1959 to 1962. But with only one game each year since 1963, this record seems absolutely untouchable.

2.

Number of pitchers used by one team—the Philadelphia A's—in the 1910 World Series. The pitchers were Jack Coombs and Chief Bender. To beat this mark, a team would have to use just one pitcher in an entire World Series. Does this seem likely?

2.

Number of hits in one inning *in his first game,* by Billy Martin, April 18, 1950, and later by others.

3.

Number of complete game shutouts thrown in one World Series (1905), by Christy Mathewson of the Giants over the Philadelphia A's.

3.

Number of big-league teams that have played at the same home stadium.

Which stadium?

The Polo Grounds. It was home to the New York Giants from 1911 to 1957 and to the Yankees from 1913 to 1922. When the Giants left for San Francisco in 1958, the stadium remained vacant until the Mets played their first two seasons there in 1962 and 1963 while Shea Stadium was being built.

3.

Number of different games in which Clyde Barnhart of the Pirates got hits *on the same day* (during the last tripleheader). October 2, 1920.

3.

Number of games worked behind the plate by one big-league umpire in one day, by Peter Harrison. Reds versus Pirates, October 2, 1920.

3.

Number of hits by Gene Stephens of the Red Sox against the Tigers in one inning, June 18, 1953.

3 + 3.

On September 23, 1995, Lance Johnson of the White Sox not only hit three triples against the Twins but also hit three singles in the same game—a double triple. The six hits were rare enough, but no other player has ever had three triples and three of any other type of hit in the same game.

4.

Number of consecutive Game 1 World Series starts in a career, by Whitey Ford of the New York Yankees: 1961 (he won), 1962 (won), 1963 (lost), 1964 (lost).

4.

Number of World Series winners played on by Joe DiMaggio of the Yankees in his first four seasons in the big leagues (1936, 1937, 1938, 1939). Joe played all 19 games in those four Series. This record has stood for over 50 years.

4.

Number of consecutive home runs in one game (by Lou Gehrig, Bobby Lowe, Rocky Colavito, and Mike Schmidt).

4.

Number of inside-the-park home runs hit in a single game—by Philadelphia's Big Ed Delahanty against Chicago, July 13, 1896. This record has stood for over 100 years. Good luck.

4.

Number of home runs in consecutive at bats in a World Series—by Reggie Jackson, Games 5 (1) and 6 (3), 1977 Series.

5.

Number of consecutive years (1937–1941) in which Joe DiMaggio hit at least 30 home runs and had more home runs than strikeouts.

	HOME RUNS	STRIKEOUTS
1937	46	37
1938	32	21

1939	30	20
1940	31	30
1941	30	13

5.

Number of times Billy Martin was hired and fired as manager of the New York Yankees. It seems unlikely that another man will serve six stints as manager of the same team.

5.

Consecutive World Series won—by the New York Yankees (1949–1953).

7.

Number of decades during which Mel Allen did baseball broadcasts (1930s–1990s). In addition to being enshrined at Cooperstown's broadcaster's wing, Allen (born Melvin Allen Israel) was elected to the Jewish Sports Hall of Fame in Israel in 1980.

7.

Number of games in the 1973 World Series in which Oakland pitcher Darold Knowles appeared.

Unless the best-of-seven World Series format is changed, this record can never be broken.

7.

The 1924 New York Giants sent this many future Hall of Famers in a row up to bat in Game 7 of the 1924 World Series, which the Giants lost to Walter Johnson's Washington Senators.

The batters were Fred Lindstrom, Frankie Frisch, Ross Youngs, George Kelly, Bill Terry, Hack Wilson, and Travis Jackson. The Giants lost the game and lost the Series 4-3.

7.

Number of consecutive complete-game World Series wins by the Cardinals' Bob Gibson. 1964, Games 5 and 7; 1967, Games 1, 4, and 7; 1968, Games 1 and 4.

8.

Number of Game 1 World Series starts in a career, by Whitey Ford, New York Yankees (1955, 1956, 1957, 1958, 1961, 1962, 1963, 1964).

8.

Number of consecutive complete World Series games for Bob Gibson of the Cardinals. 1964, Games 5 (W) and 7 (W); 1967, Games 1 (W), 4 (W), and 7 (W); 1968, Games 1 (W), 4 (W), and 7 (L).

09.

The highest uniform number ever to start with an 0. Reds' catcher Benito Santiago wore it so his number would not be obscured by his chest protector's back straps.

9.

Number of Opening Day first pitches thrown out by President Franklin D. Roosevelt.

10.

Number of World Series games won by Whitey Ford.

10.

Number of consecutive years in which all World Series games were played in the same city—New York City (1949–1958).

10.

Number of consecutive years in which Hall of Fame umpire Tom Connolly did not eject a single player or manager.

10.

Number of All-Star teams managed by Casey Stengel.

11.

Number of times Pete Reiser was carried off the field—frequently on a stretcher—with severe injuries usually incurred by crashing into unpadded concrete outfield walls.

12.

Number of perfect innings pitched against the Braves by Harvey Haddix of the Pirates on May 26, 1959, before he lost 1-0 on an error, a sacrifice, an intentional walk, and a home run (which turned into a double when Joe Adcock passed Hank Aaron on the basepaths).

According to Tim Wiles, Director of Research at the Baseball Hall of Fame Library in Cooperstown, Haddix's incredible pitching performance is itself the subject of *Twelve Perfect Innings,* an 83-page poem written by Weldon Myers in 1961.

12.

Number of consecutive World Series games won by the New York Yankees: 1927, 4-0 over the Pirates; 1928, 4-0 over the Cardinals; 1932 (the Yankees' next World Series appearance), 4-0 over the Cubs.

13.

Number of steals by the entire Washington Senators team in 1957—the lowest season total ever.

14.

Number of consecutive 20-win seasons, held by Cy Young (1891–1904).

14.

Number of men walked in one game by Giant Henry Mathewson (Christy's brother), October 5, 1906. With the advent of the reliever, it seems unlikely that any modern manager would not yank a pitcher having such a miserable outing.

15.

Joe Nuxhall's age (15 years, 10 months, 11 days) when he made his major-league debut as a relief pitcher on June 10, 1944. A younger player seems unlikely.

17.

Number of consecutive World Series games (1956–1958) in which Hank Bauer of the Yankees had at least one hit. The Yankees won in 1956 and 1958, but lost in 1957.

18.

Number of 20-game winners caught in a career, by Jim Hegan (1946–1960).

19.

Most home runs by a grandfather in a single season, achieved by 41-year-old Stan Musial in 1962, his penultimate year.

21.

Number of consecutive years coached—by Frank Crosetti of the Yankees (1947–1968). His coaching brought him $126,000 in World Series bonus money.

22.

Number of World Series games started by Whitey Ford.

23.

   Number of World Series games for which Arndt Jorgens (from Modum, Norway) of the New York Yankees was eligible but did not play. Hall of Fame catcher Bill Dickey played every inning of every World Series game in 1932, 1936, 1937, 1938, and 1939, while Jorgens warmed the bench. Jorgens' brother Orville (born in Rockford, Illinois) pitched for the Phillies for three years (1935–1937), compiling a 21-27 record.

Hey, Skip! Put me in—just once!

23.

   Number of consecutive one-year managing contracts Walter Alston had with the Dodgers (1954–1976).

23.

   Most consecutive years batting at least .300, one of the astounding records still held by Ty Cobb.

23.

   Weight, in ounces, of Eddie Gaedel's bat. What's the difference—he never swung it! He walked on four straight pitches, because owner Bill Veeck had threatened him, claiming to have a sniper ready to shoot him if he swung the bat!

25.

   Number of seasons played in the big leagues without being on a pennant winner—by Hall of Famer Bobby Wallace.

26.

   Number of seasons managed by Gene Mauch without a World Series appearance.

27.

   Number of consecutive batters retired in a World Series game—by Don Larsen.

30.

   Number of consecutive World Series games played—by Bobby Richardson (1960–1964). Richardson's games were all with the New York Yankees.

35.

Difference between RBIs and games played (minimum 100 games), set by Hack Wilson in 1930. He drove in 190 runs while playing in only 155 games, a difference of 35. Others have had more runs driven in than games played, but nobody has come close to this number.

35.

Difference between the number of home runs hit by the American League home run champion (Babe Ruth) and the runner-up. In 1920, Ruth hit 54 homers, trailed by George Sisler with 19. The very next year, Ruth improved to 59 homers, while Ken Williams and Bob Meusel tied for #2 with 24. It seems highly unlikely that such a gap between #1 and #2 will ever again exist.

36.

Consecutive batters retired in one game—by Harvey Haddix, May 26, 1959.

37.

Number of World Series games won by manager Casey Stengel.

41.

Number of victories by Hall of Fame pitcher Jack Chesbro for the Yankees in 1904.

44.

Most years for a manager without winning a pennant—by Connie Mack. Owning the team helped him keep his job at the A's helm.

44.

The number of doubleheaders played in a single season by the Chicago White Sox of 1943.

45.

Number of consecutive errorless World Series games, set by Joe DiMaggio.

46.

Most World Series games played in his hometown, by Hall of Famer Phil Rizzuto of the New York Yankees (1941–1942, 1946–1956). Twenty-six were at Yankee Stadium; 17 at Ebbets Field, home of the Brooklyn Dodgers; and 3 at the Polo Grounds, home of the New York Giants.

Were you going to guess that Lou Gehrig—another Hall of Famer from New York City—played in more World Series games at home? Sorry. Gehrig appeared in "only" seven World Series between 1926 and 1938, and played in 17 games at home.

47.

Record number of years (albeit nonconsecutive) in the uniform of one team. Held by Hall of Famer Red Schoendienst, player, coach, and manager for the St. Louis Cardinals. Red wore #2.

47.

During his 14-year career, including stints in the National and Players Leagues, and the American Association, pitcher Tim Keefe won games in 47 big-league ballparks on his way to 342 wins and a plaque in Cooperstown.

50.

Consecutive years (1901–1950) that Connie Mack managed the Philadelphia A's.

53.

Years as a big-league manager—by Connie Mack.

56.

Number of consecutive games in Joe DiMaggio's 1941 hitting streak.

65.

Most shutout losses in a career—Walter Johnson.

65.

Lowest weight in pounds for a big leaguer—Eddie Gaedel.

72.

Number of games in which Babe Ruth hit at least two home runs.

74.

Number of consecutive games in which Joe DiMaggio reached base safely in 1941.

On July 17, 1941, the day his 56-game hitting streak ended, DiMaggio drew a walk. The next day, he went on a 17-game hitting streak.

84.

In 1899, the Cleveland Spiders of the National League finished the season in last place—84 games behind Brooklyn.

96.

Number of baseballs—eight dozen—used by the Yankees and Orioles in their record four-hour, 21-minute nine-inning game on April 30, 1996 at Camden Yards. Home teams must supply five dozen balls per game, but this game went above and beyond, averaging over 10 balls per inning! The Yankees won 13-10 in a game that saw 13 walks, 28 hits, and 23 runs.

Compare that to the Cubs-Reds game played on June 29, 1913, which used just one ball!

99.

Highest uniform number worn by a player—Willie Crawford, Oakland A's, 1977; and Mitch Williams, Phillies, 1994.

100.

Percent of his team's games managed in a career—by Joe Schultz of the 1969 Seattle Pilots. Every game this team ever played—all 163—Schultz managed. Which other modern manager can make that claim?

126.

Number of at bats by Rickey Clark (pitcher, Angels, 1967–72) without an RBI.

188.

Number of consecutive *complete* games pitched in the major leagues by Jack Taylor (Cubs and Cardinals, 1901–1906).

198.

Difference between the number of games won and lost by Cy Young—511 wins, 313 losses. Nobody will ever come close.

206.

Consecutive World Series games covered by *New York Times* reporter John Drebinger (1929–1963).

In recognition of his achievements as a baseball writer, Drebinger was given the J. G. Taylor Spink Award in 1973.

259.

Career World Series at bats by Yogi Berra. Unapproachable.

295.

Weight, in pounds, of the heaviest player in baseball history—Walter "Jumbo" Brown, a 6'4" 33-31 pitcher (with 29 saves) who played for 12 years between 1925 and 1941 for the Cubs, Yankees, Indians, Reds, and Giants.

312.

Most triples in a career, by Wahoo Sam Crawford.

313.

Most games lost by a pitcher in a career—by Cy Young.

460.

Hits by two brothers for the same team in the same season, by Paul and Lloyd Waner, 1927 Pirates.

511.

Most wins in a career by a pitcher—by Cy Young. This mark seems untouchable. To surpass Young, a pitcher would first have to surpass Walter Johnson's 417, and nobody has come close. If a pitcher won 20 games a year for 20 years, he'd still be 17 wins short of Johnson's mark. Moreover, a pitcher who won 20 games a year for 25 years (or 25 games a year for 20 years) would still be 11 games short of Young's 511!

> ### Isn't there a beautiful symmetry in noting that in the history of the game, the same man won the most games and lost the most games, and that both numbers are virtually unassailable?

753.

In Chicago, on May 9, 1984, in the 25th inning of the longest game ever played in the American League, Harold Baines of the White Sox hit a game-winning home run off Milwaukee's Chuck Porter—the 753rd pitch of the game.

1,877.

Number of consecutive games in which Hall of Famer Joe Sewell used just one bat—"Black Betsy."

2,795.

Most walks surrendered in a career—by Nolan Ryan.

4,268.

Number of games Joe Torre spent in uniform (as player, coach, and manager) before his first appearance in a World Series (as the Yankees' manager: Game 1, October 20, 1996, against the Braves).

5,611.

Total hits by two brothers in a career, by Lloyd and Paul Waner.

5,714.

Most strikeouts in a career by a pitcher—Nolan Ryan.

6,856.

Total bases in a career, by Hank Aaron. This will probably last forever.

7,095.

Career outfield putouts by Willie Mays.

7,377.

Number of innings pitched in a career, by Cy Young.

01732031.

Prisoner number of Willie Mays Aikens at the federal prison at Leavenworth, Kansas, where he will serve until 2015 on a narcotics conviction.

STUFF NAMED AFTER
BALLPLAYERS

A NUMBER OF BIG LEAGUERS, including many Hall of Famers, have had structures named after them—typically streets, ballparks, or playing fields. Some have had plaques, monuments, or statues erected in their honor in their hometowns or in cities in which they played or managed. Here is a sampling. If you know of any other plaque, monument, statue, field, street, or other landmark, named for a big leaguer, please let us know—and send a photograph. We'll try to include the information in the next edition.

Who is the only .252 hitter in baseball history to have an entire town named after him?

> *Hint #1: He is not a baseball Hall of Famer.*
>
> *Hint #2: He was not born in the town, and there is no record of his ever having visited it.*

Jim Thorpe. He played for the Giants, Reds, and Braves from 1913 to 1919.

Thorpe died virtually broke on March 28, 1953. His native Oklahoma would not render any assistance in establishing a proper memorial to the 1912 Stockholm Olympic decathlon and pentathlon champion, whose records, gold medals, and trophies were taken away from him after it was learned that he had played semipro baseball for $2 a game under his own name prior to the Olympics, thus forfeiting his amateur status. Such a rule would be laughed at today. Thorpe's medals and his name in the Olympic record book were restored on January 18, 1983—70 years after he won the honors and 30 years after his death. The whereabouts of his trophies—for the pentathlon, a bronze bust of the King of Sweden presented by the King himself, and for the decathlon, a jewel-studded Viking ship presented by the Tsar—remain unknown.

Meanwhile, a fitting resting place for "The Greatest Male Athlete of the First Half of the Twentieth Century" had to be found. Thorpe's widow Patricia—his third wife—persuaded the citizens of Mauch Chunk and East Mauch Chunk in Pennsylvania's Carbon County to agree to merge all their municipal services and schools and rename the town "Jim Thorpe, Pennsylvania." In exchange, the new town would provide a dignified mausoleum. It did—in twenty tons of granite. The town also features Jim Thorpe High School—where the team is called the Olympians—Jim Thorpe National Bank (perhaps the only bank named for a ballplayer), and Jim Thorpe Fire Department. To find out more about this town, call 1-888-JIM THORPE!

A monument southwest of Prague, Oklahoma, erected by the Oklahoma Historical Society in 1995, notes the place of Thorpe's birth. Another marker was placed in front of the Historical Museum in Prague, home of the annual Kolache Festival, which includes the crowning of the Kolache Queen! (A kolache is a Czech pastry.)

# # #

A statue of **Bob Feller** is outside the Cleveland Indians' Jacobs Field.

# # #

A statue of **Stan Musial**, unveiled in 1968, is outside Busch Stadium in St. Louis.

# # #

Statues of **Ty Cobb** and **Hank Aaron** were outside Atlanta's Fulton County Stadium. They've been moved to Turner Field, the new home of the Braves, at 755 Hank Aaron Way. Another statue of Henry Aaron was unveiled in 1994 at Carson Park in Eau Claire, Wisconsin, were Aaron began his career in organized ball on June 14, 1952.

# # #

Hank Aaron was in Mobile, Alabama in January 1997 for the dedication of the 8,000-seat Hank Aaron Stadium. It is the home of the Mobile BayBears, the Padres' AA affiliate in the Southern League. Aaron threw out the first pitch at the stadium on April 17. Mobile named a street Hank Aaron Loop. Statues to

Aaron and another Mobile native, Satchel Paige, are planned for completion by 2000.

# # #

Jackie Robinson's statue is outside of the Expos' Olympic Stadium in Montreal, the city where he played for the International League's Montreal Royals in 1946 before being called up to the Dodgers.

Jackie Robinson Stadium is the home of the Daytona (Florida) Cubs in the Florida State A League.

On April 17, 1996, 50 years to the day after Robinson made his organized baseball debut (in the uniform of the Montreal Royals, then the Brooklyn Dodgers' top minor-league affiliate in the International League), Jersey City, New Jersey erected a plaque to Robinson at Society Hill, where Roosevelt Stadium stood.

On April 15, 1997, 50 years to the day after Jackie Robinson made his debut with the Brooklyn Dodgers, the name of New York City's Interboro Parkway was changed by the New York State Legislature to the Jackie Robinson Parkway. Many fans from Brooklyn use it to get to Shea Stadium in Queens.

The UCLA baseball team plays at Jackie Robinson Stadium, dedicated February 7, 1981, honoring the Bruins' first four-sport star (baseball, basketball, football, and track and field).

Although a statue of Robinson (near the concession stand) was dedicated on April 27, 1985 at UCLA, it did not just happen, nor did the school pay for it. In fact, Jackie's brother Mack Robinson, a silver medalist at the 1936 Berlin Olympic Games, raised $16,000 himself.

Models of large busts of Jackie and Mack Robinson were unveiled on April 15, 1997 (the 50th anniversary of Jackie's first game in the big leagues) across from City Hall in Pasadena, where Mack and Jackie grew up and where Mack still lives. The project is expected to cost $325,000. (Donations are being collected by the Pasadena Robinson Memorial, P.O. Box 70407, Pasadena, CA 91117-0407.) On New Year's Day, 1997, Pasadena honored Jackie with a float provided by the Simon Wiesenthal Center in the city's Tournament of Roses Parade. Pasadena has named a youth center, a post office, a park, and a ballfield for Jackie Robinson, and has installed a bronze plaque on the sidewalk outside his boyhood home at 121 Pepper Street.

In December, 1996, the school board of Grady County, Georgia, voted to approve the naming of the Cairo High School baseball field for Jackie Robinson—the first thing named for Robinson in the hometown he left when he was two. The home of the Syrupmakers also features a granite marker and bronze plaque to Robinson.

Los Angeles's Jackie Robinson Park was built in the town of Littlerock.

# # #

A statue of **Roberto Clemente** was unveiled at Three Rivers Stadium on July 8, 1994. The statue *The Great One*, by local sculptor Susan Wagner, cost $300,000.

Roberto Clemente State Park is in the Bronx, part of New York City.

There's another statue to Clemente at Roberto Clemente Park in his native Carolina, Puerto Rico. A stadium was named for him in Hato Rey.

Ruben Sierra started playing ball at Roberto Clemente City in Puerto Rico, one of thousands who have played there.

# # #

Signs on Pennsylvania Route 30 proclaim St. Thomas as the boyhood home of **Nellie Fox.** The Nellie Fox Bowling Alley (which he used to own) is still operating in nearby Chambersburg.

# # #

Joe DiMaggio was present when a 12-foot, 16,000 pound statue of him was unveiled on May 18, 1991 outside the National Italian American Sports Hall of Fame in Arlington Heights, Illinois.

Plans are under consideration to establish a Joe DiMaggio Museum in Martinez, California, his birthplace. Meanwhile, the Joe DiMaggio Complex (on Joe DiMaggio Drive) houses four sports fields. The city has also placed a plaque on a restored Chris-Craft boat that was given to DiMaggio at the marina.

There's a Joe DiMaggio Park in San Francisco.

# # #

Truxton, New York has erected a statue of its favorite son, Hall of Famer **John McGraw.**

# # #

East Brookfield, Massachusetts has erected a baseball field and a plaque in honor of its favorite son, **Connie Mack**. And there's a statue of Mr. Mack outside the Vet in Philadelphia.

Mack had a stadium named after him during his lifetime, when Shibe Park in Philadelphia was renamed Connie Mack Stadium in 1953.

# # #

Griffith Stadium (named for Hall of Famer **Clark Griffith**) was so named in 1922. A memorial to Griffith was unveiled almost a year after he died by Vice President Richard Nixon on August 8, 1956. It stood at Griffith Stadium and was later moved to Washington's RFK Stadium.

# # #

Charles Comiskey remains the only man (and consequently the only Hall of Famer) to have two stadia named after him.

# # #

September 1996 saw the unveiling of a life-size statue of **Nolan Ryan** at the ballpark in Arlington, Texas.

# # #

August 17, 1996, was **Larry Gardner** Day in Enosburg Falls, Vermont, Gardner's hometown. A state historical marker honoring "Vermont's greatest player" was dedicated in Lincoln Park. Gardner hit .289 during his big-league career with the Red Sox (1908–1917), the Philadelphia A's (1918), and the Cleveland Indians (1919–1924). He played in four World Series. The event raised over $3,000 for the renovation of the high-school ballfield where Gardner played. (Gardner was designated as the greatest player born in Vermont by the Society for American Baseball Research in 1973. Today, many would argue that Carlton Fisk is the best player born in Vermont, but *his* plaque will be in Cooperstown. Fisk was born in Bellows Falls, Vermont, because that was the location of the medical facility nearest his parents' home. He has always considered Charlestown, New Hampshire—12 miles away—his real hometown.)

# # #

Christy Mathewson's hometown of Factoryville, Pennsylvania has named a Little League park in his honor. A permanent billboard marker on Routes 6 and 11 near Keystone College proclaims: WELCOME TO FACTORYVILLE, HOME OF CHRISTY MATHEWSON. Mathewson was in the class of 1898 at what was then Keystone Academy (later a junior college, then a college). A permanent collection of Mathewson memorabilia is on display at the Gambal Athletic Center, and on September 11, 1993 the college named its field in Mathewson's honor.

A Christy Mathewson Parade was held on August 9, 1996, to celebrate Mathewson's birthday (August 12), and it may become an annual event in Factoryville.

Bucknell University, in Lewisburg, Pennsylvania, has outdone itself in honoring one of its most famous and respected alumni—Christy Mathewson, class of 1902.

A plaque at the right of the Mathewson Gate to the campus was dedicated on June 5, 1928. It notes the years and teams of Mathewson's career, and his service as a captain in the United States Army Gas and Flame Division, Allied Expeditionary Force, 1918—HE WAS ONE OF THE GREATEST FIGURES IN COMPETITIVE SPORT OF ALL TIME.

On September 10, 1989, Bucknell's sports stadium was renamed The Christy Mathewson Memorial Stadium.

Mathewson is buried in Lewisburg.

Another plaque to Mathewson was dedicated by his widow at Braves Field in Boston on May 28, 1926. (Mathewson had served as president of the Braves.) Surely one of the most artfully written of all commemorative plaques, it reads: GALLANT SPORTSMAN, COURAGEOUS SOLDIER, KINDLY GENTLEMAN. E'EN AS HE TROD THAT DAY TO GOD SO WALKED HE FROM HIS BIRTH IN SIMPLENESS AND GENTLENESS AND HONOR AND CLEAN MIRTH.

# # #

An 18-foot statue of **Honus Wagner,** situated behind the left-field wall at Forbes Field in Pittsburgh, was dedicated in 1955, shortly before Wagner's death. In 1970, the statue moved with the Pirates to Three Rivers Stadium, where it now stands outside gate C.

# # #

An eight-foot-tall granite monument featuring a bronze plaque was dedicated in 1934 to **Barney Dreyfuss,** who owned the Pirates from 1900 until his death in 1932. The monument stood on the field at Forbes Field along the right center-field wall. The monument now stands along the inner concourse between gates A and B at Three Rivers Stadium.

# # #

A plaque to **Bill Mazeroski** has been embedded in a sidewalk along Roberto Clemente Way in the Oakland section of Pittsburgh, where Forbes Field stood. The plaque shows where Mazeroski's home run in the bottom of the ninth inning of Game 7 of the 1960 World Series cleared the left-field wall and won the game and the Series for the Pirates. Mazeroski Field, a recreation facility, is nearby.

# # #

On May 17, 1994, the City Council of Jackson, Mississippi, recognizing the only native Mississippian in the Hall of Fame, unanimously passed an ordinance authorizing the naming of a street **"James Thomas 'Cool Papa' Bell Drive."**

# # #

The Pittsburgh Pirates' spring training headquarters is at McKechnie Field, named after their Hall of Fame player and manager **Bill "Deacon" McKechnie**.

# # #

Although he was born in Sylvan Lake, Hall of Famer **Dan Brouthers** grew up and played ball in nearby Wappingers Falls, New York. A Little League baseball field was dedicated there to him on May 17, 1971, and a granite monument has been erected to his memory.

# # #

The state has placed a historical marker at **Addie Joss** Park in Juneau, Wisconsin. It reads:

ADRIAN 'ADDIE' JOSS. TALL AND LANKY, WISCONSIN NATIVE ADRIAN 'ADDIE' JOSS BECAME ONE OF BASEBALL'S GREATEST PITCHERS, PRAISED FOR HIS TERRIFIC SPEED AND ACCURATE CONTROL. BORN IN NEARBY WOODLAND ON APRIL 12, 1880, HIS FAMILY MOVED HERE TO JUNEAU IN 1886, WHERE HE PLAYED SECOND BASE FOR THE HIGH SCHOOL TEAM. HE ATTENDED WATERTOWN'S SACRED HEART ACADEMY AND PLAYED BASEBALL IN THE WISCONSIN STATE LEAGUE BEFORE JOINING THE CLEVELAND 'NAPS' OF THE AMERICAN LEAGUE IN 1902. FAMOUS FOR HIS 'HIP POCKET' DELIVERY, JOSS PITCHED A PERFECT GAME AGAINST THE WHITE SOX IN 1908 AND A NO-HITTER IN 1910. HE HAD A CAREER RECORD OF 160 WINS AND 97 LOSSES, WINNING 20 OR MORE GAMES IN FOUR SUCCESSIVE SEASONS WITH A TOTAL OF 46 SHUTOUTS. HIS CAREER WAS CUT SHORT WHEN HE DIED SUDDENLY OF MENINGITIS IN 1911 AFTER HIS NINTH SEASON. THE DAY AFTER HIS FUNERAL, A CLEVELAND NEWSPAPER WROTE: 'ADDIE JOSS STILL LIVES! HIS BODY MAY BE MOLDING INTO DUST . . . BUT HIS SPIRIT REMAINS A POTENT, LIVING THING IN THE SPHERE WHERE HIS NAME WON AN HONORABLE PLACE.' HE WAS ELECTED TO BASEBALL'S HALL OF FAME IN 1978. ERECTED IN 1986.

# # #

Mrs. Henrietta (Ivy) Niekro, mother of Joe and Hall of Famer Phil, spoke to us at some length about her sons, noting that each won his 21st game of the 1979 season on the same day—September 30. She also discussed the "Hey, **Niekro** Polka" ("Please don't ask me to sing it!") and told us that there is a Little League field called Niekro Field in Bridgeport, Ohio, near her home. Consideration is now being given to rename part of U.S. Highway 40, which passes by the house in which he was born, "Phil Niekro Highway."

# # #

In exchange for $18 million, the San Diego City Council has agreed to plans to change the name of **Jack Murphy** Stadium, home of the Padres, to Qualcomm Stadium at Jack Murphy Field. Murphy, a beloved sportswriter for *The San Diego Union*, was instrumental in bringing major-league baseball and the NFL Chargers to San Diego, and in having the stadium built. His brother, Bob, is the Hall of Fame broadcaster who has broadcast every single Mets game to date. Qualcomm, a high-tech company, has agreed to donate $50,000 to erect a statue of Jack Murphy at the stadium.

# # #

John McGraw and Connie Mack collected $500 to erect a marker to replace a board at the grave of **Rube Waddell**, in San Antonio, Texas.

# # #

Gabby Street Stadium (on Gabby Street Avenue) is in Joplin, Missouri, where Street lived and died. Street caught many of Walter Johnson's games.

# # #

George "Smooth" Lyons lived and died in Nevada, Missouri, which is also the hometown of Hall of Famer Clark Griffith. Lyons (no relation to the authors) pitched 7 games for the Cardinals in 1920, and another 26 for the Browns in 1924. The town named its stadium after Lyons, and Kelly Bradham, a sportswriter for *The Nevada Daily Mail*, named the team the Griffins after both Griffith and Lyons.

# # #

Cambridge, Massachusetts has named a town square, **Timothy J. Keefe** Square, bordering Cambridge Street, but has not recognized its two other native Hall of Famers—John Clarkson and Joe Kelley.

# # #

A life-size bronze statue of Hall of Famer **Judy Johnson**—the only Hall of Famer from Delaware—was dedicated on April 14, 1995 in Wilmington, at the home of the Wilmington Blue Rocks (Carolina League, class A, Royals chain).

# # #

One of the few ballfields named for *two* Hall of Famers was dedicated in 1977 on Harrah Day, in Harrah, Oklahoma, hometown of **Paul and Lloyd Waner**. Although Paul had died in 1965, Lloyd was present (having ridden there in an open convertible) when Waner Park, home of the town's Little League team, was dedicated.

# # #

A sign outside of Binger, Oklahoma, proclaims it the hometown of **Johnny Bench.** (He was born in Oklahoma City.)

# # #

One of the most unusual historical markers relating to baseball was erected in Dunsmuir, California on June 14, 1986.

After the 1924 season, in which the Yankees finished two games behind the Senators, **Babe Ruth,** teammate **Bob Meusel,** and manager **Christy Walsh** (a well-known sportswriter who virtually created the concept of ghostwriting for athletes) barnstormed on the West Coast. Residents of Dunsmuir, in Siskiyou County, called Ruth's team in Portland, Oregon, to find out what it would take to have the players stop in Dunsmuir on their way south to play an exhibition game in San Francisco. The residents were told that if the town raised $1,000, Ruth's team would stop and play a game in Dunsmuir. The town and the local Lions Club raised the money, and a half-holiday was declared in Dunsmuir the day the big leaguers came. Ruth was proclaimed an honorary Lion.

After a power hitting exhibition, the big leaguers played a seven-inning game on October 24 with teams of locals—one led by Ruth (who played first base) and one led by Meusel. Nine hundred fans watched as the Ruths beat the Meusels 8-7. Seven dozen balls were used, as Ruth autographed and distributed ball after ball.

Two years later Ruth returned to Dunsmuir to award the trophy to the Dunsmuir high school football team, which won the league championship—by beating Yreka, the only other team in the league.

Thanks to Reva Coon (whose husband "Bones" played on the Ruths) and Joyce Davis of Dunsmuir for this delightful story of a bygone era in baseball's history.

"Harvard" Eddie Grant was a graduate of both Harvard College (1906) and Harvard Law School (1909). Grant was a battalion commander (Company H, 307th Infantry, 77th Division) whose unit was searching for the legendary "Lost Battalion" when he was killed by German machine gun fire at the Argonne on October 9, 1918–the only major leaguer killed in combat in World War I.

He had played for the Indians, Phillies, Reds, and Giants, and had appeared in the 1913 World Series.

There was a commemorative plaque to Grant at the base of the clubhouse wall at the Polo Grounds, dedicated on Memorial Day, May 30, 1921. Grantland Rice, the foremost sportswriter of the day, wrote this poem for the dedication:

Far from the Game and the cheering of old,
A cross in the Argonne will tell you the story
Where each one may read on its rain-battered mold
A final box score that is written in glory.
The final box score of a Player who gave
The flag that he fought for, his ghost–and his grave.

Green be his couch where the white lilies lean.
Crimson the poppies that keep guard above him.
Gentle the darkness that gathers between
The Player at rest and the torn hearts that love him.
God give him refuge where Life's flag is furled,
A dreamer gone back to the dust of the world.

Low be the lost winds of France that must creep
Over his rest in the Last Tavern lying.
God send Thy dreams where the Darkness is deep,
Father, Thy care when the wild storms are flying.
No monarch there–but the soul of a Man–
We speak for a Brother–for One of the Clan!

The current whereabouts of the Eddie Grant plaque are unknown. According to Joseph D. Tekulsky's fascinating article about Grant that appeared in the November/December 1993 edition of *John Harvard's Journal,* rioting fans ripped the plaque from its monument on September 29, 1957, following the Giants' last game at the Polo Grounds.

A highway in the Highbridge section of the Bronx, New York, was named for Grant. It runs from Nelson Avenue and West 172nd Street to Jerome Avenue—about seven blocks.

# # #

On October 3, 1992, a $38,000 bronze life-size statue was dedicated to Chestertown, Maryland native **Bill "Swish" Nicholson** next to Chestertown's town hall. Known for his gigantic swings (hence his nickname), which frequently yielded home runs, as a Cub Nicholson led the National League in homers and RBIs in 1943 (29, 128) and 1944 (33, 122). He played for the Philadelphia A's, the Cubs, and the Phillies (1936, 1939–1953).

# # #

On July 20, 1990, Chicago renamed part of North Michigan Avenue **Jack Brickhouse** Way. Brickhouse broadcast Cubs games from 1942 to 1982. On April 16, 1940, he broadcast the first game ever on WGN-TV—an exhibition game between the Cubs and the White Sox. The Sox won 4-1.

# # #

Donora, Pennsylvania has recognized two of its own who have played in the big leagues by naming baseball fields in Palmer Park "**Stan 'The Man' Musial** Field" and "**Ken Griffey Sr.** Field." So far, nothing has been named for Ken Griffey Jr. Be patient.

# # #

In 1927, Gettysburg College named its gym after Hall of Famer **Eddie Plank,** a native of Straban Township near Gettysburg in Adams County, Pennsylvania. According to Charles H. Glatfelter, Executive Director of the Adams County Historical Society, "although there is no record that Plank was ever enrolled in the college, he was a student in the preparatory department and sometimes played with the college baseball team."

# # #

Rodeo, California has named a baseball field for **Lefty Gomez,** its favorite son. (That's State Point of Historical Interest CCO-009 on your map.)

# # #

The varsity baseball diamond at Princeton University is named after **Bill "Boil-eryard" Clarke,** who played in the big leagues for the old Baltimore Orioles (1893–1898), the Boston Braves (1899–1900), the Washington Senators (1901–1904), and the Giants (1905). He was the Princeton baseball coach for 36 years between 1900 and 1944.

# # #

If you had to guess the only two native Georgia ballplayers who have been honored with state historical markers, which two would you pick? Ty Cobb (Narrows)? Jackie Robinson (Cairo)? Bill Terry (Atlanta)? Johnny Mize (Demorest)? Georgia has chosen to honor **Ty Cobb** (with a historic marker in front of city hall in Royston, where he lived) and **Sherry Smith.** *Sherry Smith?* Yes: his plaque at the Community Center on Main Street in Mansfield—MANSFIELD'S FAMOUS SOUTHPAW—recounts his 14 years in the majors (1911–1927, Pittsburgh, Brooklyn, Cleveland), his 1980 induction into the Georgia Sports Hall of Fame, and his amazing accomplishment of allowing just two stolen bases in 2,052 innings pitched.*

Former Mansfield Mayor Jack Roquemore told us that his grandfather had a farm adjacent to Smith's. Roquemore was responsible for the installation of the historic marker to Smith. Sherry Smith's daughter, Sara Anderson, told us that her father learned to pitch by throwing cotton balls at rabbits. We asked if she knew the names of the two men who managed to steal those two bases against her father. She told us she did not, but when asked to explain his extraordinary ability to pick runners off base, or to prevent them from stealing, she said that he "was known to walk batters so he could pick them off."

# # #

*Not meaning to throw cold water on Smith's name, memory, or plaque, our research shows that while he did indeed pitch 2,052 innings, and did indeed allow very few stolen bases, he may have allowed somewhat more than two stolen bases. We contacted the Baseball Records Committee of SABR, who contacted Pete Palmer, statistician for *Total Baseball.* Mr. Palmer writes that for several years in the 1920s, the AL actually listed stolen bases allowed by pitchers in the baseball guides. In 1922, Smith (with Cleveland) allowed one stolen base; in 1923, one; in 1924, six; and in 1925, three. That's 11 right there. So the plaque may be wrong.

On August 1, 1923, Smith, pitching for the Indians, faced the greatest left-handed slugger of his day—Babe Ruth. For reasons unknown, Ruth batted right-handed, and took the first pitch for a strike. Then he turned around to bat lefty, and hit a home run.

Auburn University's renovated baseball stadium, Plainsman Park, was renamed Hitchcock Field at Plainsman Park in honor of Auburn alumni and former big leaguers **Jimmy and Billy Hitchcock.** Jimmy played for the Red Sox in 1938, while his younger brother Billy was with the Tigers, Senators, Browns, Red Sox, and Philadelphia A's from 1942 to 1953 before managing the Tigers, Orioles, and Braves. Frank Thomas, the 1994 American League Most Valuable Player, was probably the greatest big leaguer to come out of Auburn. Another Auburn alum, Bo Jackson, was pretty good too.

# # #

The Texas Historical Survey Committee has erected a plaque in Hubbard to **Tris Speaker:**

A LEGEND IN HIS OWN TIME, TRIS SPEAKER WAS BORN, EDUCATED, AND BURIED HERE. KNOWN AS THE GREY EAGLE, HE WAS THE FIRST TEXAN NAMED TO NATIONAL BASEBALL HALL OF FAME. FIRST MAN ELEVATED TO TEXAS SPORTS HALL OF FAME. WAS ON BOSTON'S 1912 AND 1915 WORLD SERIES WINNING TEAMS. MANAGED CLEVELAND INDIANS IN THEIR FIRST PENNANT WIN 1920. AT 18 BEGAN PROFESSIONAL PLAY AT $50 A MONTH. BECAME A SMART, ABLE BUSINESSMAN, NEVER WASTED BIG MONEY OF PLAYING CAREER. ALWAYS 'CAME HOME' TO HUBBARD. HERE HE WAS A LIFETIME MEMBER OF VOLUNTEER FIRE DEPARTMENT.

# # #

In June 1969, Dartmouth named its baseball field in honor of **Red Rolfe,** a graduate of the college (he was captain of the 1931 baseball team), its baseball coach from 1954 to 1967, and also its Director of Athletics. Rolfe was the star third baseman for the Yankees from 1934 to 1942, appearing in six World Series.

# # #

The Grove Street Oval in East Orange, New Jersey, was renamed for **Monte Irvin.**

# # #

A monument to Hall of Famer **Jake Beckley** was erected in his hometown of Hannibal, Missouri.

# # #

Oakland City, Indiana has honored its most famous citizen, **"Big" Edd Roush,** with a plaque on the side of the bank building on South Main Street. The inscription beneath Roush's likeness reads:

TO EDD J. ROUSH: STAR CENTER FIELDER OF THE CINCINNATI REDS AND THE NEW YORK GIANTS AND A MEMBER OF THE NATIONAL BASEBALL HALL OF FAME AT COOPERSTOWN, N.Y., FROM THE CITIZENS OF HIS HOME TOWN, OAKLAND CITY, INDIANA, IN APPRECIATION OF HIS ABILITY AS A PLAYER IN THE NATIONAL BASEBALL LEAGUE WHERE HE ACHIEVED A LIFE-TIME BATTING AVERAGE OF .323, LED THE NATIONAL LEAGUE IN HITTING IN 1917 AND 1919, AND WAS RATED ONE OF THE GREATEST CENTER FIELDERS OF ALL TIME. THE CITIZENS OF OAKLAND CITY, INDIANA, JUNE 17, 1962.

# # #

A state commemorative marker outside of Kingston, Missouri, near Hamilton, marks the birthplace of Hall of Famer **Zack Wheat.**

# # #

New York City's Borough of Brooklyn has named a baseball field and a school after **Gil Hodges,** who played for the Dodgers.

Funds are being raised to erect a statue of Hodges in Petersburg, Indiana, where a bronze bust of Hodges was erected in 1997 in the rotunda of the Pike County Courthouse. A native of Princeton, Indiana (which has named a ballfield after him), Hodges grew up and went to school in Petersburg.

# # #

Schools have been named for **Tim McCarver, Steve Garvey, Jackie Robinson, Roberto Clemente, Walter Johnson,** and, as noted above, Gil Hodges and Jim Thorpe.

# # #

Tim McCarver Stadium, née Chicks Stadium, in Memphis, Tennessee—McCarver's hometown—home of the Memphis Chicks, of which he is a part owner, was dedicated on May 2, 1978. The Chicks are a Mariners' AA affiliate in the Southern League.

# # #

Ernie Shore Field is the home of the Winston-Salem (North Carolina) Warthogs, the Reds' affiliate in the class A Carolina League. A native of East

Bend, North Carolina, Shore pitched for the Giants, Red Sox, and Yankees from 1912 to 1920. On June 23, 1917, teammate Babe Ruth was pitching at home for the Red Sox in the first game of a twin bill against the Washington Senators when he walked the first batter. He argued the ball-four call and was ejected from the game. Shore relieved him, and, after the baserunner was caught stealing, went on to retire the next 26 batters. Thus, the Sox faced only the minimum 27 batters in one of the oddest near-perfect games ever.

# # #

Thurman Munson Stadium was the home of the Canton-Akron (Ohio) Indians, in the class AA Eastern League. Munson lived and died in Canton.

# # #

There's a **Pete Rose** Way in Rose's native Cincinnati.

# # #

A Little League park in Geneva, New York, was named for Cardinal **George "Specs" Toporcer.**

# # #

January 9 is **Harold Baines** Day, an annual event, in Baines's native St. Michael's, Maryland—where he still lives. Baines endows a scholarship program for worthy local high school graduates.

# # #

A plaque dedicated to the memory of **Pete Sheehy** adorns the far right wall of the Yankees' dugout—making Sheehy probably the only clubhouse man so honored in all of professional sports.

# # #

A tunnel under Boston was named for **Ted Williams** in 1995, as were a playground and a highway in his native San Diego.

# # #

In 1934, a monument was dedicated to **Louis Sockalexis** at his grave in the Penobscot tribal cemetery in Maine.

# # #

During the 1996 All-Star break, the host city, Philadelphia, dedicated a ball-field in **Mike Schmidt**'s name.

# # #

In 1997, New Jersey's Montclair State University named its new $10 million baseball field **Yogi Berra** Stadium. The stadium will also be home to a minor-league team in the Northeast League. The Hall of Fame catcher lives in Mont-clair.

# # #

A plaque was dedicated in 1953 at 309 East 94th Street in Manhattan, birth-place of **Lou Gehrig**. Gehrig's mother, Christine, attended.

# # #

The high school baseball field at Plant City, Florida was dedicated to former Pittsburgh pitcher **Rip Sewell**, who inspired many with his athletic activities—including playing golf—after he became a double amputee.

# # #

On September 25, 1995, in his hometown of Hoffman Estates, Illinois, a street was named after **Dave Shotkowski**, a replacement player for the Atlanta Braves who was shot and killed during an apparent attempted robbery during spring training (March 24, 1995). In February 1997, Douglas Evans, who had a long and violent criminal record, entered a plea of guilty to Shotkowski's murder in exchange for a 27-year state prison sentence.

# # #

Ney, Ohio has issued a commemorative postcard to honor native son **Ned Garver**, who had a 20-12 record for the 1951 St. Louis Browns—the only 20-game winner for any team that lost over 100 games.

# # #

Tilden, Nebraska has erected a gate proclaiming the entrance to **Richie Ash-burn** field.

# # #

The city of Minneapolis renamed a street near the Hubert Humphrey Metrodome "**Kirby Puckett** Place" on October 7, 1996. Puckett announced his retirement in the middle of the 1996 season, without having played a single game—his career ended by glaucoma.

# # #

Millville, Ohio, hometown of the first baseball commissioner, **Kenesaw Mountain Landis,** has erected two plaques to Landis on the state highway approach to the village. It has also named a street Landis Circle.

# # #

SQUEAKY WHEEL GETS THE GREASE DEPARTMENT
Berkeley, California has not recognized Chick Hafey, the only Hall of Famer born there, but in 1982 it named a ballfield after another native, **Billy Martin.**

# # #

Millerton, New York has dedicated a park in memory of Millerton native **Eddie Collins.** Collins's mother was visiting her parents when she went into labor, and Collins was born in his grandparents' house, which is now an inn.

# # #

The Committee to Preserve Troy, New York's Baseball Heritage has erected a monument to the town's seven Hall of Famers. Troy is the birthplace of Hall of Famers **King Kelly** and **Johnny Evers.** It also claims **Dan Brouthers, Roger Connor, Buck Ewing, Mickey Welch,** and **Tim Keefe,** all of whom played for Troy. In fact, Troy has sent 32 natives to the big leagues.

# # #

The Lions Clubs of Shamokin, Pennsylvania have undertaken a campaign to erect a monument to Shamokin native and Hall of Famer **Stan Coveleski,** and to erect signs at both ends of town proclaiming Shamokin as Coveleski's birthplace.

The Silver Hawks, the former White Sox class A affiliate in the Midwest League, play at Stanley Covaleski Stadium, which opened in 1988 in South Bend, Indiana.

# # #

The Phillies' Class A affiliate, the Clearwater Phillies, play at **Jack Russell** Stadium, named for a former pitcher for the Red Sox, Indians, Senators, Tigers, Cubs, and Cardinals (1926–1940). An All-Star in 1934, Russell also pitched in two World Series. He went into the oil business, was a Clearwater city commissioner from 1951 to 1955, and was instrumental in having the stadium built. It was renamed Jack Russell Memorial Stadium after Russell's 1990 death.

# # #

A plaque has been affixed to a granite slab in Rotary Park in Chatham, Ontario to honor native son and American Baseball Hall of Famer **Ferguson Jenkins.** (He's also in the Canadian Baseball Hall of Fame.) Jenkins played in Rotary Park in his youth. A roadway within the Thames Campus Sportsfields has been named Ferguson Jenkins Parkway, and there's a sign—with Jenkins's picture— at the major entrances to Chatham proclaiming it his hometown.

# # #

Newcomerstown, Ohio has gone out of its way to honor its native Hall of Famer. You would too, if **Cy Young** came from your town. The town's park is Cy Young Park, and includes a monument and baseball field named for Young. Young is buried nearby in Peoli. The local museum, The Temperance Tavern, has an entire room full of Young memorabilia, and a number of stores in the town use his name and memorabilia—as well as those of another native son who made good in sports, legendary Ohio State football coach Woody Hayes— for decoration.

On September 29, 1993, 90 years (almost to the day) after the first pitch of the first game of the first World Series was thrown by Cy Young, a 1,000-pound bronze statue of Young (and a home plate, about 60 feet away, in Churchill Hall Mall) was dedicated at Northeastern University in Boston—almost exactly on the spot where Young stood on the Huntington Avenue Baseball Grounds mound.

# # #

The Community Center at Titus, Alabama has a sign (like the one outside of town on Elmore County Road 29) proclaiming Titus the home of Hall of Famer **Joe Sewell.**

# # #

February 20, 1977 saw the dedication of a baseball field and a plaque to Hall of Famer **Red Schoendienst** in his hometown of Germantown, Illinois.

# # #

North Adams, Massachusetts has honored its native son, Hall of Famer **Jack Chesbro,** with a plaque at the Noel Field Athletic Complex on State Street, on Route 8.

# # #

October 24, 1987 was **Jimmie Foxx** Day in Foxx's hometown of Sudlersville, Maryland, which has erected a monument to the slugger. Funds are being raised to erect a statue of Foxx.

# # #

Johnny Mize Day was proclaimed on September 30, 1989 in his hometown of Demorest, Georgia, as part of Demorest's centennial celebration. A monument to the Hall of Famer was dedicated in Demorest Springs Park, where Mize lived.

# # #

The sign at the town border of Pierson, Florida proclaims: FERN CAPITAL OF THE WORLD, AND HOMETOWN OF **CHIPPER JONES.**

# # #

On September 23, 1996, the Pennsylvania Historical and Museum Commission erected a historical site marker in Pittsburgh to **Josh Gibson.** While his son, Josh Gibson Jr., and others watched—on Josh Gibson Day in Pittsburgh—the marker was dedicated in front of the field where Gibson first played pro ball, and across the street from his grave by the Macedonia Baptist Church. The marker reads:

> JOSHUA (JOSH) GIBSON 1911–1947. HAILED AS NEGRO LEAGUES' GREATEST SLUGGER, HE HIT SOME 800 HOME RUNS IN A BASEBALL CAREER THAT BEGAN HERE AT AMMON FIELD IN 1929. PLAYED FOR HOMESTEAD GRAYS AND PITTSBURGH CRAWFORDS, 1930–1946. ELECTED TO THE BASEBALL HALL OF FAME '72.

# # #

May 1996 saw the dedication of another historical marker in Pennsylvania, this one to **Roy Campanella.** One of Campanella's Brooklyn teammates, Tommy Lasorda, was present. The plaque at the Vet in Campanella's native Philadelphia reads:

ROY CAMPANELLA, 1921–1993. A RECORD-BREAKING CATCHER WITH BROOKLYN DODGERS, 1948–1957. HE BEGAN HIS PROFESSIONAL BASEBALL CAREER WHILE IN HIGH SCHOOL HERE. IN THE NEGRO LEAGUE, 1937–'42, '44–'45. MVP, NATIONAL LEAGUE, 1951, '53, '55. ALL-STAR, '49–'56. BASE-BALL HALL OF FAME, 1969.

# # #

Gretna, Louisiana marked the birthplace of the great **Mel Ott.** The park in the center of the city was named "Mel Ott Park" on April 20, 1959, and a plaque to Ott will be added to a granite column at the park when renovations are completed.

City Hall also has an exhibit of Ott photographs. The Piccadilly restaurant in Gretna displays other Ott memorabilia, and he has been the theme of Gretna's Mardi Gras Ball.

# # #

In May 1996, Byron, Illinois dedicated a bronze commemorative marker on a boulder at Second and Chestnut Streets to mark the birthplace of Hall of Famer **Albert G. Spalding.** His house is still standing there.

# # #

Hall of Famer **Sam Thompson**'s family presented a plaque with his picture to the Danville, Indiana Community High School. The plaque, in the school's trophy case, recounts Thompson's Hall of Fame career.

# # #

A plaque commemorating what was said to have been **Babe Ruth**'s longest home run ever was erected near the University of Tampa. It reads:

BABE'S LONGEST HOMER. AT TAMPA'S PLANT FIELD ON APRIL 4, 1919, 'BABE' RUTH, PLAYING FOR THE BOSTON RED SOX, AGAINST THE N.Y. GIANTS SMACKED A 567-FOOT HOME RUN THAT SET A RECORD IN A PRE-SEASON GAME. FAMED EVANGELIST BILLY SUNDAY, AN EX-MAJOR LEAGUER HIMSELF, WHO WAS CONDUCTING A TENT REVIVAL ON THE FLORIDA FAIR GROUNDS NEARBY, HAD PITCHED THE FIRST BALL OF THE GAME AND THE BAMBINO'S PACE-SETTING BALL WAS PRESENTED TO HIM. RUTH PLAYED FROM 1915 TO 1935. HE IS REGARDED AS THE MOST POPULAR PLAYER AND GREATEST SLUGGER IN HISTORY. ONE YEAR HE HIT 60 HOMERS.

# # #

Van Meter, Iowa has created the "**Bob Feller** Hometown Exhibit"—a small museum, with Feller's likeness on a brick wall—to honor one of its own. And it's "just minutes from the bridges of Madison County."

On June 20, 1961, a plaque was presented to Feller at Sec Taylor stadium in Des Moines, designating him as the first inductee into the Des Moines Demons Iowa Baseball Hall of Distinction. Feller pitched during the pregame home run hitting contest.

# # #

When it comes to museums built to honor just one player, the **Babe Ruth** Birthplace and Baseball Center in Baltimore (not far from Oriole Park at Camden Yards) stands alone. It is also the home of the Baltimore Orioles Museum and the Maryland Baseball Hall of Fame.

# # #

Lost for over 40 years, a 250-pound stone monument and 2′ × 4′ brass plaque dedicated to **Ray Chapman** of the Indians—the only man killed during a big-league game, on August 20, 1920—was found when the Indians were packing up their 17 truckloads of items in 1994 to move to the new Jacobs Field.

# # #

Franklin, Nebraska has named a ballfield for native son **Clarence Mitchell** (Tigers, Reds, Dodgers, Phillies, Cardinals, Giants, 1911, 1916–1932). Mitchell won 13 games for the Giants in 1931, when he was 40. He was considered a goodwill ambassador for baseball in Nebraska, although many recall him as the man who lined into Bill Wambsganss' unassisted triple play in the 1920 World Series. (He hit into a double play in his next at bat.)

# # #

St. Paul, Nebraska has erected a historical marker and named a baseball field for **Grover Cleveland Alexander.** The marker reads:

GROVER CLEVELAND ALEXANDER

GROVER CLEVELAND ALEXANDER, THE THIRD WINNINGEST PITCHER IN MAJOR LEAGUE BASEBALL HISTORY, WAS BORN NEAR ELBA, NEBRASKA, ON FEBRUARY 26, 1887. AFTER PITCHING FOR LOCAL AND MINOR LEAGUE TEAMS, ALEXANDER SIGNED WITH THE PHILADELPHIA PHILLIES. IN 1911, HIS FIRST SEASON, HE AMASSED TWENTY-EIGHT VICTORIES, STILL A ROOKIE RECORD. IN A CAREER THAT INCLUDED STINTS WITH THE CHICAGO CUBS

AND ST. LOUIS CARDINALS, "ALEXANDER THE GREAT" COMPILED 373 VICTORIES; NINETY SHUTOUTS, A NATIONAL LEAGUE RECORD; AND A MAJOR LEAGUE RECORD OF SIXTEEN SHUTOUTS IN A SEASON. MILITARY SERVICE AND BOUTS WITH EPILEPSY AND ALCOHOLISM PROBABLY LIMITED HIS CAREER TOTALS.

RENOWNED FOR PINPOINT CONTROL, ALEXANDER THREW ONE OF BASEBALL'S MOST FAMOUS STRIKEOUTS IN THE SEVENTH GAME OF THE 1926 WORLD SERIES. PITCHING IN RELIEF FOR THE CARDINALS, THE VETERAN RIGHTHANDER, THEN CALLED "OLD PETE", STRUCK OUT THE YANKEES' TONY LAZZERI WITH THE BASES LOADED.

IN 1938, ALEXANDER WAS AMONG THE FIRST THIRTEEN INDUCTEES TO BASEBALL'S HALL OF FAME. HE DIED IN ST. PAUL, NEBRASKA ON NOVEMBER 4, 1950. IN "THE WINNING TEAM", ALEXANDER'S 1952 FILM BIOGRAPHY, THE BASEBALL IMMORTAL WAS PORTRAYED BY RONALD REAGAN.

# # #

Commerce, Oklahoma named a Little League park after **Mickey Mantle**'s **father Mutt** (real name Elvin) in 1994. Commerce also has a Mickey Mantle Boulevard, and Mantle's home will be turned into a museum.

# # #

In April 1994, Hartford, Alabama named a baseball field after native son and Hall of Famer **Early Wynn.**

# # #

Payette, Idaho has named a road near the Payette River **Harmon Killebrew** **Drive**, and has also named a sports field at the high school for the only Payetter enshrined in Cooperstown.

# # #

It's easy to remember the name of Hall of Famer **Sam Crawford**'s hometown— it was also part of his nickname: Wahoo. (Wahoo, Nebraska is also the hometown of movie mogul Darryl F. Zanuck.) The city of Wahoo named its baseball park Wahoo Sam Crawford Field in the 1970s. (After World War II, this field was home to the Wahoo team in the Pioneer Nite League. Bob Cerv, who later played for the Yankees and the A's, played there.)

During the spring of 1996, students of Lynn Wilson, art teacher at the Wahoo Public School, painted a baseball mural on the stadium.

There's also a historical marker to Crawford and others.

# # #

John Montgomery Ward Field will be constructed in Ward's hometown of Bellefonte, Pennsylvania. A plaque marks the home where Ward lived from 1870 to 1874.

# # #

Harrisville, Michigan named a baseball park after native son and Hall of Famer **Kiki Cuyler.**

# # #

Hack Wilson Drive leads to a recreational area with a ballfield in Wilson's hometown of Ellwood City, Pennsylvania.

# # #

Baseball Hall of Famer **Warren Spahn** has also been inducted into the Greater Buffalo Sports Hall of Fame in his hometown.

# # #

Plans are under way to erect a plaque in Brainerd, Minnesota, to honor two native sons who did well in the big leagues: Hall of Famer **Charles "Chief" Bender** and **"Bullet" Joe Bush.**

# # #

Humboldt, Kansas has a display in its Historical Museum honoring the great **Walter Johnson.** A field was named in Johnson's honor.

The memorial to Johnson that stood at Washington's Griffith Stadium is now at Walter Johnson High School in Bethesda, Maryland.

# # #

Grants Pass, Oregon may erect plaques in a Wall of Fame at its new All Sports Park to honor **Ken Williams** and other sports greats from Josephine County.

# # #

Winters, Texas erected a sign at its baseball field honoring its favorite son, **Rogers Hornsby.** A commemorative softball game was held on the hundredth anniversary of Hornsby's birth on April 27, 1996, and a special postal cover was issued.

# # #

The city of Niagara Falls has erected **Sal Maglie** Stadium and has named a street **Rick Manning** Drive to honor its two big leaguers.

# # #

Tinker Field in Orlando, Florida, home of the Rays and the Cubs (class AA Southern League), is named for Hall of Famer **Joe Tinker,** who lived and died in Orlando. The field also displays a monument to **Clark Griffith,** like Tinker a Hall of Famer. The plaque reads:

CLARK C. GRIFFITH, 1869–1955. THIS MEMORIAL IS DEDICATED TO THE MEMORY OF THE LATE CLARK C. GRIFFITH, WHO BROUGHT THE WASHING-TON SENATORS TO SPRING TRAINING IN ORLANDO, FLORIDA IN 1936. HE DE-VOTED MORE THAN 65 YEARS OF HIS LIFE TO BASEBALL. A DISTINGUISHED MEMBER OF BASEBALL'S IMMORTAL HALL OF FAME, HE WON 237 GAMES AS A PITCHER; HE HELPED FOUND THE AMERICAN LEAGUE IN 1900; WAS PRESI-DENT OF THE SENATORS' PENNANT WINNING TEAMS OF 1924, '25, AND '33. CLARK GRIFFITH GAVE THE NATIONAL PASTIME GREAT DIGNITY AND RE-SPECT . . . TRULY ONE OF ITS FINEST BENEFACTORS. THE IMAGE OF BASEBALL IS EXEMPLIFIED BY THE IMMORTAL 'OLD FOX.'

# # #

San Francisco named a bridge after one of its favorite sons, **Lefty O'Doul.**

# # #

There's a **Hank Aaron** Drive near the Braves' spring training camp in West Palm Beach, Florida.

# # #

Al Kaline Drive and **Mickey Cochrane** Street are near Tiger Stadium in Detroit.

# # #

Billy Rogell Drive is near Detroit's Metropolitan Airport. Rogell was a Tiger from 1930 to 1939.

# # #

Cleveland has a **Lou Boudreau** Drive, and Boston a **(Tom) Yawkey** Way.

# # #

Going to Comiskey Park? You can drive up **Bill Veeck** Drive.

# # #

Pacific Bell Park, which will become the home of the San Francisco Giants in the year 2000, will feature a life-size statue of **Willie Mays** catching Vic Wertz's fly ball in Game 1 of the 1954 World Series.

# # #

The village office at Fowlerville, Michigan ("where agriculture and industry meet") has a plaque to Fowlerville native **Charlie Gehringer**, a Hall of Famer, noting his statistical records, his uniform number (2), and one of his nicknames—"The Fowlerville Flash."

# # #

Joe McCarthy, the first manager elected to the Hall of Fame, was honored on September 28, 1981 with a plaque dedicated on the front lawn of the home he lived in for 30 years at 459 South Ellicott Creek Road in East Amherst, New York. Hall of Famers Ernie Banks, Monte Irvin, Lefty Gomez, and others were present for the dedication of the plaque, erected by the Erie County Legislature. Later, a wreath was placed on McCarthy's nearby grave by Banks, of the Cubs; Yankee scout James Naples Sr.; and Edward F. Kenney, a Red Sox executive, representing the three teams McCarthy managed. Erie County Executive Edward J. Rutkowski and Buffalo Mayor James D. Griffin proclaimed April 21—McCarthy's birthday—Marse Joe McCarthy Day in Erie County.

The plaque reads:

A TRIBUTE TO 'MARSE' JOE McCARTHY. 1887–1978. THE GREATEST MANAGER OF ALL TIME. NINE PENNANTS, SEVEN WORLD SERIES CHAMPIONSHIPS, HALL OF FAME 1957. BORN JOSEPH VINCENT McCARTHY IN GERMANTOWN, PA., DIED IN BUFFALO, N.Y., 1978, AT THE AGE OF 91. FIRST MANAGER TO WIN PENNANTS IN BOTH MAJOR LEAGUES, McCARTHY'S YANKEES WON SEVEN PENNANTS, SIX WORLD SERIES IN A SEVEN YEAR STRETCH. McCARTHY'S YANKEES NEVER FINISHED BELOW THE FIRST DIVISION. CLAIMED BUFFALO AS HIS HOME.

THANK YOU 'MARSE' JOE,   THE PEOPLE OF ERIE COUNTY.

# # #

Leroy Satchel Paige Stadium was built in Kansas City, Missouri, where Paige had many of his triumphs for the Monarchs, one of the great teams of the old Negro Leagues. Paige was present for the dedication on June 5, 1982, but died three days later. He is buried in Kansas City.

# # #

Jimmy Hunter Drive is near the high school in Hertford, North Carolina, Hunter's hometown. The courthouse lawn features a statue of Hunter.

# # #

Boston named a street **Harry Agganis** Way on November 11, 1996. The street had previously been called Gaffney Street after another baseball personage, James E. Gaffney, who bought the Boston team in the National League and named them the Braves. He built Braves Field in Boston.

# # #

Bridgewater, Massachusetts has erected a small granite monument to **Mickey Cochrane** on the town common. It reads:

GIVEN IN MEMORY OF 'MICKEY' COCHRANE, A BRIDGEWATER NATIVE AND A MEMBER OF BASEBALL'S HALL OF FAME. IN 1952, 'MICKEY' WAS VOTED THE GREATEST CATCHER OF ALL TIME BY THE BASEBALL WRITERS OF AMERICA. MAY HIS LEADERSHIP AND FIERCE COMPETITIVE SPIRIT BE AN INSPIRATION TO THE YOUTH OF BRIDGEWATER.

A larger monument to Cochrane and a ballfield were dedicated in his honor in Bridgewater in 1997.

# # #

Lewis Fields at the University of New Hampshire in Durham are named after **Ted Lewis,** a big leaguer for the Red Sox and Braves (1896–1901) and later president of the university.

# # #

Buck O'Neil, star of the Negro Leagues, had a field named in his honor in 1995 in his hometown of Sarasota, Florida.

# # #

Just because his hometown of Palatka, Florida has done nothing to honor its native son, Hall of Famer **John Henry "Pop" Lloyd,** legendary star of the Negro Leagues, does not mean that Lloyd has not been honored elsewhere.

Pop Lloyd Stadium, in Atlantic City, New Jersey where Lloyd lived, has been lovingly restored. The Committee to Restore Pop Lloyd Stadium includes Monte Irvin, Leonard S. Coleman, Ray Dandridge, Jerry Izenberg, and Arthur Schlesinger, Jr.

A baseball fan, you're driving through Fargo, North Dakota, and you stop at the West Acres Shopping Center. Why?

To visit the **Roger Maris** Museum, not far from the Roger Maris Gardens. Although he was born in Hibbing, Minnesota, Maris grew up in Fargo, and always considered it his home. He is buried there.

# # #

Special mention must be made of the admirable Player Field Renovation Program instituted in 1995 by the Colorado Rockies. Under it, individual members of the team donate significant sums of money to refurbish public baseball fields in Colorado. The fields are then named after the ballplayers. Thirteen fields have been created. Thus far, **Andres Galarraga, Marvin Freeman, Ellis Burks, Bill Swift, Larry Walker,** and **Walt Weiss** Fields have already been dedicated. Some of the players, including **Dante Bichette,** have financed two fields. Walt Weiss provided funds for the first baseball field ever in the town of Timnath, which includes a gate and a fountain named for **Michael D. McMorris,** son of Rockies' owner Jerry McMorris. Michael died in March 1996 of cystic fibrosis.

Billy Meyer (White Sox, Philadelphia A's, 113 games, 1913–1917) had a stadium named after him. Why?

The home of the Knoxville, Tennessee Smokies (the Blue Jays affiliate in the Class AA Southern League), Billy Meyer Stadium was named after the only Knoxvillian to manage in the big leagues (he managed the Pittsburgh Pirates from 1948 through 1952, never finishing higher than fourth).

HOMETOWNS OF HALL OF FAMERS THAT HAVE DONE NOTHING TO HONOR THEM

The following towns have not erected a statue, a monument, a plaque, a WEL-COME TO ____, HOMETOWN OF ____ sign, or even named a street or baseball field after their illustrious native sons.

HALL OF FAMER	BIRTHPLACE
Cap Anson	Marshalltown, Iowa
Luke Appling	High Point, North Carolina
Home Run Baker	Trappe, Maryland
Bill Dickey	Bastrop, Louisiana
Amos Rusie	Mooresville, Indiana
Max Carey	Terre Haute, Indiana
Henry Chadwick	Exeter, England
Rollie Fingers	Steubenville, Ohio
Ford Frick	Wawaka, Indiana
Goose Goslin	Salem, New Jersey
"Sliding Billy" Hamilton	Newark, New Jersey
Ralph Kiner	Santa Rita, New Mexico
Pop Lloyd	Palatka, Florida
Ted Lyons	Lake Charles, Louisiana
Henry (Heinie) Manush	Tuscumbia, Alabama
Larry MacPhail	Cass City, Michigan
Rabbit Maranville	Springfield, Massachusetts
Eddie Mathews	Texarkana, Texas
Kid Nichols	Madison, Wisconsin
Old Hoss Radbourn	Rochester, New York
Branch Rickey	Lucasville, Ohio
Red Ruffing	Granville, Illinois
Ray Schalk	Harvey, Illinois
George Sisler	Manchester, Ohio
Pie Traynor	Framingham, Massachusetts
George Wright	Yonkers, New York
Harry Wright	Sheffield, England

Winterset, Iowa has created no memorial to Hall of Famer Fred Clarke, who was born there, but it has created a museum to another native, one Marion Michael Morrison. Why?

As an actor, he was known as John Wayne.

MARRIED AT HOME PLATE

———

DON ZIMMER, A CAREER BASEBALL MAN since 1949 and current dugout coach for the Yankees, and his wife Jean Carol Bauerle were married on August 16, 1951 at home plate in Elmira, New York, during Zimmer's minor-league career.

# # #

On September 24, 1989, before a Fan Appreciation Day crowd of 50,000, Vida Blue was married to Peggy Shannon on the pitcher's mound at Candlestick Park in San Francisco. The bride was chauffeured to the mound in a horse-drawn carriage, and threw her bridal bouquet into the stands.

Blue's best man was Hall of Famer Willie McCovey (Blue's Giant teammate 1978–80). Giving away the bride was Orlando Cepeda (Blue's teammate with the Oakland A's in 1972).

Blue pitched for the Oakland A's, the Royals, and the Giants from 1969 to 1986.

# # #

Karen Kelly and Jay Finch (catcher and pitcher, respectively, for the Tobacco Shack team) were married at home plate in Slidell, Louisiana on October 21,

1992. They walked under crossed aluminum bats held aloft by members of other teams in their Slidell Bantam Baseball Association—a cabbageball league. Instead of a veil, the bride wore a decorated white silk baseball cap.

# # #

On August 21, 1950, a quadruple wedding was held at home plate at LaGrave Field, home of the Fort Worth Texas Cats. Before a game against Oklahoma City, career minor leaguers Joe Torpey and Russ Rose, along with future big leaguers Johnny Rutherford (Dodgers' pitcher, 1952, 7-7) and Don Hoak, all of the Cats, tied the knot before 9,817 fans.

Hoak went on to an 11-year career (1954–1964) in the big leagues with the Dodgers, Cubs, Reds, Pirates, and Phillies, including an appearance in the All-Star game in 1957. Hoak's second wife was singer Jill Corey.

# # #

Art Hunt, the home run champion of the Pacific Coast League (who did not make it to the majors) and Charlotte Axelson were married on the pitcher's mound at Seattle's Civic Field on July 8, 1937. The ceremony was witnessed by 9,272 fans—the largest crowd ever to witness a wedding in Seattle. Hunt wore his baseball uniform, but substituted oxfords for spikes. The best man was former big leaguer Clarence Pickrel (1-0, Phillies and Braves, 1933–34), who homered in the game that followed, which pitted the Indians against the Sacramento Solons. (Hunt went 0-4.) The bride was walked down the aisle (a flowered path from home plate to an altar on the mound) by Washington Governor Clarence Martin. The teams marched with bats held in their right hands, in military fashion, to their positions along the base lines. The organist played "Indian Love Call," and a choir of 40 sang. After the ceremony, the couple walked under crossed bats held by both teams. Charlotte Hunt died in 1989, and Art passed away in 1996. They were married for 62 years.

# # #

Three hundred couples were married (or renewed their vows) in a Valentine's Day ceremony at The Ballpark in Arlington, Texas in 1997.

# # #

Carol Caracciol and John Zullo were married on May 16, 1997 before a crowd of 4,000 between games of a doubleheader featuring the Charleston (South Carolina) RiverDogs and the visiting Greensboro Bats.

# # #

Tim Barker, then with the San Antonio Missions, was married at their home plate in 1991.

# # #

David Sommer was married at home plate in 1991 when he was with the Williamsport Bills.

# # #

Jim Campanis, then with the Jacksonville Suns, was married at home plate in 1992.

# # #

On September 12, 1995, John Frascatore of the Louisville Redbirds was married on the pitcher's mound after Game 2 of the American Association Championship Series between Louisville and the Buffalo Pilots.

# # #

Chad Curtis (Angels, Tigers, Dodgers, Indians, Yankees, 1992–) was married to Candace Reynolds at the courthouse in Davenport, Iowa in his Quad City Angels baseball uniform at 1:30 P.M. on May 7, 1990, before a 2 P.M. game.

# # #

Harold Lloyd Griggs, who went on to pitch for the Washington Senators (1956–1959), was married on the pitcher's mound in Hickory, North Carolina before a Western Carolina League game on June 20, 1952.

# # #

Jack Swallow, general manager of the Cape Fear Crocs, the Expos' Class A affiliate in the South Atlantic League, was married at home plate in Denver's Mile High Stadium in June 1991, when he was director of sales for the Denver Zephyrs.

# # #

On June 25, 1994, Kurt Pickering and Gail Pugh were married at home plate in Princeton, West Virginia, then home of the Princeton Reds in the Appalachian League (a Rookie Advanced League.)* Pickering was the P.A. announcer for the Reds. An "invitation" was printed on page 19 of the team's scorecard book. Local merchants donated cake, rings, tents, tables, tuxedos, a limousine, first night's honeymoon lodging at a motel, wedding photos, invitations, catering, and flowers in exchange for ad space in the scorecard. According to Jim Holland, the "wedding took place at home plate just prior to a game, and the couple exited the field under crossed bats from both teams, to a reception in the third base concourse area. In the middle of the game . . . a limo came through the center-field gate and across the field to pick them up for a big exit. 1994 marked Pickering's third year as our P.A. announcer, and it would also be his last, as less than two months later, he was ejected from a game for abusing his P.A. powers toward an umpire. Pickering was dismissed by the ball club as a result of this incident, and never worked for the Princeton club again."

What did Pickering do to get ejected and subsequently fired? Holland continues: "We had a sound-mixer board with one of the sound effects being the ringing of the telephone. Pickering had the habit of using this as a 'wake up call' when umpires made a questionable call. One night, word was sent up early during a game that the phone was to stop ringing. When Pickering got wind of this, his reply was 'Oh, really!' In the late innings, he informed me . . . to be ready to take over P.A. duties. In the middle of the inning he said over the P.A. system, 'Ladies and gentlemen, as you know I am a journalist' (he was a news director at a local radio station) 'and detest any form of censorship. With this in mind,' 'I want you to know I know exactly what I'm doing.' At this point, Pickering laid his finger and held it down on the 'phone ringing' sound effect button. [Brad Campbell, the home plate umpire] promptly then turned and, looking toward the pressbox, gave Pickering the ejection theatrics."

Here's Pickering's own account, reported exclusively for *Out of Left Field*: "The term 'wake-up call' as a shot at an umpire seems to be quite common in the minor leagues, even though I've never heard it in almost 25 years as an umpire of amateur ball (everything from Little League to college and men's industrial). I saw my duties as P.A. announcer as threefold, in no particular order: keep the crowd informed, entertained, and into it. The journalist/censorship angle Jim relates is true—but it's also true that, as an umpire, I've always felt that what goes on outside the fence is no concern of mine. (The rule book

---

*For a history of baseball in Princeton, West Virginia, not only the smallest city in America (population of about 7,000) with a professional baseball team, but also the only one where both a team mascot *and* the P.A. announcer have been ejected from games, visit the Devil Rays' website: http://www.localweb.com/dcweb/PDR/Raywatch.html.

sides with me on this; the only mention of team officials specifies those whose duties place them on the playing field, and the definition of playing field does not include the stands or press box.) Hence, when I hear of P.A. announcers and organists being ejected, I always give a little shake of my head—but I've never heard of one being fired as a result. . . . My thought was that here was an opportunity to make a point about the First Amendment, the abuse of power by (not at, in my opinion) the umpires, and really get the crowd into it—all in one single move. If I knew I would have been fired, I would probably not have done it—but I didn't expect that. . . . What bothers me most is that the club neither took these factors into account nor asked me for any input."

The Princeton Reds, as they were then known (being a Cincinnati Reds affiliate at the time), went on to win the 1994 Appalachian League title—their only one. In fact, the Reds retired the number of their 1994 manager, John Stearns (#33). Stearns had an excellent 11-year major-league career (1974–1984), mostly with the Mets. The Reds also retired #34, in honor of pitching coach Brad Kelley.

Thanks to Jim Holland, General Manager of the Reds' successors, the Princeton Devil Rays, who were affiliated with the Tampa Bay Devil Rays starting in 1997, for this account of the Kurt and Gail Pickering story.

# # #

Mookie Wilson (a member of the Mets Hall of Fame) and his wife Rosa were married at home plate in Jackson, Mississippi, during his career with the AA Jackson Generals, on June 22, 1978.

# # #

Warren Hacker, who went on to pitch for the Cubs, Phillies, and White Sox (1948–1961), married Olinda Schenke at home plate at the Pampa (Texas) Oilers Baseball Park on August 1, 1946. The Oilers were a class C team in the West Texas–New Mexico League. They celebrated their 50th anniversary in 1996.

# # #

On July 14, 1996, Adrian Brown of the Lynchburg Hillcats (class A Carolina League, Pirates chain), and Lynette Lewis were married at home plate, then walked under Brown's teammates' crossed bats at Lynchburg City Stadium. Then the Hillcats lost to the Wilmington Blue Rocks. Brown had just been promoted to the class AA Carolina Mudcats, but returned to Lynchburg for the wedding.

Another Hillcat, Chris Whitehead, was also married at Lynchburg, to Kay Wilson on July 28, 1990. The couple walked under the crossed bats of the Hillcats and the Kinston (NC) Indians, and were married by Dr. Don Garlock, the team chaplain.

Rocky Nelson, another future major leaguer (Cardinals, Pirates, White Sox, Dodgers, Indians, 1949–1961) was also married at home plate as a Hillcat (to Alberta Burns), on August 25, 1947.

Thanks to Calvin Falwell, owner, and Paul Sunwalls, general manager of the Hillcats, for details of these weddings.

# # #

On August 21, 1993, Ronald Guilfoile and Karen Ehomforde were married at home plate at St. Paul, Minnesota's Municipal Stadium, before a capacity crowd of 5,100. After the game, there was cake for all. The wedding was part of a "Diamonds are a Girl's Best Friend" promotion.

ALMOST MARRIED AT HOME PLATE DEPARTMENT

Walt Cruise (Cardinals and Braves, 1914–1924) was married between games of a doubleheader in Cincinnati on August 27, 1922. He did not play in the second game against the Braves. The wedding was originally scheduled for 9 A.M. at the minister's home, but the train was late, and the bride, Lillian Lory, arrived just before the game. The couple was married in the Reds' office at Crosley Field. Best man was Braves' third baseman Tony Boeckel.

# # #

Ivan "Pudge" Rodriguez, 19, and his fiance Maribel Rivera, 18, were scheduled for a home plate wedding during Rodriguez's minor-league career with the Tulsa Drillers, the Rangers' AA affiliate in the Texas League, on June 20, 1991. Ivan and Maribel were to exchange vows between games of a doubleheader with the Shreveport Captains. The day before the scheduled wedding, Rodriguez was called up to catch for the Rangers. His fiancée learned of the change in her wedding plans only by hearing it on the radio, just hours after the on-the-field rehearsal. Rodriguez was called up during the game but couldn't call Maribel until afterward. Rangers' manager Tom Grieve offered the couple an extra day to get married, but Rodriguez did not want to delay his big-league debut. So the wedding was held at the Tulsa courthouse at 8:30 in the morning. The newlyweds caught an 11 A.M. flight to join the Rangers in Chicago. Rodriguez was inserted in the lineup, threw out two baserunners, had a hit, and drove in two runs, as the Rangers beat the White Sox 7-3.

# # #

Russ Horner, who works as Domer the Turtle, the mascot at Skydome, home of the Toronto Blue Jays, concocted an elaborate scheme to propose to flutist Susan Hoeppner five minutes before a Blue Jays–Royals game on July 18, 1993. Horner had arranged to have both families, their friends, and Hoeppner on the field as his question was read by 50,000 fans on the Jumbotron message board. In full turtle regalia, he knelt and proposed. Hoeppner accepted.

# # #

Pete Kuld of the Duluth-Superior Dukes in the independent Northern League was married at home plate at Wade Stadium in Duluth during the 1996 season.

# # #

During the summer of 1994, Warren Sawkiw of the Winnipeg Goldeyes proposed to his future wife in the infield just prior to a game. In an unrelated move, he was traded the next day to the Thunder Bay Whiskey Jacks.

# # #

Future big-league pitcher Lee Guetterman (Seattle, Yankees, Mets, 1984–1992) and Drew Robinson were married at home plate at Sam Lynn Ballpark in Bakersfield, California on July 31, 1982. Guetterman told us: "The relievers encouraged us to do it on the field, the local news covered it, and over 2,000 people were there."

Thanks to Lee Guetterman for this firsthand account of his on-the-field wedding.

Career minor leaguer Steve Klifas, a shortstop in the Dodger system, was also married at Sam Lynn.

National League umpire Doug Harvey met his future wife Joy Glasscock at the ballpark at Bakersfield, where she was a vendor.

# # #

Ken Shepard, vice president of baseball administration with the Wilmington (Delaware) Blue Rocks was married at Judy Johnson Field at Daniel S. Frawley Stadium on August 28, 1994. Skydivers brought in the wedding bands! The Blue Rocks are the Kansas City Royals' class A Advanced affiliate in the Carolina League.

# # #

The San Diego Padres have permitted a number of nonplaying fans and employees to be married on the field at Jack Murphy Stadium, including former traveling secretary Don Mattei.

# # #

Future big-league pitcher Don Mossi (Indians, Tigers, White Sox, Kansas City, 1954–1965, 101-80, 3.43 ERA, 50 saves) and Eunice Bedford were married at home plate before a game in Bakersfield, California, during Mossi's minor-league career with Bakersfield on August 27, 1950. Mossi pitched the game that followed, and told us that he had a no-hitter going into the eighth inning! The couple was married for 45 years, until Mrs. Mossi's death in 1995.

Thanks to Don Mossi for this great story.

# # #

Sharon Ayers and Jim Connors, both from Atlanta, were married before a Macon Braves game at their home park, Luther Williams Field (named after the former mayor), on June 18, 1994.

# # #

Clark Brooks and Debbie Aitchison were married at home plate at Tampa's Al Lopez Field on December 10, 1988. At the time, Debbie was the Assistant General Manager of the Tampa Tarpons, the Reds' Florida State League (class A Advanced) affiliate at the time. Clark worked next door at Tampa Stadium, home of the NFL's Buccaneers.

Among the guests were Sal Artiaga, then president of the National Association of Professional Baseball Clubs (the minor leagues), Mike Moore (the current president), and Al Lopez himself.

Clark told us in June 1997 that Tampa politics resulted in the Reds leaving Tampa for Plant City, and no team trained in Tampa in 1988. The city wanted to turn the field into a parking lot and allowed it to fall into disrepair. Nevertheless, the Tarpons signed on with the White Sox in 1988; but that was not a happy union, and the decision as made to raze the stadium. The wedding was the last real event at Al Lopez Field. Says Clark: "I don't know of many cases where a man outlives a monument named in his honor, but Al himself is still doing just fine."

The White Sox opened a new facility in Sarasota in 1989, and they bought the Tarpons and moved them to Sarasota, where they became the Sarasota White Sox (later the Brevard County Manatees). Debbie and Clark worked at the new stadium (she as general manager, and he with concession services), but they hated working at a modern-yet-charmless ballpark. They both left baseball, and now each manages a movie theater.

Thanks to Clark Brooks for this story.

# # #

Ontario (California) Orioles' outfielder Leandro Garcia was married at home plate to Dorothy Riggins on August 24, 1947, between games of a doubleheader with Anaheim, then in the Sunset League.

Fans in the stadium passed the hat and collected $105 for the happy couple. The groom went 2-4 in the first game, and walked twice with a single in the second. The Orioles split the twin bill, 3-5 and 12-1.

# # #

Beverly Hanson and Bob Upton of the Richmond Roses (Ohio State League) were married at home plate between games of a doubleheader on June 24, 1947 in Richmond, Upton's hometown, before a crowd of 2,000. Upton pitched and lost the second game to the Newark Browns 11-6.

# # #

And let's not forget the nine couples married at Atlanta-Fulton County Stadium's home plate on July 11, 1976, before the Mets-Braves game, which the Braves won 9-8. Five wrestling matches—not involving the newlyweds—followed the game.

OUT OF LEFT FIELD

———

Name two Olympians who threw no-hitters.

Jim Abbott and Hideo Nomo. Abbott was on the 1988 United States team, and Nomo was on the 1988 Japanese team.

When he was a Yankee on September 4, 1993, Abbott no-hit the Cleveland Indians at home. Nomo, of the Dodgers, threw a no-hitter against the Colorado Rockies in Denver on September 17, 1996.

You're Hank Aaron's fiancée Billye Williams (no, not Hall of Famer Billy Williams). The date is July 23, 1973, and Hank is about to hit his 700th home run—the only man besides Babe Ruth ever to reach that lofty plateau. Where are you?

Late. Ms. Williams, the host of an early morning television show in Atlanta, thought the game started at 7 P.M., rather than 6, so she missed Hank's third-inning blast (his 27th of the season) off Ken Brett. It would not have been surprising if Brett didn't know where he was either: during his 14-year career (1967–1981) he pitched for 10 different teams—the Red Sox, Brewers, Phillies, Pirates, Yankees, White Sox, Angels, Twins, Dodgers, and Royals.

Two New York players led their respective leagues in triples and homers in the same year—1955. Who were they?

Mickey Mantle, Yankees: 37 homers, 11 triples (tied for lead).

Willie Mays, Giants: 51 homers, 13 triples (also tied).

What position did Joe DiMaggio play in the big leagues besides the outfield?

DiMaggio played 1,721 games in the outfield, and just 1 at another position—first base. On July 3, 1950, DiMaggio played first as part of manager Casey Stengel's plan to turn Hank Bauer into a regular outfielder, but DiMaggio injured his ankle sliding into second base and was taken to the hospital for x-rays. Thereafter, DiMaggio returned to center field, and Johnny Mize filled in for Bauer at first.

He played major-league baseball for 11 years (Red Sox, White Sox, A's) as a catcher. Later, he became a coach and then an American League umpire for 20 years. In 1958, he umpired in the Yankees-Braves World Series *and* officiated in the December 28, 1958 NFL sudden-death championship game between the Giants and the Colts (Colts 24, Giants 17). Who was he?

Charlie Berry.

Which of Willie Mays' records will probably last forever?

All-Star total bases—40? No. 24 All-Star Games? Maybe. But our money is on career putouts by an outfielder: 7,095, set over 22 years.

Tris Speaker, "The Grey Eagle," who pioneered shallow outfield play during the dead-ball era and once participated in an incredible 1-3-8 double play, holds the American League record with 6,794.

With the advent of the designated hitter, it seems unlikely that any man will play the outfield for 20 years—and certainly not like Mays.

Name an umpire buried in Cooperstown.

Emmett Ashford (American League, 1966–1970).

This man had six hits in a row over four games. Big deal. But they were all home runs. That *is* a big deal. Who is he?

Moises Alou, Expos, July 6–9, 1993.

In 1962, two home-team pitchers threw no-hitters in the same stadium. But they played for different teams in different leagues. Explain.

Bo Belinsky of the Angels no-hit Baltimore on May 5, 1962—the first no-hitter on the West Coast. The Los Angeles (later California, then Anaheim) Angels shared Dodger Stadium with the Dodgers until their own stadium in Anaheim was built. (The first game in Anaheim was April 19, 1966.) During the three years the Angels played in Dodger Stadium, they called it by its geographic name, Chavez Ravine, rather than mention their rivals' name.

On June 30, 1962, also at Dodger Stadium, Dodger Sandy Koufax pitched his first no-hitter, beating the Mets 5-0.

Who had the longest hitless streak at the start of his big-league career?

Up until 1995, this dubious record was thought to have been held by pitcher Ron Herbel of the Giants, who went hitless in his first 55 plate appearances in 1964–1965. But Padres pitcher Joey Hamilton went 0-for-57—including 0-for-1994 in 40 at-bats—before smacking his first hit: a double off Pete Harnish of the Mets on June 9, 1995. Hamilton was 7-for-65 in 1995 (.108) after finding his batting stroke, and then went 11-for-68 (.162) with one home run in 1996.

Which man was in uniform the longest without a World Series appearance?

Joe Torre. As a player and nine-time All-Star with the Milwaukee and Atlanta Braves, the Cardinals, and the Mets, he appeared in 2,209 games. He then managed the Mets (in 1977 as a player-manager), the Braves, and the Cardinals before becoming the Yankees' skipper in 1996. In all, Torre was in uniform for 4,268 games before his debut in the World Series on October 20, 1996 against the Braves.

Every member of his World Champion 1996 Yankee coaching staff had World Series experience, either as a player or as a coach. The staff included Willie Randolph, Tony Cloninger, Chris Chambliss, Don Zimmer, Mel Stottlemyre, and José Cardenal.

When was the first game with a grand total of just one hit?

September 9, 1965—Sandy Koufax's perfect game, Dodgers versus Cubs. The only hit was a double by Dodger Sweet Lou Johnson off Cubs' pitcher Bob Hendley. Johnson was the only baserunner, and scored the only run.

IGNOMINIOUS ENDS TO SPECIAL DAYS DEPARTMENT

What did George Brett do immediately after getting his 3,000th hit—a single off the Angels' Tim Fortugno—on September 30, 1992?

He was picked off first base by Fortugno. Ouch!

Mr. Brett, please say hello to John Franco of the Mets—ejected from the game on May 11, 1996 (John Franco Day at Shea Stadium)—and Felipe Alou, ejected on May 12, 1996 (his 61st birthday).

Not football, hockey, or basketball. Only in baseball does the manager wear a uniform. Except for four men.

Name the four men who managed in business suits—not uniforms—and were therefore prohibited from stepping onto the field during a game.

Burt Shotton: Phillies, 1928–1933; Reds, 1934, 1947–1948; Dodgers, 1947–1948, 1949–1950.

Connie Mack: Pittsburgh Pirates, 1894–1896; Philadelphia Athletics, 1901–1950.

George Stallings: Phillies, 1897–1898; Tigers, 1901; Yankees, 1909–1910; Braves, 1913–1920.

Bill Armour: Indians, 1902–1904; Tigers, 1905–1906.

"Judge" Emil Fuchs, Boston Braves, 1929. Although he was a lawyer, he was never a judge.

Were you going to say Ted Turner? *Wrong!* Although he did manage his Atlanta Braves on May 11, 1977, he did so in uniform.

He's the only player who had more runs scored than games played. Who was he?

Hall of Famer "Sliding Billy" Hamilton—1,690 runs, 1,591 games.

Who hit home runs for the most different teams?

Tommy Davis. During his 18-year career (1959–1976), he homered for nine different teams: the Dodgers, Mets, White Sox, Pilots, Astros, Athletics, Cubs, Orioles, and Angels. Total homers: 153.

Who scored the most runs in a career without ever scoring 100 in a single season?

Luis Aparicio. He scored 1,335 during his 18-year career with the White Sox, Red Sox, and Orioles but never scored more than 98, a high he reached in 1959.

Who succeeded Roberto Clemente in right field for the Pittsburgh Pirates?

Manny Sanguillen. Primarily a catcher, he did not last long in right. Dave Parker—"The Cobra"—soon followed.

Who held the record for most stolen bases in a season before Ty Cobb broke it by stealing 96 in 1915?

Clyde Milan, 1912 Senators: 88.

How many trees does Hillerich and Bradsby cut each season to make Louisville Slugger baseball bats?

About 40,000, spread over 5,000 acres in Pennsylvania.

What was the lowest number of stolen bases in the American League to win the stolen base title? Who did it and when?

In 1950, Boston's Dom DiMaggio led the American League with 15 stolen bases. The very next year, Minnie Minoso, playing for Cleveland and Chicago, more than doubled that number by stealing 31 bases.

BAD STREAK DEPARTMENT

What was Burleigh's Grimes's worst streak at the plate in 1925?

He hit into two double plays and one triple play *in succession!* Three swings, seven outs!

What was Kenesaw Mountain Landis's salary during 1921, his first year as Commissioner of Baseball?

$50,000.

Who had the most putouts in his career—for any position?

Hall of Famer Jake Beckley—23,696. Beckley played 2,377 games at first base between 1888 and 1907 for the Pirates, Giants, Reds, and Cardinals in the National League, and the Pittsburgh Burghers in the Players' League. He was reputed to have bunted occasionally with his bat turned upside down.

Name three things which were unusual about the 1944 World Series.

- The teams were in the same city—the St. Louis Browns against the Cardinals.
- All six games were played at Sportsman's Park, which the teams shared—the last one-park Series.
- The rival managers, Luke Sewell of the Browns and Billy Southworth of the Cardinals, shared a one-bedroom apartment.

The Cardinals won four games to two, completing the Series in six days (October 4–8).

In 1934, Lou Gehrig won the Triple Crown, batting .363 with 49 home runs and 165 RBIs. What was his salary in 1935?

He earned $23,000, roughly what one of today's superstars earns *per game*.

In 1996, Rickey Henderson had a clause in his Padres contract guaranteeing him—in addition to his base salary—$4,100 for every plate appearance over 299. He wound up with 602 plate appearances (465 at bats, 125 walks, two sacrifice flies, and 10 times hit by pitched balls). That's a $1,242,300 bonus.

Who was the first manager of a New York American League team?

Hall of Famer Clark Griffith, of the New York Highlanders, in 1903. The name was changed to *Yankees* in 1913.

MEL OTT, 32, NAMED TO MANAGE THE NEW YORK GIANTS. Big news at the time, right? But not for long. Why?

The announcement was made December 6, 1941, the day before Pearl Harbor was attacked and the United States entered World War II.

Where did the Seattle Pilots play?

Sicks Stadium, which held 25,400 and was deemed below major-league standards—much like the Pilots themselves. No matter—the Pilots (64-98) lasted only one season (1969).

The league home-run champion must have lots of RBIs—at least 100, right? But one Hall of Famer led the American League in home runs in three years in which he had fewer than 100 RBIs. Who was he?

Mickey Mantle: 1955 (37 homers, 99 RBIs); 1958 (42 homers, 97 RBIs); 1960 (40 homers, 94 RBIs).

In how many seasons did Mantle lead the league in home runs and have *more* than 100 RBIs?

Just one—1956, his Triple Crown year, when he had 52 homers and 130 RBIs.

Which batting champion had the fewest RBIs in the year he won the batting crown?

Matty Alou of the Pirates, in 1966. His batting average was .342, but even with his 183 hits he drove in only 27 runs. The Pirates' team batting average that year was .279.

What is a play called a "John Anderson"?

Stealing an already-occupied base. It is named for one of only two Norwegian-born Yankees. Heinie Mueller once accomplished this dubious feat, as did Lou Novikoff—with the bases loaded. Hall of Famer Red Faber did it in the 1917 World Series, with Buck Weaver already on third base.

What happened on the day Derrel "Bud" Harrelson, the Mets shortstop and later their manager, was born?

The Allies invaded France. Harrelson was born on D Day (June 6, 1944). Yogi Berra—who also managed the Mets—was in the third wave to hit Omaha Beach that day. On the 50th anniversary of D Day, Berra described it as "a lot of noise—like Opening Day."

Thanks to Mort Fleischner for this quote.

Of the 19 men to date who have had 3,000 hits, how many got number 3,000 on a home run?

None.

Which 3,000-hit man had the fewest stolen bases?

Stan Musial—78.

Which 3,000-hit man had the most RBIs?

Hank Aaron—2,297.

Which 3,000-hit man had more stolen bases than RBIs?

Lou Brock—938 stolen bases, only 900 RBIs. In fact, he has the fewest RBIs of any member of the 3,000 hit club.

Which 3,000-hit man scored the fewest runs?

Rod Carew—1,015.

How many games did Kansas City win in 1968?

None. There was no Kansas City team that year. The A's left in 1967 for Oakland, and the Royals' first year was 1969.

Where was the National League's Roosevelt Stadium?

Jersey City, New Jersey. The Brooklyn Dodgers played 15 games there in 1955 and 1956 to dramatize their need for a new stadium. They finally got one—in Los Angeles.

In 1954, the St. Louis Browns moved to Baltimore to become the Orioles. Who were they before they became the Browns?

The Milwaukee Brewers (1901).

Willie Mays was considered one of the premier center fielders of all time. How many times did he lead National League center fielders in fielding average?

He never did. The all-time outfield putout leader had a lifetime fielding average of .981.

Who is the first man to lead his league in stolen bases during his first four full seasons in the big leagues?

Bob Bescher, Reds (1909–1912).

Luis Aparicio, Tim Raines, Vince Coleman, and Kenny Lofton (who weighed just three pounds at birth) have also accomplished this feat.

The late songwriter Irving Gordon wrote "Unforgettable" for Nat King Cole. He won a Grammy award for the song in 1992, when Cole's daughter Natalie rerecorded it as a duet with the voice of her late father. Which of Gordon's other writings is in the National Baseball Museum at Cooperstown?

"Who's on First?" He wrote the classic comedy bit for Abbott and Costello.

Which is the northernmost city in the major leagues?

Toronto? No (latitude 43°65′). How about Montreal? Again, no (45°52′). The correct answer is Seattle, at 47°60′.

It's 1916, and you're the owner of the New York Giants. For reasons which in hindsight seem unimaginable, you trade away three future Hall of Famers. In exchange, you get Wade "Red" Killefer (7 years, 3 home runs, .248) and Buck Herzog (13 years, 20 home runs, .259). Whom did you trade?

Christy Mathewson, Bill McKechnie, and Big Edd Roush.

How long did Honus Wagner manage in the big leagues?

Although he is still considered the standard by which all shortstops are judged, he never measured up as a manager. He managed the Pirates for a mere five games in 1917, winning one and losing four.

On his retirement following the 1963 season, after 22 years with the Cardinals, Stan Musial held every Cardinal batting record but one. Which one?

He led all Cardinals in homers, hits, doubles, triples, slugging average, and on-base percentage. But Rogers Hornsby achieved the highest single-season batting average for any Cardinal when he hit .424 in 1924—still the major-league record. Musial's highest average was .376, which led the National League in 1948.

How long was Wee Willie Keeler's bat?

30½″. It weighed a mere 29 ounces.

Just how wee was Wee Willie?

5′4″, 140 pounds.

Which major-league stadiums closed in 1970?

Crosley Field, Cincinnati; Forbes Field, Pittsburgh; and Connie Mack Stadium (formerly Shibe Park), Philadelphia.

What was the last stadium in the American League to add lights for night games?

Briggs (later Tiger) Stadium, in 1948.

During his eight-year career between 1903 and 1910, Ed Killian pitched 213 games (1,598.1 innings). How many home runs did he surrender?

Nine—approximately one every 20 nine-inning games.

Joe DiMaggio scored over 100 runs in eight different seasons. How many times did he lead the American League in runs scored?

Only once—in 1937, when he scored 151 runs.

In one inning of the Red Sox–Tigers game on June 18, 1953, 16 major-league records were broken or tied. How?

During that 48-minute seventh inning, the Tigers sent 23 batters to the plate and scored 17 runs. They had six walks plus 14 hits—a homer, two doubles, and 11 singles.

Steve Gromek was charged with nine earned runs in the 27-hit game, which the Tigers won 23-2.

The otherwise undistinguished Gene Stephens (.240 lifetime average, 37 homers) set a record in that game that seems unlikely ever to be tied, much less broken.

What was it?

He had three hits in that seventh inning! (A single, a double, and another single.)

Pee Wee Reese, Ted Williams, Duke Snider, and George Kell—to name just a few—have also come to bat three times in an inning, but not even these Hall of Famers had three hits in a single inning. In fact, Kell had his three at bats in the same game as did Stephens, but he could manage only one hit—a double. Sammy White, Tom Umphlett, and Johnny Lipon also came to bat three times in that inning. White and Lipon each had two singles and a walk. On May 21, 1952, Reese of the Dodgers reached base three times in a single inning, with a single and two walks.

The Minnesota Twins and the Oakland A's did something on June 8, 1996 that no other teams in the big leagues did that year. What was it?

They played a scheduled doubleheader. (A few other twin bills were played that year, but only as makeups for rainouts.)

On April 11, 1959, the White Sox got only one hit in the seventh inning against the Kansas City A's. But the inning lasted 45 minutes. How many runs did the Sox score in that inning?

Eleven! Only 2 of the 11 runs were earned. The Sox had 10 walks, a stolen base, a sacrifice, and one hit batsman—Johnny Callison had the only hit!

Who is the only player to lead his league in homers and fewest strikeouts in the same season?

Tommy Holmes of the Boston Braves, in 1945. In his 636 at bats that season, he hit 28 home runs but struck out only nine times.

This team boasted two Triple Crown winners in the same year and still finished second. Who were the players and what was the team?

Sorry, this is a trick question. One player won the Triple Crown of batting, and the other won the Triple Crown of pitching.

The team is the 1934 Yankees, who finished second to Detroit. That season Lou Gehrig batted .363, hit 49 home runs, and drove in 165 runs. Lefty Gomez won 26 games, had an ERA of 2.33, and struck out 158.

On July 19, 1909, in the second inning, Cleveland Naps Shortstop Neal Ball hit his first—and only—home run of the season in a game against Boston. What else did he do in that game?

He turned the first unassisted triple play in major league history—also in the second inning!

Name the five National League catchers who were All-Stars in their rookie seasons.

Johnny Bench (Reds, 1968), Gary Carter (Expos, 1975), Greg Olson (Braves, 1990), Mike Piazza (Dodgers, 1995), Jason Kendall (Pirates, 1996).

Name a date in modern big-league history when all games were canceled (not by any strike or lockout).

D Day, June 6, 1944.

Outfielder Chuck Klein had an amazing year for the Phillies in 1930, batting .386 with 44 assists and leading the National League with 59 doubles, and 158 runs scored—still the National League record.

He played every inning of all 156 games the Phillies played that season—except for one inning. Why?

He was ejected on July 24, in the eighth inning, for arguing balls and strikes with umpire Lou Jorda.

Bob Davis was a catcher for the Padres, Blue Jays, and Angels from 1973 to 1981. What was his hobby?

Snake hunting.

Which big leaguer was born on October 8, 1956, the day Don Larsen pitched the only perfect game in a World Series?

Jeff Lahti, Cardinals' pitcher (1982–1986).

One man holds his team's single-season records in the following categories—all achieved in the same season!

Most games in a season	148
Most at-bats	537
Most hits	126
Most singles	105
Most walks	95
Most strikeouts	90
Most stolen bases	73
Most times caught stealing	18

Who was the player and why won't these records ever be broken?

These marks, belonging to Tommy Harper, 1969 Seattle Pilots, will stand forever because the Pilots moved to Milwaukee in 1970 to become the Brewers.

In 1950, the desperate St. Louis Browns signed David Tracy to help their team. But all his efforts were for naught. The team finished 58-96, in seventh place. What did Tracy do?

He was a hypnotist.

Which catcher stole the most bases in his career?

Hall of Famer Ray Schalk—176. This record has stood since 1929!

In 1923, Hall of Famer Joe Sewell of the Cleveland Indians played every inning of all 153 games. He had 553 at bats, hit .353, drove in 109 runs, and struck out only 12 times!

What was his salary for the year?

$6,000—less than $40 per game! Today's stars make $6,000 per at-bat! (In 1996, Angels' pitcher Mark Langston earned $26,000 per day.)

Sewell struck out only 114 times in his 14-year playing career, covering 1,903 games and 7,132 at bats. His high for strikeouts was 20, in 1922, and he had nine full years in which he struck out fewer than 10 times. Only twice in his career did he strike out twice in one game. No pitcher ever struck him out more than four times. (Among those who accomplished this titanic feat were Hall of Famers Waite Hoyt and Walter Johnson.)

He won the American League RBI crown in 1955, 1958, and 1959. He sat out 1960, and retired after playing the 1961 season. Who was he, and why did he retire?

Jackie Jensen. He retired because he hated flying. Jensen (Yankees, Senators, Red Sox, 1950–1961) was married to two-time Olympian Zoe Ann Olsen, who won a silver medal in 1948 in London and a bronze medal in 1952 in Helsinki in springboard diving.

Name three catchers who played in four decades.

Carlton Fisk (1969–1993, Red Sox, White Sox), Tim McCarver (1959–1980, Cardinals, Phillies, Expos, Red Sox), and Rick Dempsey (1969–1992, Twins, Yankees, Orioles, Indians, Dodgers, Brewers).

Which players were teammates the longest?

Detroit's Alan Trammell and Lou Whitaker. 1995 marked their 19th and final season together.

When he retired in 1975, he had hit over 500 home runs, had played five positions, and had never been thrown out of any of the 2,435 games in which he played. Who was he?

Harmon Killebrew. Total homers: 573, #5 on the all-time list.

How many times in his career did Killebrew bunt—either to sacrifice or for a hit?

Never.

Who was the first player to hit a *pinch-hit* home run in his first major-league at bat?

Eddie Morgan, Cardinals, April 14, 1936, in the seventh inning. His .212 batting average (in 66 career at bats) assured him an otherwise undistinguished career.

ED REULBACH, ONLY MAN TO THROW TWO SHUTOUTS THE SAME DAY (CUBS, SEPTEMBER 26, 1954) DIES

This headline from July 17, 1961 wasn't the biggest baseball news that day. Why?

Ty Cobb also died on July 17, 1961.

Who is the only big leaguer born on June 2, 1941, the day Lou Gehrig died?

Bob Saverine—Orioles, Senators, 1959–1967.

Was October 7, 1925, a happy day or a sad day for baseball?

Both: the World Series between the Pirates and the Senators opened, and the beloved Christy Mathewson died. (He was gassed during World War I, and his lungs never healed.) The presence of Mathewson, a graduate of Bucknell College, in the big leagues helped make baseball a respectable career. One of his nicknames symbolizes his status as an icon of the game: "The Christian Gentleman."

Which player displayed the name of his hometown on his back?

Bill Voiselle (Giants, Braves, 1942–1950), from the town of Ninety Six, South Carolina, wore number 96.

Lee King, of Hundred, West Virginia (Pirates, Giants, Phillies, 1916–1922), did not wear his hometown's name on his back.

Where did the 1911 Yankees hold their spring training?

Bermuda.

During a 20-year, 2,317-game career that landed him in Cooperstown, Jimmie Foxx played every position except one. Which one?

Second base.

On August 21, 1979, Jeff Leonard, "Penitentiary Face," flied out twice and singled *in one at bat*. How?

He came to bat at Shea Stadium with two outs in the top of the ninth inning and his Astros losing 5-0 to the Mets. He flied out to center field. Game over, right? No. The Mets' shortstop had called time just before the pitch, so Leonard returned to the batter's box. This time, he singled. The on-deck batter was up next, right? No. Met first baseman Ed Kranepool thought that Leonard had been retired (and the game completed) on the fly ball, so he was not on the field when Leonard singled—thus leaving the Mets with only eight men on the field. (This *is* the Mets we're talking about!) No good. So the single was erased, and Leonard trudged back to the batter's box for a third try. This time, he flied out to left. *Now*, the game was really over, right? *Wrong!* National League President Chub Feeney upheld the Astros' protest and ruled that time was not out when Kranepool had left the field. So Leonard's single stood. The game was replayed the next day from that point: two outs, Leonard on first. José Cruz then grounded out, and the game was finally, officially, and incontrovertibly over. Houston lost.

What is the significance of Sid Fernandez's choice of uniform number—50?

He's from Hawaii, the 50th state.

How many games did Lou Gehrig play at positions other than first base?

Ten—nine in the outfield, and one at shortstop in 1934. He was listed at shortstop in the lineup the day after he broke Everett Scott's record for consecutive games played. He singled and was pinch run for by Red Rolfe, who went in to play short. Jack Saltzgaver played first base that game.

Perhaps overlooked in the wake of the publicity given to Carl Hubbell for striking out Babe Ruth, Lou Gehrig, Jimmie Foxx, Al Simmons, and Joe Cronin in order—truly one of baseball's most memorable moments—in the 1934 All-Star game was a lineup change that happened in that game and may have happened in only one big-league game since. What was it?

One man substituted for two different players in the same game!

Pinch-hitting for the National League's Hubbell in the third inning, Billy Herman popped out. But in the seventh inning, Frankie Frisch went down with an injury, and Herman went in for him, too. (American League manager Joe Cronin had to approve National League manager Bill Terry's request that Herman reappear, which he did at second base.) The modern All-Star rule permits a second appearance only for catchers.

Who is the only man to win 300 games and ground into two triple plays?

Hall of Famer Phil Niekro. Both came when he was with the Braves.

On April 11, 1978, in San Diego, Niekro came to bat with the bases loaded (with Dale Murphy, Rod Gilbreath, and Pat Rockett) and no outs. Niekro hit a grounder between short and third. Third baseman Bill Almon fielded it and tagged Gilbreath (out 1), then threw to Derrell Thomas at second base to retire Rockett (out 2). Thomas then threw to Gene Richards at first base to retire Niekro (out 3) 5-4-3. Niekro was the losing pitcher.

On July 23, 1979, at Pittsburgh, Niekro won a game 8-0, to lead the National League in wins at 14—tied with his brother Joe, then with the Astros. In the second inning, Phil hit into his second triple play, which went from Bill Madlock to Phil Garner to Willie Stargell.

At the end of the season, the Niekro brothers tied for most wins in the National League—21.

Burleigh Grimes also hit into two triple plays, as did fellow Hall of Famers Lloyd Waner, Billy Williams, Roberto Clemente, Kiki Cuyler, and Max Carey.

In 1964, two rookies had 200 hits. Who were they?

Tony Oliva, Twins (217). Richie Allen, Phillies (201).

Which fielder, active in 1997, has turned the most triple plays?

Gary Gaetti—seven.

Sunny Jim Bottomley also participated in seven triple plays during his Hall of Fame career.

Both teams in the same city finished dead last three years in a row. What teams and what years?

Philadelphia Phillies and A's, 1940–42.

Who is the only man to lead his league in stolen bases one year, but steal only 100 in his entire career?

Dom DiMaggio. He led the American League with 15 stolen bases in 1950, yet stole only 100 in his entire career.

In 1930, Hack Wilson set the National League record of 56 home runs in a season. How many were grand slams?

None. Thus, Wilson also holds two brand-new records, created especially for this book: most home runs in a National League season without a grand slam, and most RBIs in a single season (190) without a grand slam.

When Gene Mauch set the record for managing in the big leagues for the most years (22) without a pennant, who held the record he broke?

Jimmy Dykes—20 years—White Sox, 1934–1946; Philadelphia A's, 1951–1953; Baltimore Orioles, 1954; Cincinnati Reds, 1958; Detroit Tigers, 1959–1960; Cleveland Indians, 1960–1961.

Mauch managed the Philadelphia Phillies, 1960–1968; the Montreal Expos, 1969–1975; the Minnesota Twins, 1976–1980; and the California Angels, 1981–1982 and 1985–1987.

Every baseball player dreams about it. Ossee Schreckengost did it twice. What is it?

Playing in a perfect game. But Schreckengost was on the losing end of both. Schreckengost played for the Philadelphia A's when Boston's Cy Young pitched a perfect game against them on May 5, 1904, and lost again when Cleveland's Addie Joss beat Schreckengost's White Sox on October 2, 1908.

Was there ever a year in which there was a Triple Crown winner in both leagues?

Yes: 1933. In fact, the winners played in the same city—Philadelphia (Chuck Klein of the Phillies in the National League, Jimmie Foxx of the Athletics in the American).

From 1959 to 1962, two All-Star Games were played each year.
Which league won the second 1961 All-Star Game, played in Fenway Park on July 31, 1961?

Neither. A heavy rain in the bottom of the ninth inning forced the game to end as a 1-1 tie—the only tie in All-Star history.

Romer Carl Grey, of Zanesville, Ohio, did not have much of a major-league career—just two games for the 1902 Pirates. He may have spent his spare time reading Westerns. Why?

His brother, Zane Grey—himself a minor-league outfielder for the Wheeling, West Virginia team—wrote them.

Federal judge Kenesaw Mountain Landis became the first Commissioner of Baseball in January, 1921, to restore the integrity of the game after the Black Sox scandal. When did he resign as a judge?

A year later.

After nine years with the Cubs, he sat out the 1909 season to pursue a billiards career after winning the world championship in pocket billiards. Who was he?

Johnny Kling—inevitably nicknamed "Peaches."

What are Fenway Park's seats made of?

Oak.

Before the Colorado Rockies entered the big leagues, which stadium was the highest?

Atlanta's Fulton County Stadium—"The Launching Pad"—1,000 feet above sea level.

On July 25, 1933, the St. Louis Cardinals released Rogers Hornsby as a player. The very next day Hornsby signed to manage another team, but did not have to relocate to the new team's city. Why?

He became the new manager of the St. Louis Browns.

What's wrong with this sentence? "The Dodgers hosted the 1942 All-Star Game at Ebbets Field on July 6, 1942."

Proceeds from the 1942 game were to go to the war effort; so while the Dodgers were the official hosts of the game, it was held at the Giants' home, the Polo Grounds, whose larger seating capacity would hold more fans and thus raise more money. But it rained before the game, and attendance was only 33,694. The American League won 3-1.

Whose initials are always displayed on the Fenway Park scoreboard?

Former team owners Thomas A. Yawkey and his wife, Jean R. Yawkey. Their initials, TAY and JRY, appear in Morse code.

Who was the first National League manager to win pennants in his first two seasons?

Tommy Lasorda, Los Angeles Dodgers, 1977–1978.

What did Angels' third baseman Felix Torres do in the 10 games between June 14 and 23, 1963?

Nothing. He played all 10 games without a putout!

When were the last forfeits in the American and National Leagues?

National League: on Ball Day at Dodger Stadium, August 10, 1995, fans (presumably 14 and under) threw souvenir baseballs onto the field to protest what they considered bad calls by the umpires. Sensing a dangerous situation, first base umpire Bob Davidson declared a forfeit to the visiting Cardinals in the ninth inning.

American League: the White Sox forfeited the second game of a double-header to the Tigers on July 12, 1979 because Comiskey Park was in un-playable condition following a "Disco Demolition" record-burning between games. Gary Meier and Steve Dahl, then of WLUP, were the DJs.

Who was the first big leaguer to become a sportscaster?

Jack Graney. After his 14-year career with the Indians ended in 1922, he became a play-by-play broadcaster for the team. Born in Ontario, Canada, he thus became the first Canadian big leaguer to broadcast in the United States.

Who is the only man called for a balk in a big-league game who was neither a pitcher nor a catcher?

Red Sox' second baseman Jerry Remy. In the bottom of the fourth inning of a 4-2 Red Sox–Tigers game on May 1, 1984, Manny Castillo grounded past third base for a double. Remy played behind Mike Easler at first base to back up the throw from pitcher Bruce Hurst. The Red Sox claimed that Castillo missed first base, but first base umpire Rocky Roe ruled him safe. Then Tigers' manager Sparky Anderson claimed that Remy had played in foul territory—a vi-olation of the rules. Agreeing with him, home plate umpire Ken Kaiser then called a balk on Remy and waved Castillo to third.

But the rules say only that all players except the catcher must be in fair ter-ritory when the ball is pitched. No penalty is mentioned. If this play were to be repeated today, according to Marty Springstead, supervisor of American League umpires, play would be halted, and Remy would not be permitted to stand in foul territory.

The balk was subsequently credited to Sox pitcher Bruce Hurst, and the Tigers won 11-2.

Thanks to Dick Bresciani of the Red Sox for his analysis of this unique play.

Every American League manager in 1925 was ultimately enshrined in Cooperstown—except one. Name the managers and their teams.

Only Lee Fohl, who guided (if that's the right word) the Red Sox to a 47-105 record, is not a Hall of Famer. The others are Bucky Harris, Senators; Connie Mack, A's; George Sisler, Browns; Ty Cobb, Tigers; Eddie Collins, White Sox; Tris Speaker, Indians; and Miller Huggins, Yankees.

When was the first All-Star Game without any walks?

July 9, 1996, in Philadelphia.

"I once hit into four consecutive double plays in one nine-inning game—still the American League record. No matter—I'm a Hall of Famer. Who am I?"

Goose Goslin of the Tigers set this dubious mark (since tied) on April 28, 1934.

When did the legendary (but mediocre) Cubs double play combination of Tinker, Evers, and Chance first play together?

September 13, 1902. The Cubs beat the Cardinals in Chicago, 12-0.

Who are the only father and son to play in perfect games?

Hint—both were shortstops.

Dick J. Schofield and his son Dick C.

Dick J. was the Pirate shortstop when teammate Harvey Haddix pitched 12 perfect innings, but lost to the Milwaukee Braves, on May 26, 1959.

Dick C. was the Angels' shortstop during teammate Mike Witt's perfect game on September 30, 1984.

Before the 1994 strike began on August 12, when was the earliest end to a major-league season?

Labor Day, September 2, 1918—because of World War I. The World Series was held between September 5 and 11.

Were colored baseballs ever used in a real major-league game?

Yes. On August 2, 1938, yellow baseballs were used in a game between the Dodgers and Cardinals at Ebbets Field. The reviews were mixed, and the experiment was not repeated.

When Eddie Murray got his 3,000th hit on June 30, 1995, he joined teammate Dave Winfield in the 3,000 hit club. Who were the only other 3,000 hit club member teammates before them?

Eddie Collins, Ty Cobb, and Tris Speaker, 1928 Philadelphia A's. The A's finished second, 2½ games behind the Yankees.

You're Hank Aaron. On Opening Day, April 4, 1974, in Cincinnati, you tied Babe Ruth's 39-year-old record for home runs in a career with your 714th. Now it's April 8. You're going to break that record tonight, and notch another place for yourself in the record book when you slam your 715th home run.

But you've already set a titanic record in this game. What is it?

Most runs scored in a National League career. In the April 4 game, Aaron scored two runs to tie Willie Mays at 2,062. In the April 8 at bat before he hit #715, Aaron walked and scored—breaking Mays' record. In his next at bat, he broke Ruth's record. Not a bad night.

Aaron finished his National League career with a record 2,107 runs scored (since broken by Pete Rose's 2,165). Aaron also scored 67 runs in the American League, thus bringing his career total for runs scored to 2,174.

Where did the Yankees finish in 1925, Lou Gehrig's rookie season?

Seventh (69-85). Gehrig played in 126 games and hit .295 with 20 homers and 68 RBIs. Washington won the pennant. The Yankees finished a dismal 28½ games back.

For which team did Pete Rose play when he tied Ty Cobb's record for most singles in a career?

The Montreal Expos—July 26, 1984, #3,052.

Who is the only man to lead his league in strikeouts by a pitcher one year, and in batting average in another?

Cy Seymour. With the Giants in 1898, he struck out 244 batters. When an injury ended his career as a pitcher, he led the National League in batting as a Red in 1905, with a .377 average.

Who is the only man to be in uniform for both the first and last regular season games at Atlanta–Fulton County Stadium?

Felipe Alou. He played an exhibition game there for the Braves in 1965 against the Tigers, and was the first Brave to bat in 1966.

On September 23, 1996, he was there as the Montreal Expos' manager for the Braves' last regular season home game there. (The final game at Atlanta–Fulton County Stadium was Game 5 of the 1996 World Series, which Atlanta lost 1-0 to the Yankees on October 24, 1996.)

What did Rangers' shortstop Toby Harrah do in the field during a double-header against the White Sox on June 25, 1976?

Nothing. He played both games—all 18 innings—and never fielded the ball. Texas won the first game 8-4 and lost the nightcap 14-9.

ARTICLES I SHOULD HAVE WAITED JUST A LITTLE LONGER TO WRITE DEPARTMENT

"The Game I'll Never Forget," by Bill Buckner. *Baseball Digest,* April 1981.

Buckner recounts his game for the Cubs on August 19, 1977, when he hit two home runs and drove in five against the team that had traded him, the Dodgers.

Bill, isn't there another game you'll never forget?

Catfish Hunter's pregame ritual included eating fish—flounder, if he could get it. Wade Boggs is well known for combining gastronomy and superstition—he eats chicken at precisely the same time before every game (7:17 before a night game). Hey, it's working: his lifetime batting average is .334, and he has won five American League batting titles and three Gold Gloves at third base.

Ben McDonald eats a can of mustard sardines before he pitches.

Vic Davalillo (.279) liked to *pet* chickens before games.

To what food did Texas designated hitter Mickey Tettleton attribute his (more modest .242) success?

Froot Loops cereal.

Where is the biggest bat in the world?

It stands outside the Hillerich and Bradsby headquarters in Louisville, Kentucky. Made of metal painted to look like wood, it's 120 feet tall and weighs 68,000 pounds.

"Before my baseball career started, I was a bodyguard for Tina Turner. Who am I?"

Lance Parrish.

Mel Ott hit 511 home runs and appeared in 11 All-Star Games. How many All-Star homers did he hit?

None. In fact, the lifetime .304 hitter was only 5-for-23 (.217) in his All-Star Games, going hitless in six games. On the other hand, playing in 11 All-Star Games is quite an accomplishment in itself.

Who hit the most triples in a season without hitting a double?

George Twombly of the 1914 Reds. He had five triples.

Who hit the most doubles in a season without hitting a triple?

Edgar Martinez of the 1995 Seattle Mariners. Although he had 29 homers and 52 doubles, he had no triples.

What was Jackie Robinson's salary in 1947, his rookie year?

The major-league minimum—$5,000. He played in 151 games that season (when he was selected as the first Rookie of the Year), hit .297, and stole a league-leading 29 bases.

That's $172 per stolen base, or $33 per game!

Who is the only man to play in four College World Series?

Daryl Arenstein, University of Southern California, 1970–73. He did not play in the big leagues.

How can a team turn a triple play without any fielder touching the ball?

With runners on first and second and no outs, the batter hits a high pop-up in the infield. The infield fly rule is invoked—one out. The runner on first thinks it's a hit, and passes the runner on second for the second out. The ball drops untouched, but the runner on second thinks it was caught, so he runs off the field (or is hit in the head by the ball) for the third out.

Which baseball team broadcasts all of its games in London?

The Toronto Blue Jays. Their games are broadcast on 1410 on the AM dial in beautiful London, Ontario.

Who was the first African-American to homer in the American League?

Hint #1: Not Larry Doby.

Hint #2: He hit it off a future Hall of Famer.

Willard Brown, St. Louis Browns, August 13, 1947, off Hal Newhouser of the Tigers. In fact, it was his only major-league home run. Larry Doby's first homer (for the Indians) was on April 23, 1948, off Fred Hutchinson, also of the Tigers.

Complete this sentence: Babe Ruth's final career home run (the last of three he hit on May 25, 1935) was also the first home run . . .

. . . hit out of Pittsburgh's Forbes Field, which opened in 1909.

TRICK QUESTION DEPARTMENT

Who is the best royal pitcher?

(Notice that this question did not say "Royal" or "Royals" pitcher.) The answer is Masako Owada. She was a devoted baseball fan in Japan. As a high school student at Belmont High School in Massachusetts while her father was in the Japanese consular corps in Boston, the former third baseman pitched and batted cleanup for the coed consulate softball team. In June 1993, she married Crown Prince Naruhito and became Princess Masako.

The grounds crew in San Diego was so excited about the Padres having won the National League West Championship in 1996 that, when they raised that pennant at Jack Murphy Stadium on April 3, 1997, they ____.

Raised it upside down.

Which team had the highest-ever winning percentage over five consecutive years?

The Chicago Cubs, 1906–1910. Their combined won-lost record was 530-235, for an incredible .692!

When Jackie Robinson broke the color barrier in baseball, and played his first game for the Brooklyn Dodgers on April 15, 1947, he was the only black man on the team.

How many blacks were on the Dodgers on April 15, 1997, exactly 50 years later?

Just one—Wayne Kirby.

ON THE COVER

THE MAN PICTURED ON THE COVER is Danny Gardella. This unusual photo was taken in the Giants' Miami training camp on February 14, 1946, after manager Mel Ott notified Gardella that he would not be with the Giants that year.

After parts of two seasons with the Giants in 1944–45, Gardella jumped to the Mexican League in 1946. In an exclusive interview in the fall of 1997, he recalled meeting Babe Ruth in Mexico. Ruth asked Gardella for a cigar, but Gardella had only one. So he broke it in half and shared it with the Babe. Gardella also sang for us—a few bars of the song "Van Lingle Mungo," which consists of the names of former ballplayers, including Danny Gardella.

Because his sojourn in the Mexican League was seen as a threat to the reserve clause, Gardella was suspended by big-league baseball for five years, and was able to find work only as a hospital orderly and a trainer at a gym. He sued in Federal court, challenging baseball's antitrust exemption. Although Gardella lost at the trial-court level, a Federal appellate court found in his favor. Rather than risk a further appeal to the Supreme Court of the United States, which might have upheld the judgment, thereby destroying the only legal monopoly in the United States, baseball settled with Gardella and he was back in the big leagues—but for just one at bat with the 1950 St. Louis Cardinals.

Gardella told us that he was something of a "show-off." He was one of the first big leaguers to train with weights. That, walking on his hands, and other such acrobatic tricks strengthened his forearms enormously and gave him the power and balance required to do the handstand shown on the cover.

Gardella told us that when the Giants traveled by train, he was assigned to bunk with future Hall of Famer Ernie Lombardi. This was considered an initiation rite by the team, because Lombardi, a great catcher and perhaps the hardest hitter in the game, was also considered the loudest snorer on the team. (His nickname was "Schnozz.")

Gardella's teammates included future Hall of Famers Mel Ott, Joe Medwick, Red Schoendienst, Enos Slaughter, and Stan Musial.

Like Billy Sunday, Johnny Berardino, Joe Garagiola, Bob Uecker, and Chuck Connors, Gardella was better known for his off-the-field activities than for his accomplishments as a ballplayer.

ABOUT THE AUTHORS

Jeffrey Lyons is the nationally known entertainment critic for New York's WNBC-TV. He was co-host of *Sneak Previews* on PBS, and hosts *The Lyons Den* syndicated radio report and the film seminar "Coming Attractions."

Jeffrey Lyons has been a Boston Red Sox fan since his birth in 1944, even though the Sox finished in fourth place that year. He lives in New York with his wife and two children, and is the author of *Jeffrey Lyons' 101 Great Movies for Kids.*

Douglas B. Lyons, Jeffrey's brother, is a criminal lawyer. He lives in Scarsdale, New York, with his wife and four children. When Jeffrey was three, his first words to Douglas—age four days—were: "Are you a Dodger fan?"